Mastering NGINX

Second Edition

An in-depth guide to configuring NGINX for your everyday server needs

Dimitri Aivaliotis

[PACKT] open source*
PUBLISHING   community experience distilled

BIRMINGHAM - MUMBAI

Mastering NGINX
Second Edition

First published: March 2013

Second edition: July 2016

Production reference: 1220716

Published by Packt Publishing Ltd.
Livery Place
35 Livery Street
Birmingham B3 2PB, UK.

ISBN 978-1-78217-331-1

www.packtpub.com

Credits

Author
Dimitri Aivaliotis

Reviewer
Markus Jelsma

Acquisition Editor
Kevin Colaco

Content Development Editor
Rashmi Suvarna

Technical Editors
Naveenkumar Jain

Novina Kewalramani

Copy Editor
Vikrant Phadke

Project Coordinator
Judie Jose

Proofreader
Safis Editing

Indexer
Hemangini Bari

Graphics
Kirk D'Penha

Production Coordinator
Shantanu N. Zagade

Cover Work
Shantanu N. Zagade

About the Author

Dimitri Aivaliotis is a production engineer in Silicon Valley. His career has taken him from building a Linux-based computer network for a school up through multi-datacenter, high-availability infrastructures for banks and popular websites. He has spent over a decade solving his customers' problems and learned NGINX along the way.

Dimitri graduated summa cum laude with a BS in Physics from Rensselaer Polytechnic Institute and received an MS in Management Information Systems at Florida State University.

One would think that a second edition should be easy to write, correcting the errors of the first and updating the content. On the one hand, there is much less to write from scratch, but on the other hand, everything must be re-evaluated. It's not as easy as it may seem at first.

I'd like to thank all the reviewers for keeping me honest and pointing out where things are not clear. Any remaining errors are, of course, my own.

Thank you Packt for giving me this opportunity to have another go at writing this book.

Thank you Nginx Inc. for creating a product so flexible and performant that it's still in wide use today.

About the Reviewer

Markus Jelsma is the CTO and co-owner of Openindex B.V, a Dutch company specializing in open source search and crawl solutions. As a committer and PMC member of Apache Nutch, he's an expert in search engine technology and web crawling solutions.

www.PacktPub.com

eBooks, discount offers, and more

Did you know that Packt offers eBook versions of every book published, with PDF and ePub files available? You can upgrade to the eBook version at `www.PacktPub.com` and as a print book customer, you are entitled to a discount on the eBook copy. Get in touch with us at `customercare@packtpub.com` for more details.

At `www.PacktPub.com`, you can also read a collection of free technical articles, sign up for a range of free newsletters and receive exclusive discounts and offers on Packt books and eBooks.

`https://www2.packtpub.com/books/subscription/packtlib`

Do you need instant solutions to your IT questions? PacktLib is Packt's online digital book library. Here, you can search, access, and read Packt's entire library of books.

Why subscribe?

- Fully searchable across every book published by Packt
- Copy and paste, print, and bookmark content
- On demand and accessible via a web browser

For Katja. You mean the world to me.

Table of Contents

Preface

NGINX is a high-performance web server designed to use very few system resources. There are many how-to guides and example configurations floating around the Web. This guide will serve to clarify the murky waters of NGINX configuration. In doing so, you will learn how to tune NGINX for various situations, what some of the more obscure configuration options do, and how to design a decent configuration to match your needs.

You will no longer feel the need to copy-paste a configuration snippet because you will understand how to construct a configuration file to do exactly what you want it to do. This is a process and there will be bumps along the way, but with the tips explained in this book, you will feel comfortable writing an NGINX configuration file by hand. In case something doesn't work as expected, you will be able to debug the problem yourself, or at least be capable of asking for help without feeling like you haven't given it a try yourself.

This book is written in a modular fashion. It is laid out to help you get to the information you need as quickly as possible. Each chapter is pretty much a standalone piece. Feel free to jump in anywhere you feel you need to get more in-depth about a particular topic. If you feel you have missed something major, go back and read the earlier chapters. They are constructed in a way to help you grow your configuration piece by piece.

What this book covers

Chapter 1, *Installing NGINX and Third-Party Modules*, teaches you how to install NGINX on your operating system of choice and how to include third-party modules in your installation.

Chapter 2, *A Configuration Guide*, explains the NGINX configuration file format. You will learn what each of the different contexts is for, how to configure global parameters, and what a location is used for.

Chapter 3, Using the mail Module, explores NGINX's mail proxy module, detailing all aspects of its configuration. An example authentication service is included in the code for this chapter.

Chapter 4, NGINX as a Reverse Proxy, introduces the concept of a reverse proxy and describes how NGINX fills that role.

Chapter 5, Reverse Proxy Advanced Topics, delves deeper into using NGINX as a reverse proxy to solve scaling issues and performance problems.

Chapter 6, The NGINX HTTP Server, describes how to use the various modules included with NGINX to solve common *webserving* problems.

Chapter 7, NGINX for the Application Developer, shows how NGINX can be integrated with your application to deliver content to your users more quickly.

Chapter 8, Integrating Lua with NGINX, provides a brief look at how to extend NGINX functionality using the embedded Lua scripting language.

Chapter 9, Troubleshooting Techniques, investigates some common configuration problems, how to debug a problem once it arises, and makes some suggestions for performance tuning.

Appendix A, Directive Reference, provides a handy reference for the configuration directives used throughout the book, as well as a selection of others not previously covered.

Appendix B, The Rewrite Rule Guide, describes how to use the NGINX rewrite module and describes a few simple steps for converting Apache-style rewrite rules into ones NGINX can process.

Appendix C, The NGINX Community, introduces you to the online resources available to seek more information.

Appendix D, Persisting Solaris Network Tunings, details what is necessary to persist different network tuning changes under Solaris 10 and above.

What you need for this book

Any modern Linux PC should be sufficient to run the code samples in the book. The installation instructions are given in each chapter that uses code samples. Basically, it boils down to:

- The build environment (compiler, header files, and so on)
- NGINX (the most recent version should be fine)

- Ruby (best installed from https://rvm.io)
- Perl (the default version should be fine)

Who this book is for

You are an experienced systems administrator or systems engineer, familiar with installing and configuring servers to meet specific needs. You do not need experience using NGINX.

Conventions

In this book, you will find a number of text styles that distinguish between different kinds of information. Here are some examples of these styles and an explanation of their meaning.

Code words in text, database table names, folder names, filenames, file extensions, pathnames, dummy URLs, user input, and Twitter handles are shown as follows: "This section will be placed at the top of the nginx.conf configuration file."

A block of code is set as follows:

```
http {
    include         /opt/local/etc/nginx/mime.types;
    default_type    application/octet-stream;
    sendfile on;
    tcp_nopush on;
    tcp_nodelay on;
    keepalive_timeout  65;
    server_names_hash_max_size 1024;
}
```

Any command-line input or output is written as follows:

```
$ mkdir $HOME/build
$ cd $HOME/build && tar xzf nginx-<version-number>.tar.gz
```

New terms and **important words** are shown in bold. Words that you see on the screen, for example, in menus or dialog boxes, appear in the text like this: "Clicking the **Next** button moves you to the next screen."

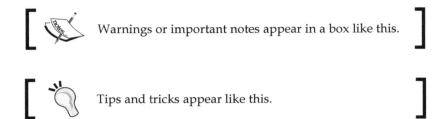

Warnings or important notes appear in a box like this.

Tips and tricks appear like this.

Reader feedback

Feedback from our readers is always welcome. Let us know what you think about this book—what you liked or disliked. Reader feedback is important for us as it helps us develop titles that you will really get the most out of.

To send us general feedback, simply e-mail feedback@packtpub.com, and mention the book's title in the subject of your message.

If there is a topic that you have expertise in and you are interested in either writing or contributing to a book, see our author guide at www.packtpub.com/authors.

Customer support

Now that you are the proud owner of a Packt book, we have a number of things to help you to get the most from your purchase.

Downloading the example code

You can download the example code files for this book from your account at http://www.packtpub.com. If you purchased this book elsewhere, you can visit http://www.packtpub.com/support and register to have the files e-mailed directly to you.

You can download the code files by following these steps:

1. Log in or register to our website using your e-mail address and password.
2. Hover the mouse pointer on the **SUPPORT** tab at the top.
3. Click on **Code Downloads & Errata**.
4. Enter the name of the book in the **Search** box.
5. Select the book for which you're looking to download the code files.

6. Choose from the drop-down menu where you purchased this book from.
7. Click on **Code Download**.

Once the file is downloaded, please make sure that you unzip or extract the folder using the latest version of:

- WinRAR / 7-Zip for Windows
- Zipeg / iZip / UnRarX for Mac
- 7-Zip / PeaZip for Linux

Downloading the color images of this book

We also provide you with a PDF file that has color images of the screenshots/ diagrams used in this book. The color images will help you better understand the changes in the output. You can download this file from `http://www.packtpub.com/ sites/default/files/downloads/Bookname_ColorImages.pdf`.

Errata

Although we have taken every care to ensure the accuracy of our content, mistakes do happen. If you find a mistake in one of our books—maybe a mistake in the text or the code—we would be grateful if you could report this to us. By doing so, you can save other readers from frustration and help us improve subsequent versions of this book. If you find any errata, please report them by visiting `http://www.packtpub. com/submit-errata`, selecting your book, clicking on the **Errata Submission Form** link, and entering the details of your errata. Once your errata are verified, your submission will be accepted and the errata will be uploaded to our website or added to any list of existing errata under the Errata section of that title.

To view the previously submitted errata, go to `https://www.packtpub.com/books/ content/support` and enter the name of the book in the search field. The required information will appear under the **Errata** section.

Piracy

Piracy of copyrighted material on the Internet is an ongoing problem across all media. At Packt, we take the protection of our copyright and licenses very seriously. If you come across any illegal copies of our works in any form on the Internet, please provide us with the location address or website name immediately so that we can pursue a remedy.

Please contact us at copyright@packtpub.com with a link to the suspected pirated material.

We appreciate your help in protecting our authors and our ability to bring you valuable content.

Questions

If you have a problem with any aspect of this book, you can contact us at questions@packtpub.com, and we will do our best to address the problem.

1
Installing NGINX and Third-Party Modules

NGINX was first conceived to be an HTTP server. It was created to solve the C10K problem, described by Daniel Kegel on http://www.kegel.com/c10k.html, in designing a web server to handle 10,000 simultaneous connections. NGINX can do this through its event-based connection-handling mechanism and will use the OS-appropriate event mechanism in order to achieve this goal.

Before we begin exploring how to configure NGINX, we will first install it. This chapter details how to install NGINX and how to get the correct modules installed and configured. NGINX is modular by design and there is a rich community of third-party module developers who have added functionality to the core NGINX server by creating modules that can be compiled into the server and installed along with it.

In this chapter, we will cover the following topics:

- Installing NGINX using a package manager
- Installing NGINX from source
- Configuring for a web or mail service
- Configuring SSL support
- Enabling various modules
- Finding and installing third-party modules
- Adding support for Lua
- Putting it all together

Installing NGINX using a package manager

Chances are that your operating system of choice already provides `nginx` as a package. Installing it is as simple as using your package manager's commands:

- Linux (deb-based)

  ```
  sudo apt-get install nginx
  ```

- Linux (rpm-based)

  ```
  sudo yum install nginx
  ```

- FreeBSD

  ```
  sudo pkg_install -r nginx
  ```

 The `sudo` command is representative of what you need to execute on your operating system to achieve superuser (*root*) privileges. If your operating system supports **role-based access control (RBAC)**, then you would use a different command, such as *pfexec*, to achieve the same goal.

These commands will install NGINX into standard locations, specific to your operating system. This is the preferred installation method if you need to use your operating system's packages.

The NGINX core team also provides binaries of the stable version, available from `http://nginx.org/en/download.html`. Users of distributions without an `nginx` package (such as CentOS) can use the following instructions to install pre-tested and pre-compiled binaries.

Installing NGINX on CentOS

Add the NGINX repository to your `yum` configuration by creating the following file:

```
sudo vi /etc/yum.repos.d/nginx.repo
[nginx]
name=nginx repo
baseurl=http://nginx.org/packages/centos/7/$basearch/
gpgcheck=0
enabled=1
```

Then install `nginx` by executing the following command:

```
sudo yum install nginx
```

Alternative instructions for installing an `nginx-release` package are available at the preceding URL.

Installing NGINX on Debian

Let's install NGINX on Debian using the following steps:

1. Install the NGINX signing key by downloading it from `http://nginx.org/keys/nginx_signing.key` and adding it to the apt keyring:

    ```
    sudo apt-key add nginx_signing.key
    ```

2. Append the nginx.org repository to the end of `/etc/apt/sources.list`:

    ```
    vi /etc/apt/sources.list
    deb http://nginx.org/packages/debian/ jessie nginx
    deb-src http://nginx.org/packages/debian/ jessie nginx
    ```

3. Then install `nginx` by executing the following command:

    ```
    sudo apt-get update
    sudo apt-get install nginx
    ```

If your operating system does not include `nginx` in its list of available packages, the version is too old for what you would like to do, the packages at nginx.org don't serve your needs, you would like to use the *development* release of NGINX, or if you want to enable/disable specific modules, then compiling NGINX from source is the only other option.

Installing NGINX from source

NGINX downloads are available for two separate branches of NGINX code—mainline and stable. The mainline branch is the one in which active development is taking place. Here is where new features will be found and integrated before finding their way into the stable branch. When a *mainline* version is released, it has undergone the same QA and a similar set of functional tests as the stable branch, so either branch may be used on production systems. The major difference between the two branches lies in the support of third-party modules. The internal API may change in the mainline release, whereas it stays the same on the stable branch, so backward compatibility for third-party modules is only available for stable releases.

Preparing a build environment

In order to compile NGINX from source, certain requirements need to be met on your system. Besides a compiler, you also need the OpenSSL and **Perl Compatible Regular Expressions** (**PCRE**) libraries and development headers if you want to enable SSL support and be able to use the rewrite module, respectively. The rewrite module is enabled by default, so if you don't have PCRE libraries and headers, you'll need to disable the rewrite module during the configuration phase. Depending on your system, these requirements may already be met in the default installation. If not, you will need to both locate the appropriate package and install it, or download the source, unpack it, and point NGINX's configure script to this location.

NGINX will attempt to build a dependent library statically if you include a `--with-<library>=<path>` option to configure. You might do this if you want to ensure that NGINX is not dependent on any other part of the system and/or would like to squeeze that extra bit of performance out of your `nginx` binary. If you are using features of external libraries that are only available from a certain version onwards (for example, the next protocol negotiation TLS extension available from OpenSSL Version 1.0.1), then you have to specify the path to the unpacked sources of that particular version.

There are other, optional, packages that you can provide support for, if you like. These include MD5 and SHA-1 hashing algorithm support, `zlib` compression, and `libatomic` library support. The hashing algorithms are used in many places in NGINX, for example, to compute the hash of a URI to determine a cache key. The `zlib` compression library is used for delivering `gzipped` content. If the `atomic_ops` library is available, NGINX will use its atomic memory update operations to implement high-performance memory-locking code.

Compiling from source

NGINX can be downloaded from `http://nginx.org/en/download.html`. Here you will find the source of either branch in `.tar.gz`, or `.zip` format. Unpack the archive into a temporary directory as follows:

```
$ mkdir $HOME/build
$ cd $HOME/build && tar xzf nginx-<version-number>.tar.gz
```

Configure it using the following command:

```
$ cd $HOME/build/nginx-<version-number> && ./configure
```

And compile it as follows:

```
$ make && sudo make install
```

When compiling your own `nginx` binary, you are much more free to include only what you need. Can you already say under which user NGINX should run? Do you want to specify the default log file locations so that they don't need to be explicitly set in the configuration? The following table of configure options will help you design your own binary. These are options that are valid for NGINX, independent of which module is activated.

Table – Common configure options

Option	Explanation
`--prefix=<path>`	The root of the installation. All other installation paths are relative to this one.
`--sbin-path=<path>`	The path to the `nginx` binary. If not specified, this will be relative to the prefix.
`--conf-path=<path>`	The path to where `nginx` will look for its configuration file, if not specified on the command line.
`--error-log-path=<path>`	This is where nginx will write its error `logfile`, unless configured otherwise.
`--pid-path=<path>`	This is where `nginx` will write the `pid` file of the master process, usually under `/var/run`.
`--lock-path=<path>`	The path to the shared memory `mutex` lock file.
`--user=<user>`	The user under which the worker processes should run.
`--group=<group>`	The group under which the worker processes should run.
`--with-file-aio`	Enables asynchronous I/O for FreeBSD 4.3+ and Linux 2.6.22+.
`--with-debug`	This option will enable debug logging. Not recommended for production systems.

You are also able to compile with optimizations that you may not get in a packaged installation. This is where the following options can be especially useful:

Table – Configure options for optimization

Option	Explanation
`--with-cc=<path>`	If you would like to set a C compiler that is not in your default PATH.
`--with-cpp=<path>`	This is the corresponding path to the C preprocessor.
`--with-cc-opt=<options>`	Here is where the path to the necessary `include` files may be indicated (`-I<path>`), as well as optimizations (`-O4`) and specifying a 64-bit build.
`--with-ld-opt=<options>`	The options to the linker include library path (`-L<path>`) and run path (`-R<path>`).
`--with-cpu-opt=<cpu>`	A build specific to a particular CPU family may be specified with this option.

Configuring for web or mail service

NGINX is unique among high-performing web servers in that it was also designed to be a mail proxy server. Depending on your goals in building NGINX, you can configure it for web acceleration, a web server, a mail proxy, or all three. It may be beneficial to have one package that you can install on any server in your infrastructure and be able to set NGINX's role through configuration, or it may serve your needs better to have a slimmed-down binary to use in high-performance environments where every extra KB counts.

Configure options for a mail proxy

The following table specifies configuration options that are unique to the mail module.

Table: Mail configure options

Option	Explanation
`--with-mail`	This will enable the `mail` module, which is not activated by default.
`--with-mail_ssl_module`	In order to proxy any kind of `mail` transaction that uses SSL/TLS, this module will need to be activated.
`--without-mail_pop3_module`	When enabling the `mail` module, the POP3 module may be disabled separately.
`--without-mail_imap_module`	When enabling the `mail` module, the IMAP module may be disabled separately.

Option	Explanation
`--without-mail_smtp_module`	When enabling the `mail` module, the SMTP module may be disabled separately.
`--without-http`	This option will completely disable the `http` module; use it if you know you only want to compile in `mail` support.

For a typical mail proxy, I would recommend configuring NGINX as follows:

```
$ ./configure --with-mail --with-mail_ssl_module --with-openssl=${BUILD_DIR}/openssl-1.0.1p
```

SSL/TLS is needed nowadays on almost every mail installation and not having it enabled on a mail proxy robs users of expected functionality. I've recommended compiling OpenSSL statically so that there are no dependencies on the operating system's OpenSSL library. This does mean, though, that you will have to be vigilant and ensure that your statically-compiled OpenSSL is kept up-to-date and rebuild your binary when necessary. The `BUILD_DIR` variable referenced in the preceding command would of course have to be set beforehand.

Configure options to specify paths

The following table shows what configuration options are available to the `http` module, from activating the Perl module to specifying the location of temporary directories.

Table – HTTP configuration options

Option	Explanation
`--without-http-cache`	When using the upstream module, NGINX can be configured to cache the contents locally. This option disables that cache.
`--with-http_perl_module`	NGINX configuration can be extended by using Perl code. This option activates that module. (Use of this module, however, degrades performance when blocking I/O is done.)
`--with-perl_modules_path=<path>`	This option specifies the path to additional Perl modules needed for using the embedded Perl interpreter. It may also be specified as a configuration option.
`--with-perl=<path>`	The path to Perl (Version 5.6.1 and higher), if not found on the default path.
`--http-log-path=<path>`	The default path to the HTTP access log.

Option	Explanation
`--http-client-body-temp-path=<path>`	When receiving the request from the client, this is the directory used as a temporary location for the body of that request. If the WebDAV module is enabled, it is recommended to set this path to be on the same filesystem as the final destination.
`--http-proxy-temp-path=<path>`	When proxying, this is the directory used as a location to store temporary files.
`--http-fastcgi-temp-path=<path>`	The location for FastCGI temporary files.
`--http-uwsgi-temp-path=<path>`	The location for uWSGI temporary files.
`--http-scgi-temp-path=<path>`	The location for SCGI temporary files.

Configuring SSL support

NGINX uses the OpenSSL Project for TLS/SSL protocols. More information about this Open Source toolkit can be found at `https://www.openssl.org`. Support for SSL can be had from either the OS or directly from a separate copy of the toolkit. If you use either `--with-http_ssl_module` or `--with-mail_ssl_module` without `--with-ssl`, you're using the OpenSSL library that is installed on the machine where you executed the `configure` command. If you'd like to compile against a specific version of OpenSSL, download the distribution, unpack it in a directory, and then specify the path to that directory as the argument to `--with-openssl`. Use the `--with-openssl-opt` option to specify additional build options for OpenSSL itself.

For example, to build NGINX with an OpenSSL that has optimized elliptic curves, you would use a command such as the following:

```
$ ./configure --with-http_ssl_module --with-openssl=${BUILD_DIR}/openssl-
1.0.1p --with-openssl-opt=enable-ec_nistp_64_gcc_128
```

Enabling various modules

Besides the `http` and `mail` modules, there are a number of other modules included in the NGINX distribution. These modules are not activated by default, but may be enabled by setting the appropriate configuration option:

```
--with-<module-name>_module
```

Table – HTTP module configure options

Option	Explanation
`--with-http_ssl_module`	If you need to encrypt web traffic, you will need this option to be able to use URLs beginning with `https`. (Requires the OpenSSL library.)
`--with-http_realip_module`	If your NGINX is behind an L7 load balancer or other device that passes the client's IP address in an HTTP header, you will need to enable this module. For use in situations where multiple clients appear to come from one IP address.
`--with-http_addition_module`	This module works as an output filter, enabling you to add content of a different location before or after that of the location itself.
`--with-http_xslt_module`	This module will handle transformations of XML responses, based on one or more XSLT stylesheets. (Requires the libxml2 and libxslt libraries.)
`--with-http_image_filter_module`	This module is able to act as a filter on images, processing them before handing them over to the client. (Requires the `libgd` library.)
`--with-http_geoip_module`	With this module, you are able to set various variables to use in configuration blocks to make decisions based on the geographic location found for a client's IP address. (Requires the `MaxMind GeoIP` library and the corresponding precompiled database files.)
`--with-http_sub_module`	This module implements a substitution filter, replacing one string in the response with another. (A word of caution: using this module implicitly disables the caching of headers.)
`--with-http_dav_module`	Enabling this module will activate the configuration directives for using WebDAV. Note that this module should only be enabled on a need-to-use basis, as it could present security problems if configured incorrectly.

Option	Explanation
`--with-http_flv_module`	If you need to be able to stream Flash video files, this module will provide pseudo-streaming.
`--with-http_mp4_module`	This module supports pseudo-streaming for H.264/AAC files.
`--with-http_gzip_static_ module`	Use this module if you would like to support sending pre-compressed versions of static files when the resource is called without the `.gz` ending.
`--with-http_gunzip_ module`	This module will decompress pre-compressed content for clients that do not support `gzip` encoding.
`--with-http_random_ index_module`	If you would like to serve an index file chosen at random from the files in a directory, then this module needs to be enabled.
`--with-http_secure_link_ module`	This module provides a mechanism to hash a link to a URL, so that only those with the proper password would be able to calculate the link.
`--with-http_stub_status_ module`	Enabling this module will help you gather statistics from NGINX itself. The output can be graphed using `RRDtool` or something similar.

As you can see, these are all modules that build upon the `http` module, providing extra functionality. Enabling the modules at compile time should not affect runtime performance at all. Using the modules later in the configuration is where performance may be impacted.

I would therefore recommend the following `configure` options for a web accelerator/proxy:

```
$ ./configure --with-http_ssl_module --with-http_realip_module --with-http_geoip_module --with-http_stub_status_module --with-openssl=${BUILD_DIR}/openssl-1.0.1p
```

And the following for a web server:

```
$ ./configure --with-http_stub_status_module
```

The difference lies in where NGINX will be faced with clients. The web acceleration role takes care of terminating SSL requests as well as dealing with proxied clients and making decisions based on where a client came from. The web server role only needs to provide default file serving capability.

I would recommend always enabling the `stub_status` module, as it provides a means of gathering metrics on how your NGINX is performing.

Disabling unused modules

There are also a number of `http` modules that are normally activated, but may be disabled by setting the appropriate configuration option `--without-<module-name>_module`. If you have no use for these modules in your configuration, you can safely disable them.

Table – Disable configure options

Option	Explanation
`--without-http_charset_module`	The `charset` module is responsible for setting the `Content-Type` response header, as well as converting from one `charset` to another.
`--without-http_gzip_module`	The `gzip` module works as an output filter, compressing content as it's delivered to the client.
`--without-http_ssi_module`	This module is a filter that processes Server Side Includes. If the Perl module is enabled, an additional SSI command (`perl`) is available.
`--without-http_userid_module`	The `userid` module enables NGINX to set cookies that can be used for client identification. The variables `$uid_set` and `$uid_got` can then be logged for user tracking.
`--without-http_access_module`	The `access` module controls access to a location based on IP address.
`--without-http_auth_basic_module`	This module limits access via HTTP Basic Authentication.
`--without-http_autoindex_module`	The `autoindex` module enables NGINX to generate a directory listing for directories that have no `index` file.
`--without-http_geo_module`	This module enables you to set up configuration variables based on a client's IP address and then take action on the value of those variables.
`--without-http_map_module`	The map module enables you to map one variable to another.
`--without-http_split_clients_module`	This module creates variables that can be used for A/B testing.
`--without-http_referer_module`	This module enables NGINX to block requests based on the Referer HTTP header.
`--without-http_rewrite_module`	The `rewrite` module allows you to change URIs based on various conditions.

Option	Explanation
`--without-http_proxy_module`	The proxy module allows NGINX to pass requests onto another server or group of servers.
`--without-http_fastcgi_ module`	The FastCGI module enables NGINX to pass requests to a FastCGI server.
`--without-http_uwsgi_module`	This module enables NGINX to pass requests to a uWSGI server.
`--without-http_scgi_module`	The SCGI module enables NGINX to pass requests to an SCGI server.
`--without-http_memcached_ module`	This module enables NGINX to interact with a memcached server, placing responses to queries into a variable.
`--without-http_limit_conn_ module`	This module enables NGINX to set connection limits based on certain keys, usually an IP address.
`--without-http_limit_req_ module`	With this module, NGINX can limit the request rate per key.
`--without-http_empty_gif_ module`	The empty GIF module produces a 1 x 1-pixel in-memory transparent GIF.
`--without-http_browser_ module`	The browser module allows for configurations based on the User-Agent HTTP request header. Variables are set based on the version found in this header.
`--without-http_upstream_ip_ hash_module`	This module defines a set of servers that may be used in conjunction with the various proxy modules.

Finding and installing third-party modules

As with many open source projects, there is an active developer community surrounding NGINX. Thanks to NGINX's modular nature, this community is able to develop and publish modules to provide additional functionality. They cover a wide range of applications, so it pays to take a look at what is available before embarking on developing your own module.

The procedure for installing a third-party module is fairly straightforward:

1. Locate the module you would like to use (either search on `https://github.com` or see `http://wiki.nginx.org/3rdPartyModules`).
2. Download the module.
3. Unpack the source.

4. Read the README file, if included. See if there are any dependencies that you will need to install.

5. Configure NGINX to use the module as follows:

```
./configure --add-module=<path>
```

This procedure will give you an nginx binary with the additional functionality of that module.

Keep in mind that many third-party modules are of an experimental nature. Test using a module first before rolling it out on production systems and remember that the mainline releases of NGINX may have API changes that can cause problems with third-party modules.

Adding support for Lua

Special mention should be made here of the ngx_lua third-party module. The ngx_lua module serves to enable Lua instead of Perl as a configuration time embedded scripting language. The great advantage this module has over the perl module is its non-blocking nature and tight integration with other third-party modules. The installation instructions are fully described at https://github.com/openresty/lua-nginx-module#installation. We will be using this module as an example of installing a third-party module in the next section.

Putting it all together

Now that you have gotten a glimpse at what all the various configuration options are for, you can design a binary that precisely fits your needs. The following example specifies the prefix, user, group, paths, disables some modules, enables some others, and includes a couple of third-party modules:

```
$ export BUILD_DIR=`pwd`
$ export NGINX_INSTALLDIR=/opt/nginx
$ export VAR_DIR=/home/www/tmp
$ export LUAJIT_LIB=/opt/luajit/lib
$ export LUAJIT_INC=/opt/luajit/include/luajit-2.0

$ ./configure \
        --prefix=${NGINX_INSTALLDIR} \
        --user=www \
        --group=www \
```

```
        --http-client-body-temp-path=${VAR_DIR}/client_body_temp \
        --http-proxy-temp-path=${VAR_DIR}/proxy_temp \
        --http-fastcgi-temp-path=${VAR_DIR}/fastcgi_temp \
        --without-http_uwsgi_module \
        --without-http_scgi_module \
        --without-http_browser_module \
        --with-openssl=${BUILD_DIR}/../openssl-1.0.1p \
        --with-pcre=${BUILD_DIR}/../pcre-8.32 \
        --with-http_ssl_module \
        --with-http_realip_module \
        --with-http_sub_module \
        --with-http_flv_module \
        --with-http_gzip_static_module \
        --with-http_gunzip_module \
        --with-http_secure_link_module \
        --with-http_stub_status_module \
        --add-module=${BUILD_DIR}/ngx_devel_kit-0.2.17 \
        --add-module=${BUILD_DIR}/ngx_lua-0.7.9
```

Following a lot of output showing what configure was able to find on your system, a summary is printed out as follows:

```
Configuration summary
  + using PCRE library: /home/builder/build/pcre-8.32
  + using OpenSSL library: /home/builder/build/openssl-1.0.1p
  + md5: using OpenSSL library
  + sha1: using OpenSSL library
  + using system zlib library


  nginx path prefix: "/opt/nginx"
  nginx binary file: "/opt/nginx/sbin/nginx"
  nginx configuration prefix: "/opt/nginx/conf"
  nginx configuration file: "/opt/nginx/conf/nginx.conf"
  nginx pid file: "/opt/nginx/logs/nginx.pid"
  nginx error log file: "/opt/nginx/logs/error.log"
  nginx http access log file: "/opt/nginx/logs/access.log"
  nginx http client request body temporary files: "/home/www/tmp/
client_body_temp"
  nginx http proxy temporary files: "/home/www/tmp/proxy_temp"
  nginx http fastcgi temporary files: "/home/www/tmp/fastcgi_temp"
```

As you can see, configure found all the items we were looking for, and acknowledged our preferences for certain paths. Now you can build your nginx and install it, as mentioned at the beginning of the chapter.

Summary

This chapter has introduced you to the various modules available for NGINX. By compiling your own binary, you are able to tailor what functionality your nginx will provide. Building and installing software will not be new to you, so not a lot of time was spent on creating a build environment or making sure that all dependencies were present. An NGINX installation should be one that fits your needs, so feel free to enable or disable modules as you see fit.

Next up, we will present an overview of basic NGINX configuration, to get a feel for how to configure NGINX in general.

2
A Configuration Guide

The NGINX configuration file follows a very logical format. Learning this format and how to use each section is one of the building blocks that will help you create a configuration file by hand. Constructing a configuration involves specifying global parameters as well as directives for each individual section. These directives and how they fit into the overall configuration file is the main subject of this chapter. The goal is to understand how to create the right configuration file to meet your needs.

This chapter will help you reach this goal by explaining the following topics:

- The basic configuration format
- NGINX global configuration parameters
- Using the `include` files
- The HTTP server section
- The virtual server section
- Locations — where, when, and how?
- The mail server section
- Full sample configuration

The basic configuration format

The basic NGINX configuration file is set up in a number of sections. Each section is delineated as shown:

```
<section> {

    <directive> <parameters>;

}
```

It is important to note that each directive line ends with a semicolon (;). This marks the end of line. The curly braces ({}) actually denote a new configuration context, but we will read these as sections for the most part.

NGINX global configuration parameters

The global section is used to configure the parameters that affect the entire server and is an exception to the format shown in the preceding section. The global section may include configuration directives, such as user and worker_processes, as well as sections, such as events. There are no open and closing braces ({}) surrounding the global section.

The most important configuration directives in the global context are shown in the following table. These configuration directives will be the ones that you will be dealing with for the most part.

Global configuration directives	Explanation
user	The user and group under which the worker processes run is configured using this parameter. If the group is omitted, a group name equal to that of the user is used.
worker_processes	This directive shows the number of worker processes that will be started. These processes will handle all the connections made by the clients. Choosing the right number depends on the server environment, the disk subsystem, and the network infrastructure. A good rule of thumb is to set this equal to the number of processor cores for CPU-bound loads and to multiply this number by 1.5 to 2 for the I/O bound loads.
error_log	This directive is where all the errors are written. If no other error_log is given in a separate context, this log file will be used for all errors, globally. A second parameter to this directive indicates the level at which (debug, info, notice, warn, error, crit, alert, and emerg) errors are written in the log. Note that the debug-level errors are only available if the --with-debug configuration switch is given at compilation time.
pid	This directive is the file where the process ID of the main process is written, overwriting the compiled-in default.

Global configuration directives	Explanation
use	This directive indicates the connection processing method that should be used. This will overwrite the compiled-in default and must be contained in an events context, if used. It will not normally need to be overridden, except when the compiled-in default is found to produce errors over time.
worker_connections	This directive configures the maximum number of simultaneous connections that a worker process may have opened. This includes, but is not limited to, client connections and connections to upstream servers. This is especially important on reverse proxy servers—some additional tuning may be required at the operating system level in order to reach this number of simultaneous connections.

Here is a small example using each of these directives:

```
# we want nginx to run as user 'www'
user www;

# the load is CPU-bound and we have 12 cores
worker_processes  12;

# explicitly specifying the path to the mandatory error log
error_log  /var/log/nginx/error.log;

# also explicitly specifying the path to the pid file
pid        /var/run/nginx.pid;

# sets up a new configuration context for the 'events' module
events {

    # we're on a Solaris-based system and have determined that
        nginx
    # will stop responding to new requests over time with the
        default
    # connection-processing mechanism, so we switch to the
        second-best
    use /dev/poll;
    # the product of this number and the number of
        worker_processes
    # indicates how many simultaneous connections per IP:port pair
        are
    # accepted
    worker_connections  2048;

}
```

This section will be placed at the top of the `nginx.conf` configuration file.

Using the include files

The `include` files can be used anywhere in your configuration file to help it be more readable and to enable you to reuse parts of your configuration. To use them, make sure that the files themselves contain the syntactically correct NGINX configuration directives and blocks; then specify a path to those files:

```
include /opt/local/etc/nginx/mime.types;
```

A wildcard may appear in the path to match multiple files:

```
include /opt/local/etc/nginx/vhost/*.conf;
```

If the full path is not given, NGINX will search relative to its main configuration file.

A configuration file can easily be tested by calling NGINX as follows:

```
nginx -t -c <path-to-nginx.conf>
```

This command will test the configuration, including all files separated out into the `include` files, for syntax errors.

The HTTP server section

The HTTP server section, or the HTTP configuration context, is available unless you have built NGINX without the HTTP module (`--without-http`). This section controls all aspects of working with the HTTP module and will probably be the one that you will use the most.

The configuration directives found in this section deals with handling the HTTP connections. As such, there are quite a number of directives defined by this module. We will divide these directives up by type, to be able to talk about them more easily.

Client directives

This set of directives deals with the aspects of the client connection itself, as well as with different types of client.

The HTTP client directives	Explanation
`chunked_transfer_encoding`	This directive allows disabling the standard HTTP/1.1 chunked transfer encoding in responses to clients.
`client_body_buffer_size`	This directive is used to set a buffer size for the client request body that is larger than the default two memory pages, in order to prevent temporary files from being written to disk.
`client_body_in_file_only`	This directive is used for debugging or further processing of the client request body. This directive can be set to `on` to force save the client request body to a file.
`client_body_in_single_buffer`	This directive forces NGINX to save the entire client request body in a single buffer to reduce the copy operations.
`client_body_temp_path`	This directive defines a directory path for saving the client request body.
`client_body_timeout`	This directive specifies the length of time between the successive read operations of the client body.
`client_header_buffer_size`	This directive is used for specifying a buffer size for the client request header, when this needs to be larger than the default size of 1 KB.
`client_header_timeout`	This timeout is the length of time for reading the entire client header.
`client_max_body_size`	This directive defines the largest allowable client request body, before a `413` (`Request Entity Too Large`) error is returned to the browser.
`keepalive_disable`	This directive disables `keepalive` request for certain browser types.
`keepalive_requests`	This directive defines how many requests may be made over one `keepalive` connection before it is closed.

The HTTP client directives	Explanation
`keepalive_timeout`	This directive specifies how long a `keepalive` connection will stay open. A second parameter may be given to set a `keepalive` header in the response.
`large_client_header_buffers`	This directive defines the maximum number and size of a large client request header.
`msie_padding`	This directive enables the disabling of adding comments to responses with a status greater than 400 for MSIE clients, in order to pad the response size to 512 bytes.
`msie_refresh`	This directive enables the sending of a `refresh` instead of a `redirect` for the MSIE clients.

File I/O directives

File I/O directives control how NGINX delivers static files and/or how it manages file descriptors.

HTTP file I/O directives	Explanation
`aio`	This directive enables the use of asynchronous file I/O. It is available on all modern versions of FreeBSD and distributions of Linux. On FreeBSD, `aio` may be used to preload data for `sendfile`. Under Linux, `directio` is required, which automatically disables `sendfile`.
`directio`	This directive enables the operating system specific flag or function for serving files larger than the given parameter. It's required when using `aio` on Linux.
`directio_alignment`	This directive sets the alignment for `directio`. The default value of `512` is usually enough, although it's recommended to increase this to 4 K when using XFS on Linux.
`open_file_cache`	This directive configures a cache that can store open file descriptors, directory lookups, and file lookup errors.
`open_file_cache_errors`	This directive enables the caching of file lookup errors by `open_file_cache`.

HTTP file I/O directives	Explanation
`open_file_cache_min_uses`	This directive configures the minimum number of uses for a file within the inactive parameter to `open_file_cache` for the file descriptor to remain open in the cache.
`open_file_cache_valid`	This directive specifies the time interval between validity checks for items in `open_file_cache`.
`postpone_output`	This directive specifies the minimum size of data for NGINX to send to the client. If possible, no data will be sent until this value is reached.
`read_ahead`	If possible, the kernel will pre-read files up to the size parameter. It's supported on current FreeBSD and Linux (the size parameter is ignored on Linux).
`sendfile`	This directive enables using `sendfile(2)` to directly copy the data from one file descriptor to another.
`sendfile_max_chunk`	This directive sets the maximum size of data to copy in one `sendfile(2)` call, to prevent a worker from seizing.

Hash directives

The set of hash directives controls how large a range of static memory NGINX allocates to certain variables. NGINX will calculate the minimum size needed on startup and reconfiguration. You will, most likely, only need to adjust one of the `*_hash_max_size` parameters by setting the appropriate directive when NGINX emits a warning to that effect. The `*_hash_bucket_size` variables are set by default to a multiple of the processor's cache line size to minimize the lookups needed to retrieve the entry and therefore should not normally be changed. Refer to `http://nginx.org/en/docs/hash.html` for additional details.

HTTP hash directives	Explanation
`server_names_hash_bucket_size`	This directive specifies the bucket size used to hold the `server_name` hash tables.
`server_names_hash_max_size`	This directive specifies the maximum size of the `server_name` hash tables.
`types_hash_bucket_size`	This directive specifies the bucket size used to hold the `types` hash tables.
`types_hash_max_size`	This directive specifies the maximum size of the `types` hash tables.
`variables_hash_bucket_size`	This directive specifies the bucket size used to hold the remaining variables.
`variables_hash_max_size`	This directive specifies the maximum size of the hash that holds the remaining variables.

Socket directives

Socket directives describe how NGINX can set various options on the TCP sockets it creates.

HTTP socket directives	Explanation
lingering_close	This directive specifies how a client connection will be kept open for more data.
lingering_time	In connection with the lingering_close directive, this directive will specify how long a client connection will be kept open for processing more data.
lingering_timeout	Also in conjunction with lingering_close, this directive indicates how long NGINX will wait for additional data before closing the client connection.
reset_timedout_connection	With this directive enabled, connections that have been timed out will immediately be reset, freeing all associated memory. The default is to leave the socket in the FIN_WAIT1 state, which will always be the case for keepalive connections.
send_lowat	If nonzero, NGINX will try to minimize the number of send operations on client sockets. It is ignored on Linux, Solaris, and Windows.
send_timeout	This directive sets a timeout between two successive write operations for a client receiving a response.
tcp_nodelay	This directive enables or disables the TCP_NODELAY option for keepalive connections.
tcp_nopush	This directive is relevant only when sendfile is used. It enables NGINX to attempt to send response headers in one packet, as well as sending a file in full packets.

Sample configuration

The following code is an example of an HTTP configuration section:

```
http {

    include      /opt/local/etc/nginx/mime.types;

    default_type application/octet-stream;
```

```
    sendfile on;

    tcp_nopush on;

    tcp_nodelay on;

    keepalive_timeout   65;

    server_names_hash_max_size 1024;

}
```

This context block would go after any global configuration directives in the `nginx.conf` file.

The virtual server section

Any context beginning with the keyword `server` is considered a virtual server section. It describes a logical separation of a set of resources that will be delivered under a different `server_name` directive. These virtual servers respond to the HTTP requests, and are contained within the `http` section.

A virtual server is defined by a combination of the `listen` and `server_name` directives. The `listen` directive defines an IP address/port combination or path to a UNIX-domain socket:

```
listen address[:port];
listen port;
listen unix:path;
```

The `listen` directive uniquely identifies a socket binding under NGINX. There are a number of optional parameters that `listen` can take:

The listen parameters	Explanation	Comments
default_server	This parameter defines this address/port combination as being the default value for the requests bound here.	
setfib	This parameter sets the corresponding FIB for the listening socket.	This parameter is only supported on FreeBSD and not for UNIX-domain sockets.

The listen parameters	Explanation	Comments
backlog	This parameter sets the backlog parameter in the listen() call.	This parameter defaults to -1 on FreeBSD and 511 on all other platforms.
rcvbuf	This parameter sets the SO_RCVBUF parameter on the listening socket.	
sndbuf	This parameter sets the SO_SNDBUF parameter on the listening socket.	
accept_filter	This parameter sets the name of the accept filter to either dataready or httpready.	This parameter is only supported on FreeBSD.
deferred	This parameter sets the TCP_DEFER_ACCEPT option to use a deferred accept() call.	This parameter is only supported on Linux.
bind	This parameter makes a separate bind() call for this address/port pair.	A separate bind() call will be made implicitly if any of the other socket-specific parameters are used.
ipv6only	This parameter sets the value of the IPV6_ONLY parameter.	This parameter can only be set on a fresh start and not for UNIX-domain sockets.
ssl	This parameter indicates that only the HTTPS connections will be made on this port.	This parameter allows for a more compact configuration.
so_keepalive	This parameter configures the TCP keepalive connection for the listening socket.	

The server_name directive is fairly straightforward and it can be used to solve a number of configuration problems. Its default value is "", which means that a server section without a server_name directive will match a request that has no Host header field set. This can be used, for example, to drop requests that lack this header:

```
server {

    listen 80;

    return 444;

}
```

The nonstandard HTTP code, `444`, used in this example will cause NGINX to immediately close the connection.

Besides a normal string, NGINX will accept a wildcard as a parameter to the `server_name` directive:

- The wildcard can replace the subdomain part: `*.example.com`
- The wildcard can replace the top-level domain part: `www.example.*`
- A special form will match the subdomain or the domain itself: `.example.com` (matches `*.example.com` as well as `example.com`)

A regular expression can also be used as a parameter to `server_name` by prepending the name with a tilde (~):

```
server_name ~^www\.example\.com$;
server_name ~^www(\d+).example\.(com)$;
```

The latter form is an example using captures, which can later be referenced (as `$1`, `$2`, and so on) in further configuration directives.

NGINX uses the following logic when determining which virtual server should serve a specific request:

1. Match the IP address and port to the `listen` directive.
2. Match the `Host` header field against the `server_name` directive as a string.
3. Match the `Host` header field against the `server_name` directive with a wildcard at the beginning of the string.
4. Match the `Host` header field against the `server_name` directive with a wildcard at the end of the string.
5. Match the `Host` header field against the `server_name` directive as a regular expression.

6. If all the `Host` headers match `fail`, direct to the `listen` directive marked as `default_server`.

7. If all the `Host` headers match `fail` and there is no `default_server`, direct to the first server with a `listen` directive that satisfies step 1.

This logic is expressed in the following flowchart:

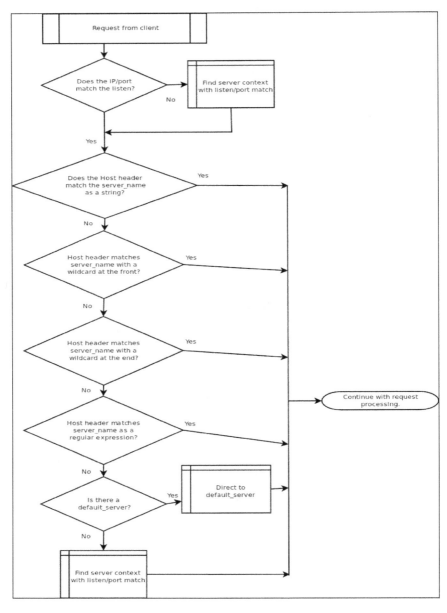

The `default_server` parameter can be used to handle requests that would otherwise go unhandled. It is therefore recommended to always set `default_server` explicitly so that these unhandled requests will be handled in a defined manner.

Besides this usage, `default_server` may also be helpful in configuring a number of virtual servers with the same `listen` directive. Any directives set here will be the same for all matching server blocks.

Locations – where, when, and how

The `location` directive may be used within a virtual server section and indicates a URI that comes either from the client or from an internal redirect. Locations may be nested with a few exceptions. They are used for processing requests with as specific configuration as possible.

A location is defined as follows:

```
location [modifier] uri {...}
```

Or it can be defined for a named location:

```
location @name {…}
```

A named location is only reachable from an internal redirect. It preserves the URI as it was before entering the location block. It may only be defined at the server context level.

The modifiers affect the processing of a location in the following way:

Location modifiers	Handling
=	This modifier uses exact match and terminate search.
~	This modifier uses case-sensitive regular expression matching.
~*	This modifier uses case-insensitive regular expression matching.
^~	This modifier stops processing before regular expressions are checked for a match of this location's string, if it's the most specific match. Note that this is not a regular expression match—its purpose is to preempt regular expression matching.

When a request comes in, the URI is checked against the most specific location as follows:

- Locations without a regular expression are searched for the most-specific match, independent of the order in which they are defined.
- Regular expressions are matched in the order in which they are found in the configuration file. The regular expression search is terminated on the first match. The mostspecific location match is then used for request processing.

The comparison match described here is against decoded URIs; for example, "a %20 in a URI" will match against a " " (space) specified in a location.

A named location may only be used by internally redirected requests.

The following directives are found only within a location:

Location-only directives	Explanation
alias	This directive defines another name for the location, as found on the filesystem. If the location is specified with a regular expression, alias should reference captures defined in that regular expression. The alias directive replaces the part of the URI matched by the location so that the rest of the URI not matched will be searched for in that filesystem location. Using the alias directive is fragile when moving bits of the configuration around, so using the root directive is preferred, unless the URI needs to be modified in order to find the file.
internal	This directive specifies a location that can only be used for internal requests (redirects defined in other directives, rewrite requests, error pages, and so on).
limit_except	This directive limits a location to the specified HTTP verb(s) (GET also includes HEAD).

Additionally, a number of directives found in the http section may also be specified in a location. Refer to *Appendix A*, *Directive Reference*, for a complete list.

The `try_files` directive deserves a special mention here. It may also be used in a server context, but will most often be found in a location. The `try_files` directive will do just that—try files in the order given as parameters; the first match wins. It is often used to match potential files from a variable and then pass processing to a named location, as shown in the following example:

```
location / {

    try_files $uri $uri/ @mongrel;

}
location @mongrel {
    proxy_pass http://appserver;

}
```

Here, an implicit directory index is tried if the given URI is not found as a file and then processing is passed on to `appserver` via a proxy. We will explore how best to use `location`, `try_files`, and `proxy_pass` to solve specific problems throughout the rest of the book.

Locations may be nested except in the following situations:

- When the prefix is =
- When the location is a named location

Best practice dictates that regular expression locations be nested inside the string-based locations. An example of this is as follows:

```
# first, we enter through the root
location / {

    # then we find a most-specific substring
    # note that this is not a regular expression
    location ^~ /css {

        # here is the regular expression that then gets matched
        location ~* /css/.*\.css$ {

        }

    }

}
```

Full sample configuration

What follows is a sample configuration file, including the different sections discussed in this chapter. Please note that this should not be copy-pasted and used as-is. It will most likely not fit your needs. This code is shown here only to give an idea of the structure of a complete configuration file:

```
user www;

worker_processes 12;

error_log /var/log/nginx/error.log;

pid /var/run/nginx.pid;

events {

    use /dev/poll;

    worker_connections  2048;

}
http {

    include       /opt/local/etc/nginx/mime.types;

    default_type  application/octet-stream;

    sendfile on;

    tcp_nopush on;

    tcp_nodelay on;

    keepalive_timeout  65;

    server_names_hash_max_size 1024;

    server {

        listen 80;

        return 444;

    }
```

```
server {

    listen 80;

    server_name www.example.com;

    location / {

        try_files $uri $uri/ @mongrel;

    }

    location @mongrel {

        proxy_pass http://127.0.0.1:8080;

    }

}

}
```

Summary

In this chapter, we saw how a NGINX configuration file is built. Its modular nature is a reflection, in part, of the modularity of NGINX itself. A global configuration block is responsible for all aspects that affect the running of NGINX as a whole. There is a separate configuration section for each protocol that NGINX is responsible for handling. We may further define how each request is to be handled by specifying servers within those protocol configuration contexts (either http or mail) so that requests are routed to a specific IP address/port. Within the http context, locations are then used to match the URI of the request. These locations may be nested, or otherwise ordered to ensure that requests get routed to the right areas of the filesystem or application server.

What we did not cover in this chapter are the configuration options provided by the various modules that may be compiled into your nginx binary. These additional directives will be touched upon throughout the book, as that particular module is used to solve a problem. Also absent was an explanation of the variables that NGINX makes available for its configuration. These too will be discussed later in this book. This chapter's focus was on the basics of configuring NGINX.

In the next chapter, we will explore configuring NGINX's mail module to enable e-mail proxying.

3
Using the mail Module

NGINX was designed not only to serve web traffic, but also to provide a means of proxying e-mail services. In this chapter, you will learn how to configure NGINX as an e-mail proxy for POP3, IMAP, and SMTP services. The mail module is useful to those who need to accept a lot of connections, but the backend mailbox infrastructure either isn't capable of handling the load or needs to be protected from direct access to the Internet. The chapter also covers topics such as the authentication service, caching, and interpreting log files, that are of general use, even if an e-mail service doesn't fit your needs.

We will examine running NGINX as a mail proxy server in the following sections:

* Basic proxy service
* Authentication service
* Combining with memcached
* Interpreting log files
* Operating system limits

Basic proxy service

The NGINX mail proxy module was originally developed for FastMail. They needed to provide a single IMAP endpoint for their users, while hosting the actual e-mail account on one of the number of upstream mail servers. Typical proxying programs of the time used the classic Unix forking model, which meant that a new process was forked for each connection. IMAP has very long-lived connections, which means that these processes would stay around for a very long time. This would then lead to very sluggish proxy servers, as they would have to manage these processes for the lifetime of each connection. NGINX's event-based process model was a better fit for this type of service. As an e-mail proxy, NGINX is able to direct traffic to any number of mailbox servers where the actual e-mail account is hosted. This provides the ability to communicate one endpoint to customers, while scaling the number of mailbox servers up with the number of users. Both commercial and opensource e-mail solutions, such as Atmail and Zimbra, are built around this model.

The following diagram will help visualize how this works:

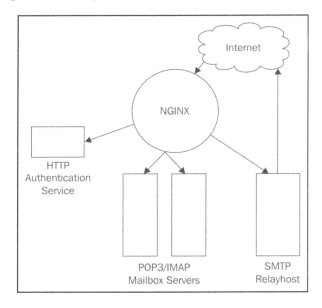

An incoming request will be handled on a per-protocol basis. The mail proxy module may be configured differently for POP3, IMAP, or SMTP. For each protocol, NGINX queries an authentication service with the username and password. If the authentication is successful, the connection is proxied to the mail server indicated in the response from the authentication service. If the authentication was unsuccessful, the client connection is terminated. The authentication service thus determines which clients can use the POP3/IMAP/SMTP services and which mail server they may use. As any number of the mail servers may be handled in this way, NGINX can provide a proxy service for all of them through one central gateway.

A proxy acts on behalf of someone or something else. In this case, NGINX is acting on behalf of the e-mail client, terminating the connection and opening a new one to the upstream server. This means that there is no direct communication between the e-mail client and the actual mailbox server or SMTP relay host.

If there are any e-mail rules based on information contained in the client connection, these rules will not work, unless the e-mail software is able to support an extension, such as XCLIENT for SMTP.

This is an important point in designing an architecture that contains a proxy server — the proxy host will need to be able to support more connections than a typical upstream server. Not as much processing power or memory as a mailbox server would be needed, but the number of persistent connections needs to be taken into account.

The mail server configuration section

The mail server section, or the e-mail configuration context, is available only if you've built NGINX with the mail module (--with-mail). This section controls all aspects of working with the mail module.

The mail module allows for configuration directives that affect all aspects of proxying e-mail connections, as well as for specifying them per server. The server context also accepts the listen and server_name directives that we saw under the http server section in the previous chapter.

NGINX can proxy the IMAP, POP3, and SMTP protocols. The following table lists the directives that are available to this module:

The mail module directives	Explanation
auth_http	This directive specifies the server used for authenticating the POP3/IMAP user. The functionality of this server will be discussed in detail in this chapter.
imap_capabilities	This directive indicates the IMAP4 capabilities that are supported by the backend server.
pop3_capabilities	This directive indicates the POP3 capabilities that are supported by the backend server.
protocol	This directive indicates the protocol that is supported by this virtual server context.
proxy	This directive will simply enable or disable e-mail proxying.
proxy_buffer	This directive allows setting the size of the buffer used for the proxy connection beyond the default of one page.
proxy_pass_error_message	This directive is useful in situations where the backend authentication process emits a useful error message to the client.
proxy_timeout	If a timeout beyond the default of 24 hours is required, this directive can be used.
xclient	The SMTP protocol allows checking based on IP/HELO/LOGIN parameters, which are passed via the XCLIENT command. This directive enables NGINX to communicate this information.

If NGINX was compiled with the SSL support (--with-mail_ssl_module), the following directives will be available in addition to the previous ones:

Mail SSL directives	Explanation
ssl	This directive indicates if this context should support the SSL transactions.
ssl_certificate	This directive specifies the path to the PEM-encoded SSL certificate(s) for this virtual server.
ssl_certificate_key	This directive specifies the path to the PEM-encoded SSL secret key for this virtual server.
ssl_ciphers	This directive specifies the ciphers that should be supported in this virtual server context (the OpenSSL format).

Mail SSL directives	Explanation
ssl_prefer_server_ciphers	This directive indicates that the SSLv3 and TLSv1 server ciphers are preferred over the client's ciphers.
ssl_protocols	This directive indicates which SSL protocols should be enabled.
ssl_session_cache	This directive specifies an SSL cache, and whether or not it should be shared among all worker processes.
ssl_session_timeout	This directive specifies how long the client can use the same SSL parameters, provided they are stored in the cache.

POP3 service

The **Post Office Protocol (POP3)** is an Internet standard protocol used to retrieve e-mail messages from a mailbox server. The current incarnation of the protocol is Version 3, thus POP3. The e-mail clients will typically retrieve all new messages on a mailbox server in one session, and then close the connection. After closing, the mailbox server will delete all messages that have been marked as retrieved.

In order for NGINX to act as a POP3 proxy, some basic directives need to be configured:

```
mail {
  auth_http localhost:9000/auth;

  server {
    listen 110;
    protocol pop3;
    proxy on;
  }
}
```

This configuration snippet enables the `mail` module and configures it for the POP3 service, querying an authentication service running on port 9000 on the same machine. NGINX will listen on port 110 on all local IP addresses, providing a POP3 proxy service. You will note that we do not configure the actual `mail` servers here—it is the job of the authentication service to tell NGINX which server a particular client should be connected to.

If your `mail` server only supports certain capabilities (or you only want to advertise certain capabilities), NGINX is flexible enough to announce these:

```
mail {
  pop3_capabilities TOP USER;
}
```

Capabilities are a way of advertising support for optional commands. For POP3, the client can request the supported capabilities before or after authentication, so it is important to configure these correctly in NGINX.

You may also specify which authentication methods are supported:

```
mail {
  pop3_auth apop cram-md5;
}
```

If the APOP authentication method is supported, the authentication service needs to provide NGINX with the user's password in clear text so that it can generate the MD5 digest.

IMAP service

The **Internet Message Access Protocol (IMAP)** is also an Internet-standard protocol used to retrieve the e-mail messages from a mailbox server. It provides quite a bit of extended functionality over the earlier POP protocol. Typical usage leaves all messages on the server, so that multiple e-mail clients can access the same mailbox. This also means that there may be many more persistent connections to an upstream mailbox server from clients using IMAP than those using POP3.

To proxy the IMAP connections, a configuration similar to the POP3 NGINX snippet used before can be used:

```
mail {
  auth_http localhost:9000/auth;

  imap_capabilities IMAP4rev1 UIDPLUS QUOTA;
  imap_auth login cram-md5;

  server {
    listen 143;
    protocol imap;
    proxy on;
  }
}
```

Note that we did not need to specify the `protocol` directive, as `imap` is the default value. It is included here for clarity.

The `imap_capabilities` and `imap_auth` directives function similarly to their POP3 counterparts.

SMTP service

The **Simple Mail Transport Protocol (SMTP)** is the Internet standard protocol for transferring the e-mail messages from one server to another or from a client to a server. Although authentication was not at first conceived for this protocol, `smtp_auth` is supported as an extension.

As you have seen, the logic of configuring the `mail` module is fairly straightforward. This holds for SMTP proxying as well:

```
mail {
  auth_http localhost:9000/auth;

  smtp_capabilities PIPELINING 8BITMIME DSN;
  smtp_auth login cram-md5;

  server {
    listen 25;
    protocol smtp;
    proxy on;
  }
}
```

Our proxy server will only advertise `smtp_capabilities` that we set; otherwise, it will only list which authentication mechanisms it accepts, because the list of extensions is sent to the client when it sends the `HELO`/`EHLO` command. This may be useful when proxying to the multiple SMTP servers, each having different capabilities. You could configure NGINX to list only the capabilities that all of these servers have in common. It is important to set these to only the extensions that the SMTP server itself supports.

Due to `smtp_auth` being an extension to SMTP, and not necessarily supported in every configuration, NGINX is capable of proxying an SMTP connection that does no authentication whatsoever. In this case, only the `HELO`, `MAIL FROM`, and `RCPT TO` parts of the protocol are available to the authentication service for determining which upstream should be chosen for a given client connection. For this setup, ensure that the `smtp_auth` directive is set to `none`.

Using SSL/TLS

If your organization requires e-mail traffic to be encrypted, or if you yourself want more security in your e-mail transfers, you can enable NGINX to use TLS to provide POP3 over SSL, IMAP over SSL, or SMTP over SSL. To enable TLS support, either set the `starttls` directive to `on` for the STLS/STARTTLS support or set the `ssl` directive to `on` for the pure SSL/TLS support and configure the appropriate `ssl_*` directives for your site:

```
mail {
    # allow STLS for POP3 and STARTTLS for IMAP and SMTP
    starttls on;
    # prefer the server's list of ciphers, so that we may determine
      security
    ssl_prefer_server_ciphers on;
    # use only these protocols
    ssl_protocols TLSv1 SSLv3;
    # use only high encryption cipher suites, excluding those
    # using anonymous DH and MD5, sorted by strength
    ssl_ciphers HIGH:!ADH:!MD5:@STRENGTH;
    # use a shared SSL session cache, so that all workers can
    # use the same cache
    ssl_session_cache shared:MAIL:10m;
    # certificate and key for this host
    ssl_certificate /usr/local/etc/nginx/mail.example.com.crt;
    ssl_certificate_key /usr/local/etc/nginx/mail.example.com.key;
}
```

Navigate to `https://www.fastmail.fm/help/technology_ssl_vs_tls_starttls.html` for a description of the differences between a pure SSL/TLS connection and upgrading a plain connection to an encrypted one with SSL/TLS.

Using OpenSSL to generate an SSL certificate

If you have never generated an SSL certificate before, the following steps will help you create one.

Create a certificate request:

```
$ openssl req -newkey rsa:2048 -nodes -out mail.example.
com.csr -keyout mail.example.com.key
```

This command should generate the following output:

```
Generating a 2048 bit RSA private key
.........................................................
.......................................................++
+
...................+++
writing new private key to 'mail.example.com.key'
-----
You are about to be asked to enter information that will be
incorporated
into your certificate request.
What you are about to enter is what is called a
Distinguished Name or a DN.
There are quite a few fields but you can leave some blank
For some fields there will be a default value,
If you enter '.', the field will be left blank.
-----
Country Name (2 letter code) [AU]:CH
State or Province Name (full name) [Some-State]:Zurich
Locality Name (eg, city) []:ZH
Organization Name (eg, company) [Internet Widgits Pty
Ltd]:Example Company
Organizational Unit Name (eg, section) []:
Common Name (e.g. server FQDN or YOUR name) []:mail.example.
com
Email Address []:
Please enter the following 'extra' attributes
to be sent with your certificate request
A challenge password []:
An optional company name []:
```

You can get this certificate signing request (mail.example.com.csr) signed by a certificate authority, such as Verisign or GoDaddy, or you can sign it yourself:

```
$ openssl x509 -req -days 365 -in mail.example.com.csr
-signkey mail.example.com.key -out mail.example.com.crt
```

You will see the following response:

```
Signature ok
subject=/C=CH/ST=Zurich/L=ZH/O=Example Company/CN=mail.
example.com
Getting Private key
```

Please note, though, that a self-signed certificate will generate an error in a client that connects to your server. If you are deploying this certificate on a production server, make sure that you get it signed by a recognized authority.

The signed certificate is shown in the following screenshot:

```
-----BEGIN CERTIFICATE-----
MIIDPDCCAiQCCQDdPKFcY1X35jANBgkqhkiG9w0BAQUFADBgMQswCQYDVQQGEwJD
SDEPMA0GA1UECAwGWnVyaWNoMQswCQYDVQQHDAJaSDEYMBYGA1UECgwPRXhhbXBs
ZSBDb21wYW55MRkwFwYDVQQDDBBtYWlsLmV4YW1wbGUuY29tMB4XDTEyMDgzMTE0
MjczMloXDTEzMDgzMTE0MjczMlowYDELMAkGA1UEBhMCQ0gxDzANBgNVBAgMBlp1
cmljaDELMAkGA1UEBwwCWkgxGDAWBgNVBAoMD0V4YW1wbGUgQ29tcGFueTEZMBcG
A1UEAwwQbWFpbC5leGFtcGxlLmNvbTCCASIwDQYJKoZIhvcNAQEBBQADggEPADCC
AQoCggEBAN8WUGzQIKR+iuTxtLPko/zSR+DbjDYqbMo4PdNvEN46nTFMkktvOsIk
1kfk9l2jzVcmUUSZayLp3woDgxRpkpQ5eRpB7yeifsZwPJlXfVPTgfXtQkktfPVn
uz0Mf7Ogd2Xt8uI6n0AtODAr8+CxebIpRwIwZBXPrWwFFjQvy4/qD7EXs33+x5U8
9CMxkGo2FPqCSYE39jN3JtIZ9YibnZh01NALHRvnqyw3mdzR340mu5WNFjl/NElp
M0yFL7+5wzI4ktgmAo+Mic6JnXC0bSjrL1xZjWfn/5TQiYQVzUit4jd1CswWtCHw
tv67TRQ3edgvssvzfZlm7QfBbdYGjkUCAwEAATANBgkqhkiG9w0BAQUFAAOCAQEA
TDfdngMRk2w/1KCGbxrg9bVmfKXUSIfpWyt0hG02EtLx83TZajqwtOKhmPh9Q/lc
GZdF1PGscdJ2Bc0eJBUGyt6mevEi2Dg4h727yVvnacnViQvzyLxQgmeC5rDEj4EC
yDzzi4n0I/rddjPeQO+cMFHz26scsKYoRemzp0yHT8JhK8AF2iOioLzwaMqxC+ll
U7lkinHdTaG6nT4WpH05HtSBno8Xco/ujY6xIrShiP0naOd/B4TRCmB96KYhyMdd
AyrOZgLqsskKeAlnmuSJA/7zbplLwHarvUVFpzKed73554lfJ5kpyOciHrIfyj/2
dM/tjsDVjpE2B/meYBx8Kg==
-----END CERTIFICATE-----
```

Complete mail example

The e-mail services are often combined on one gateway. The following configuration will enable NGINX to service POP3, IMAP, and SMTP traffic (as well as their encrypted variants) from one authentication service, while offering clients the option to use STLS/STARTTLS on unencrypted ports:

```
events {
  worker_connections 1024;
}

mail {
  server_name mail.example.com;
  auth_http localhost:9000/auth;

  proxy on;
```

```
ssl_prefer_server_ciphers on;
ssl_protocols TLSv1 SSLv3;
ssl_ciphers HIGH:!ADH:!MD5:@STRENGTH;
ssl_session_cache shared:MAIL:10m;
ssl_certificate /usr/local/etc/nginx/mail.example.com.crt;
ssl_certificate_key /usr/local/etc/nginx/mail.example.com.key;

pop3_capabilities TOP USER;
imap_capabilities IMAP4rev1 UIDPLUS QUOTA;
smtp_capabilities PIPELINING 8BITMIME DSN;

pop3_auth apop cram-md5;
imap_auth login cram-md5;
smtp_auth login cram-md5;

server {
  listen 25;
  protocol smtp;
  timeout 120000;
}
server {
  listen 465;
  protocol smtp;
  ssl on;
}
server {
  listen 587;
  protocol smtp;
  starttls on;
}
server {
  listen 110;
  protocol pop3;
  starttls on;
}
server {
  listen 995;
  protocol pop3;
  ssl on;
}
server {
  listen 143;
  protocol imap;
  starttls on;
```

```
    }
  server {
    listen 993;
    protocol imap;
    ssl on;
  }
}
```

As you can see, we declared the name of this server at the top of the `mail` context. This is because we want each of our e-mail services to be addressed as `mail.example.com`. Even if the actual hostname of the machine on which NGINX runs is different, and each `mail` server has its own hostname, we want this proxy to be a single point of reference for our users. This hostname will in turn be used wherever NGINX needs to present its own name, for example, in the initial SMTP server greeting.

The `timeout` directive was used in the `smtp` server context in order to double its default value because we knew this particular upstream SMTP relay host inserted an artificial delay in order to dissuade spammers from trying to send e-mails via this server.

Authentication service

We mentioned the authentication service quite a few times in the previous section, but what exactly is the authentication service and what does it do? When a user makes a POP3, IMAP, or SMTP request to NGINX, authenticating the connection is one of the first steps. NGINX does not perform this authentication itself, but rather makes a query to an authentication service that will fulfill the request. NGINX then uses the response from the authentication service to make the connection to the upstream `mail` server.

This authentication service may be written in any language. It need only conform to the authentication protocol required by NGINX. The protocol is similar to HTTP, so it will be fairly easy for us to write our own authentication service.

NGINX will send the following headers in its request to the authentication service:

- Host
- Auth-Method
- Auth-User
- Auth-Pass
- Auth-Salt
- Auth-Protocol

- Auth-Login-Attempt
- Client-IP
- Client-Host
- Auth-SMTP-Helo
- Auth-SMTP-From
- Auth-SMTP-To

The meaning of each of these headers should be fairly self-explanatory, and not each header will be present in every request. We will go over these as we write our authentication service.

We choose Ruby as the language for this authentication service implementation. If you do not currently have Ruby installed, don't worry about doing so now. Ruby as a language is very clear to read, so just try to follow along with the commented code below. Adapting it to your environment and running it is outside the scope of this book. This example will give you a good starting point in writing your own authentication service.

 A good resource to help you get Ruby installed easily is located at https://rvm.io.

Let us first examine the request part of the HTTP request/response dialogue.

We first collect the values we need from the headers NGINX sends:

```ruby
# the authentication mechanism
meth = @env['HTTP_AUTH_METHOD']
# the username (login)
user = @env['HTTP_AUTH_USER']
# the password, either in the clear or encrypted,
  depending on the
# authentication mechanism used
pass = @env['HTTP_AUTH_PASS']
# need the salt to encrypt the cleartext password, used for some
# authentication mechanisms, not in our example
salt = @env['HTTP_AUTH_SALT']
# this is the protocol being proxied
proto = @env['HTTP_AUTH_PROTOCOL']
# the number of attempts needs to be an integer
attempt = @env['HTTP_AUTH_LOGIN_ATTEMPT'].to_i
# not used in our implementation, but these are
  here for reference
client = @env['HTTP_CLIENT_IP']
host = @env['HTTP_CLIENT_HOST']
```

What are all these @ symbols about?

The @ symbol is used in Ruby to denote a class variable. We'll use them in our example to make it easier to pass around variables. In the preceding snippet, we are referencing the environment (@env) as passed into the Rack request. Besides all the HTTP headers that we need, the environment contains additional information relating to how the service is being run.

Now that we know how to handle each of the headers NGINX may send, we need to do something with them and send NGINX a response. The following headers are expected in the response from the authentication service:

- Auth-Status: In this header, anything but OK is an error
- Auth-Server: This header is the IP address to which the connection is proxied
- Auth-Port: This header is the port to which the connection is proxied
- Auth-User: This header is the user that will be used to authenticate with the mail server
- Auth-Pass: This header is the plaintext password used for APOP
- Auth-Wait: This header tells how many seconds to wait before another authentication attempt is made
- Auth-Error-Code: This header is an alternative error code to return to the client

The three headers used most often are Auth-Status, Auth-Server, and Auth-Port. The presence of these in a response is typically all that is needed for a successful authentication session.

As we will see in the following snippet, additional headers may be used, depending on the situation. The response itself consists of simply emitting the relevant headers with the appropriate values substituted in.

We first check if there have been too many tries:

```
# fail if more than the maximum login attempts are tried
if attempt > @max_attempts
@res["Auth-Status"] = "Maximum login attempts exceeded"
return
end
```

Then, we return the appropriate headers and set the values obtained from our authentication mechanism:

```
@res["Auth-Status"] = "OK"
@res["Auth-Server"] = @mailhost
# return the correct port for this protocol
@res["Auth-Port"] = MailAuth::Port[proto]
# if we're using APOP, we need to return the password in
  cleartext
if meth == 'apop' && proto == 'pop3'
@res["Auth-User"] = user
@res["Auth-Pass"] = pass
end
```

If the authentication check has failed, we need to tell NGINX:

```
# if authentication was unsuccessful, we return an appropriate
  response
@res["Auth-Status"] = "Invalid login or password"
# and set the wait time in seconds before the client may make
# another authentication attempt
@res["Auth-Wait"] = "3"
# we can also set the error code to be returned
  to the SMTP client
@res["Auth-Error-Code"] = "535 5.7.8"
```

Not every header is required in the response, but as we can see, some are dependent on the status of the authentication query and/or any error condition that may exist.

> One interesting use of the Auth-User header is to return a different username than the one given in the request. This can prove useful, for example, when migrating from an older upstream mail server that accepted a username without the domain to a newer upstream mail server that requires the username to have a domain. NGINX will then use this username when connecting to the upstream server.

The authentication database may take any form, from a flat text file, to an LDAP directory, to a relational database. It does not have to necessarily be the same store that your e-mail service uses to access this information, but should be in sync with that store to prevent any errors due to stale data.

Our example authentication database is a simple hash for this example:

```
@auths = { "test:1234" => '127.0.1.1' }
```

The mechanism used to verify a user is a simple hash lookup:

```
# this simply returns the value looked-up by the 'user:pass' key
if @auths.key?("#{user}:#{pass}")
@mailhost = @auths["#{user}:#{pass}"]
return true
# if there is no such key, the method returns false
else
return false
end
```

Tying these three parts together, we have the complete authentication service:

```
#!/usr/bin/env rackup

# This is a basic HTTP server, conforming to the authentication
  protocol
# required by NGINX's mail module.
#
require 'logger'
require 'rack'

module MailAuth

# setup a protocol-to-port mapping
Port = {
  'smtp' => '25',
  'pop3' => '110',
  'imap' => '143'
}

class Handler

def initialize
# setup logging, as a mail service
@log = Logger.new("| logger -p mail.info")
# replacing the normal timestamp by the service name and pid
@log.datetime_format = "nginx_mail_proxy_auth pid: "
# the "Auth-Server" header must be an IP address
@mailhost = '127.0.0.1'
# set a maximum number of login attempts
@max_attempts = 3
# our authentication 'database' will just be a fixed hash for
  # this example
```

```
  # it should be replaced by a method to connect to LDAP or a
    # database
  @auths = { "test:1234" => '127.0.1.1' }
  end
```

After the preceding setup and module initialization, we tell `Rack` (the middleware server we're using to run this service) which requests we would like to have handled and define a `get` method to respond to requests from NGINX:

```
def call(env)
# our headers are contained in the environment
@env = env
# set up the request and response objects
@req = Rack::Request.new(env)
@res = Rack::Response.new
# pass control to the method named after the HTTP verb
# with which we're called
self.send(@req.request_method.downcase)
# come back here to finish the response when done
@res.finish
end

def get
# the authentication mechanism
meth = @env['HTTP_AUTH_METHOD']
# the username (login)
user = @env['HTTP_AUTH_USER']
# the password, either in the clear or encrypted, depending on
# the authentication mechanism used
pass = @env['HTTP_AUTH_PASS']
# need the salt to encrypt the cleartext password, used for some
# authentication mechanisms, not in our example
salt = @env['HTTP_AUTH_SALT']
# this is the protocol being proxied
proto = @env['HTTP_AUTH_PROTOCOL']
# the number of attempts needs to be an integer
attempt = @env['HTTP_AUTH_LOGIN_ATTEMPT'].to_i
# not used in our implementation, but these are here for
  reference
client = @env['HTTP_CLIENT_IP']
host = @env['HTTP_CLIENT_HOST']

# fail if more than the maximum login attempts are tried
if attempt > @max_attempts
```

```
@res["Auth-Status"] = "Maximum login attempts exceeded"
return
end


# for the special case where no authentication is done
# on smtp transactions, the following is in nginx.conf:
# smtp_auth none;
# may want to setup a lookup table to steer certain senders
# to particular SMTP servers
if meth == 'none' && proto == 'smtp'
helo = @env['HTTP_AUTH_SMTP_HELO']
# want to get just the address from these two here
from = @env['HTTP_AUTH_SMTP_FROM'].split(/: /)[1]
to = @env['HTTP_AUTH_SMTP_TO'].split(/: /)[1]
@res["Auth-Status"] = "OK"
@res["Auth-Server"] = @mailhost
# return the correct port for this protocol
@res["Auth-Port"] = MailAuth::Port[proto]
@log.info("a mail from #{from} on #{helo} for #{to}")
# try to authenticate using the headers provided
elsif auth(user, pass)
@res["Auth-Status"] = "OK"
@res["Auth-Server"] = @mailhost
# return the correct port for this protocol
@res["Auth-Port"] = MailAuth::Port[proto]
# if we're using APOP, we need to return the password in
  cleartext
if meth == 'apop' && proto == 'pop3'
@res["Auth-User"] = user
@res["Auth-Pass"] = pass
end
@log.info("+ #{user} from #{client}")
# the authentication attempt has failed
else
# if authentication was unsuccessful, we return an appropriate
  response
@res["Auth-Status"] = "Invalid login or password"
# and set the wait time in seconds before the client may make
# another authentication attempt
@res["Auth-Wait"] = "3"
# we can also set the error code to be returned to the SMTP
  client
@res["Auth-Error-Code"] = "535 5.7.8"
@log.info("! #{user} from #{client}")
end


end
```

The next section is declared `private` so that only this class may use the methods declared afterwards. The `auth` method is the workhorse of the authentication service, checking the username and password for validity. The `method_missing` method is there to handle invalid methods, responding with a `Not Found` error message:

```
private

# our authentication method, adapt to fit your environment
def auth(user, pass)
# this simply returns the value looked-up by the 'user:pass' key
if @auths.key?("#{user}:#{pass}")
@mailhost = @auths["#{user}:#{pass}"]
return @mailhost
# if there is no such key, the method returns false
else
return false
end
end


# just in case some other process tries to access the service
# and sends something other than a GET
def method_missing(env)
@res.status = 404
end


end # class MailAuthHandler
end # module MailAuth
```

This last section sets up the server to run and routes the `/auth` URI to the proper handler:

```
# setup Rack middleware
use Rack::ShowStatus
# map the /auth URI to our authentication handler
map "/auth" do
run MailAuth::Handler.new
end
```

This listing may be saved as a file, `nginx_mail_proxy_auth.ru`, and called with a `-p <port>` parameter to tell it on which port it should run. For more options and more information about the `Rack` web server interface, visit `https://rack.github.io`.

Combining with memcached

Depending on the frequency of clients accessing the e-mail services on your proxy and how many resources are available to the authentication service, you may want to introduce a caching layer into the setup. To this end, we will integrate memcached as an in-memory store for authentication information.

NGINX can look up a key in memcached, but only in the context of a location in the http module. Therefore, we will have to implement our own caching layer outside of NGINX.

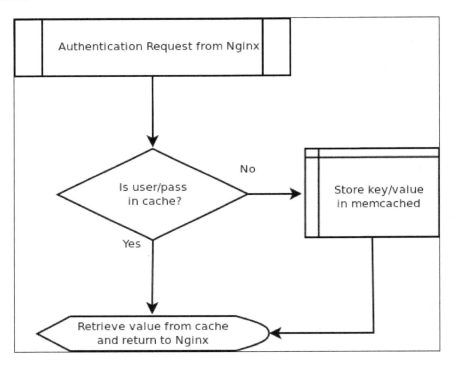

As the flowchart shows, we will first check whether or not this username/password combination is already in the cache. If not, we will query our authentication store for the information and place the key/value pair into the cache. If it is, we can retrieve this information directly from the cache.

 Zimbra has created a memcache module for NGINX that takes care of this directly within the context of NGINX. To date, though, this code has not been integrated into the official NGINX sources.

The following code will extend our original authentication service by implementing a caching layer (admittedly, a little overkill for our implementation, but this is to provide a basis for working with a networked authentication database):

```
# gem install memcached (depends on libsasl2 and gettext
  libraries)
require 'memcached'

# set this to the IP address/port where you have memcached running
@cache = Memcached.new("localhost:11211")

def get_cache_value(user, pass)
resp = ''
begin
# first, let's see if our key is already in the cache
resp = @cache.get("#{user}:#{pass}")
rescue Memcached::NotFound
# it's not in the cache, so let's call the auth method
resp = auth(user, pass)
# and now store the response in the cache, keyed on 'user:pass'
@cache.set("#{user}:#{pass}",resp)
end
# explicitly returning the response to the caller
return resp
end
```

In order to use this code, you will of course have to install and run memcached. There should be a prebuilt package for your operating system:

- Linux (deb-based)

  ```
  sudo apt-get install memcached
  ```

- Linux (rpm-based)

  ```
  sudo yum install memcached
  ```

- FreeBSD

  ```
  sudo pkg_add -r memcached
  ```

The memcached command is configured simply by passing parameters to the binary when running it. There is no configuration file that is read directly, although your operating system and/or packaging manager may provide a file that is parsed to make passing these parameters easier.

The most important parameters for memcached are as follows:

- -l: This parameter specifies the address(es) on which memcached will listen (default is all). It is important to note that for the greatest security, memcached shouldn't listen on an address that is reachable from the Internet because there is no authentication.

- -m: This parameter specifies the amount of RAM to use for the cache (in megabytes).

- -c: This parameter specifies the maximum number of simultaneous connections (default is 1024).

- -p: This parameter specifies the port on which memcached will listen (default is 11211).

Setting these parameters to reasonable values will be all you need to do to get memcached up and running.

Now, by substituting the elsif auth(user, pass) with elsif get_cache_value(user, pass) in our nginx_mail_proxy_auth.ru service, you should have an authentication service running with a caching layer, to help serve as many requests as quickly as possible.

Interpreting log files

The log files provide some of the best clues as to what is going on when a system doesn't act as expected. Depending on the verbosity level configured and whether or not NGINX was compiled with debugging support (--enable-debug), the log files will help you understand what is going on in a particular session.

Each line in the error log corresponds to a particular log level, configured using the error_log directive. The different levels are debug, info, notice, warn, error, crit, alert, and emerg, in order of increasing severity. Configuring a particular level will include messages for all of the more severe levels above it. The default log level is error.

In the context of the mail module, we would typically want to configure a log level of info so that we can get as much information about a particular session as possible without having to configure debug logging. Debug logging, in this case, would be useful only for following function entry points, or seeing what password was used for a particular connection.

Since e-mail is extremely dependent upon a correctly-functioning DNS, many errors can be traced back to invalid DNS entries or expired cache information. If you believe you may have a case that could be explained by a name resolution error, you can get NGINX to tell you what IP address a particular hostname is resolved to by configuring debug logging. Unfortunately, this requires a recompile if your `nginx` binary was not initially compiled with debugging support.

A typical proxy connection is logged, as in the following example of a POP3 session.

First, the client establishes a connection to the proxy:

```
<timestamp> [info] <worker pid>#0: *<connection id> client <ip address>
connected to 0.0.0.0:110
```

Then, once the client has completed a successful login, a statement listing all relevant connection information is logged:

```
<timestamp> [info] <worker pid>#0: *<connection id> client logged in,
client: <ip address>, server: 0.0.0.0:110, login: "<username>", upstream:
<upstream ip>:<upstream port>, [<client ip>:<client port>-<local ip>:110]
<=> [<local ip:<high port>-<upstream ip>:<upstream port>]
```

You will note that the section before the double arrows, `<=>`, relates to the client-to-proxy side of the connection, whereas the section after the double arrows describes the proxy-to-upstream part of the connection. This information is again repeated once the session is terminated:

```
<timestamp> [info] <worker pid>#0: *<connection id> proxied session done,
client: <ip address>, server: 0.0.0.0:110, login: "<username>", upstream:
<upstream ip>:<upstream port>, [<client ip>:<client port>-<local ip>:110]
<=> [<local ip:<high port>-<upstream ip>:<upstream port>]
```

In this way, we see the ports that are in use on all sides of the connection, to help debug any potential problems or to perhaps correlate the log entry with what may appear in a firewall log.

Other log entries at the `info` level pertain to timeouts or invalid commands/responses sent by either the client or upstream.

Entries at the `warn` log level are typically configuration errors:

```
<timestamp> [warn] <worker pid>#0: *<connection id> "starttls" directive
conflicts with "ssl on"
```

Many errors that are reported at the `error` log level are indicative of problems with the authentication service. You will note the text `while in http auth state` in the following entries. This shows where in the connection state the error has occurred:

```
<timestamp> [error] <worker pid>#0: *<connection id> auth http server
127.0.0.1:9000 timed out while in http auth state, client: <client ip>,
server: 0.0.0.0:25
```

```
<timestamp> [error] <worker pid>#0: *<connection id> auth http server
127.0.0.1:9000 sent invalid response while in http auth state, client:
<client ip>, server: 0.0.0.0:25
```

If the authentication query is not successfully answered for any reason, the connection is terminated. NGINX doesn't know to which upstream the client should be proxied, and therefore closes the connection with an `Internal server error` with the protocol-specific response code.

Depending on whether or not the username is present, the information will appear in the log file. Here's an entry from an authenticated SMTP connection:

```
<timestamp> [error] <worker pid>#0: *<connection id> auth http server
127.0.0.1:9000 did not send server or port while in http auth state,
client: <client ip>, server: 0.0.0.0:25, login: "<login>"
```

Note that the previous two entries are missing in the `login` information.

An `alert` log level event will indicate that NGINX was not able to set a parameter as expected, but will otherwise operate normally.

Any log entry at the `emerg` level, however, will prevent NGINX from starting: either the situation has to be corrected or the configuration must be changed. If NGINX is already running, it will not restart any worker process until the change has been made:

```
<timestamp> [error] <worker pid>#0: *<connection id> no "http_auth" is
defined for server in /opt/nginx/conf/nginx.conf:32
```

Here we need to define an authentication service using the `http_auth` directive.

Operating system limits

You may run into a situation in which NGINX does not perform as you expect. Either connections are being dropped or warning messages are printed in the log file. This is when it is important to know what limits your operating system may place on NGINX and how to tune them to get the best performance out of your server.

The area in which an e-mail proxy is most likely to run into problems is a connection limit. To understand what this means, you first have to know how NGINX handles client connections. The NGINX master process starts a number of workers, each of which runs as a separate process. Each process is able to handle a fixed number of connections, set by the `worker_connections` directive. For each proxied connection, NGINX opens a new connection to the `mail` server. Each of these connections requires a file descriptor and for each `mail` server IP/port combination, a new TCP port is required from the ephemeral port range (see the following explanation).

Depending on your operating system, the maximum number of open file descriptors is tunable in a resource file or by sending a signal to a resource-management daemon. You can see what the current value is set to by entering the following command at the prompt:

```
ulimit -n
```

If by your calculations, this limit is too low, or you see a message in your error log that `worker_connections exceed open file resource limit`, you'll know that you need to increase this value. First, tune the maximum number of open file descriptors at the operating system level, either for just the user that NGINX runs as or globally. Then, set the `worker_rlimit_nofile` directive to the new value in the main context of the `nginx.conf` file. Sending `nginx` a configuration reload signal (HUP) will then be enough to raise this limit without restarting the main process.

If you observe a connection limit due to the exhaustion of available TCP ports, you will need to increase the ephemeral port range. This is the range of TCP ports that your operating system maintains for the outgoing connections. It can default to as few as 5,000, but is typically set to a range of 16,384 ports.

A good description of how to increase this range for various operating systems is provided at `http://www.ncftp.com/ncftpd/doc/misc/ephemeral_ports.html`.

Summary

In this chapter, we saw how NGINX can be configured to proxy POP3, IMAP, and SMTP connections. Each protocol may be configured separately, announcing support for various capabilities in the upstream server. Encrypting e-mail traffic is possible by using TLS and providing the server with an appropriate SSL certificate.

The authentication service is fundamental to the functioning of the `mail` module, as no proxying can be done without it. We have detailed an example of such an authentication service, outlining the requirements of both what is expected in the request and how the response should be formed. With this as a foundation, you should be able to write an authentication service that fits your environment.

Understanding how to interpret log files is one of the most useful skills a system administrator can develop. NGINX gives fairly detailed log entries, although some may be a bit cryptic. Knowing where to place the various entries within the context of a single connection and seeing the state NGINX is in at that time is helpful in deciphering the entry.

NGINX, like any other piece of software, runs within the context of an operating system. It is therefore extremely useful to know how to increase any limits the OS may place on NGINX. If it is not possible to increase the limits any further, an architectural solution must be found by either multiplying the number of servers on which NGINX runs, or using some other technique to reduce the number of connections a single instance must handle.

In the next chapter, we will see how to configure NGINX to proxy HTTP connections.

4
NGINX as a Reverse Proxy

A reverse proxy is a web server that terminates connections with clients and makes new ones to upstream servers on their behalf. An upstream server is defined as a server that NGINX makes a connection with in order to fulfill the client's request. These upstream servers can take various forms, and NGINX can be configured differently to handle each of them.

NGINX configuration, which you have been learning about in detail, can be difficult to understand at times. There are different directives that may be used to fulfill similar configuration needs. Some of these options should not really be used, as they can lead to unexpected results.

At times, an upstream server may not be able to fulfill a request. NGINX has the capability to deliver an error message to the client, either directly from this upstream server, from its local disk, or as a redirect to a page on a completely different server.

Due to the nature of a reverse proxy, the upstream server doesn't obtain information directly from the client. Some of this information, such as the client's real IP address, is important for debugging purposes, as well as tracking requests. This information may be passed to the upstream server in the form of headers.

We will cover these topics, as well as an overview of some proxy module directives, in the following sections:

- Introducing reverse proxying
- Types of upstream servers
- Load balancing
- Converting an if-fy configuration to a more modern interpretation
- Using error documents to handle upstream problems
- Determining the client's real IP address

Introducing reverse proxying

NGINX can serve as a reverse proxy by terminating requests from clients and opening new ones to its upstream servers. On the way, the request can be split up according to its URI, client parameters, or some other logic, in order to best respond to the request from the client. Any part of the request's original URL can be transformed on its way through the reverse proxy.

The most important directive when proxying to an upstream server is the proxy_pass directive. This directive takes one parameter — the URL to which the request should be transferred. Using proxy_pass with a URI part will replace the request_uri variable with this part. For example, /uri in the following example will be transformed to /newuri when the request is passed on to the upstream:

```
location /uri {

  proxy_pass http://localhost:8080/newuri;
}
```

There are two exceptions to this rule, however. First, if the location is defined with a regular expression, no transformation of the URI occurs. In this example, the URI, /local, will be passed directly to the upstream, and not be transformed to /foreign as intended:

```
location ~ ^/local {

  proxy_pass http://localhost:8080/foreign;
}
```

The second exception is that if within the location a rewrite rule changes the URI, and then NGINX uses this URI to process the request, no transformation occurs. In this example, the URI passed to the upstream will be /index.php?page=<match>, with <match> being whatever was captured in the parentheses, and not /index, as indicated by the URI part of the proxy_pass directive:

```
location / {

  rewrite /(.*)$ /index.php?page=$1 break;

  proxy_pass http://localhost:8080/index;
}
```

The break flag to the rewrite directive is used here to immediately stop all processing of rewrite module directives.

In both of these cases, the URI part of the `proxy_pass` directive is not relevant, so the configuration would be complete without it:

```
location ~ ^/local {

  proxy_pass http://localhost:8080;
}

location / {

  rewrite /(.*)$ /index.php?page=$1 break;

  proxy_pass http://localhost:8080;
}
```

The proxy module

The following table summarizes some of the commonly used directives in the `proxy` module:

The proxy module directives	Explanation
proxy_connect_timeout	This directive specifies the maximum amount of time NGINX will wait for its connection to be accepted when making a request to an upstream server.
proxy_cookie_domain	This directive replaces the domain attribute of the Set-Cookie header from the upstream server; the domain to be replaced can either be a string, a regular expression, or a reference variable.
proxy_cookie_path	This directive replaces the path attribute of the Set-Cookie header from the upstream server; the path to be replaced can either be a string, a regular expression, or a reference variable.
proxy_headers_hash_bucket_size	This directive specifies the maximum size of header names.
proxy_headers_hash_max_size	This directive specifies the total size of headers received from the upstream server.
proxy_hide_header	This directive specifies a list of header fields that should not be passed on to the client.

The proxy module directives	Explanation
proxy_http_version	This directive specifies the HTTP protocol version used to communicate with the upstream servers (use 1.1 for the keepalive connections).
proxy_ignore_client_abort	If this directive is set to on, NGINX will not abort the connection to an upstream server if the client aborts the connection.
proxy_ignore_headers	This directive sets the headers that can be disregarded when processing the response from the upstream server.
proxy_intercept_errors	If this directive is enabled, NGINX will display a configured error_page error instead of the response directly from the upstream server.
proxy_max_temp_file_size	This directive specifies the maximum size of the overflow file written when the response doesn't fit into memory buffers.
proxy_pass	This directive specifies the upstream server to which the request is passed, in the form of a URL.
proxy_pass_header	This directive overrides the disabled headers set in proxy_hide_header, allowing them to be sent to the client.
proxy_pass_request_body	This directive prevents sending the body of the request to the upstream server if set to off.
proxy_pass_request_headers	This directive prevents sending the headers of the request to the upstream server if set to off.
proxy_read_timeout	This directive specifies the length of time that needs to elapse between two successive read operations from an upstream server, before the connection is closed. This directive should be set to a higher value if the upstream server processes requests slowly.
proxy_redirect	This directive rewrites the Location and Refresh headers received from the upstream servers; it's useful for working around assumptions made by an application framework.

The proxy module directives	Explanation
`proxy_send_timeout`	This directive specifies the length of time that needs to elapse between two successive `write` operations to an upstream server, before the connection is closed.
`proxy_set_body`	The body of a request sent to an upstream server may be altered by setting this directive.
`proxy_set_header`	This directive rewrites the contents of headers sent to an upstream server; it may also be used to not send certain headers by setting its value to the empty string.
`proxy_temp_file_write_size`	This directive limits the amount of data buffered to a temporary file at one time, so that NGINX will not block too long on a single request.
`proxy_temp_path`	This directive specifies a directory where temporary files may be buffered as they are proxied from the upstream server, optionally multilevel deep.

The following listing brings many of these directives together in a file that can be included in the configuration within the same location as the `proxy_pass` directive. The contents of `proxy.conf` are shown in this code:

```
proxy_redirect off;

proxy_set_header Host $host;

proxy_set_header X-Real-IP $remote_addr;

proxy_set_header X-Forwarded-For $proxy_add_x_forwarded_for;

client_max_body_size 10m;

client_body_buffer_size 128k;
proxy_connect_timeout 30;

proxy_send_timeout 15;

proxy_read_timeout 15;

proxy_send_lowat 12000;
```

```
proxy_buffer_size 4k;

proxy_buffers 32 4k;

proxy_busy_buffers_size 64k;

proxy_temp_file_write_size 64k;
```

We are setting a number of common directives to values that we think would be useful for reverse proxying scenarios:

- The proxy_redirect directive has been set to off because there is no need to rewrite the Location header in most situations.

- The Host header is set so the upstream server can map the request to a virtual server or otherwise make use of the host portion of the URL the user entered.

- The X-Real-IP and X-Forwarded-For headers serve similar purposes — to relay the information about the connecting client's IP address to the upstream server.

- The $remote_addr variable used in the X-Real-IP header is the IP address of the client as NGINX perceives it.

- The $proxy_add_x_forwarded_for variable contains the contents of the X-Forwarded-For header field from the client's request, followed by the $remote_addr variable.

- The client_max_body_size directive, while not strictly a proxy module directive, is mentioned here because of its relevance to proxy configurations. If this value is set too low, uploaded files will not make it to the upstream server. When setting this directive, keep in mind that files uploaded via a web form will usually have a larger file size than that shown in the filesystem.

- The proxy_connect_timeout directive indicates how long NGINX will wait when establishing initial contact with the upstream server.

- The proxy_read_timeout and proxy_send_timeout directives define how long NGINX will wait between successive operations with the upstream server.

- The proxy_send_lowat directive is only effective on FreeBSD systems and specifies the number of bytes the socket send buffer should hold before passing the data on to the protocol.

- The `proxy_buffer_size`, `proxy_buffers`, and `proxy_busy_buffers_size` directives will be discussed in detail in the next chapter. Suffice it to say that these buffers control how quickly NGINX appears to respond to user requests.

- The `proxy_temp_file_write_size` directive controls how long a worker process blocks while spooling data: the higher the value, the longer the process blocks.

These directives are included in a file as follows, and may be used multiple times in the same configuration:

```
location / {

    include proxy.conf;

    proxy_pass http://localhost:8080;
}
```

If one of these directives should have a different value than what's in the `include` file, override it in that particular location.

```
location /uploads {

    include proxy.conf;

    client_max_body_size 500m;

    proxy_connect_timeout 75;

    proxy_send_timeout 90;

    proxy_read_timeout 90;

    proxy_pass http://localhost:8080;
}
```

 The order is important here. If there is more than one occurrence of a directive in a configuration file (or `include`), NGINX will take the value of the directive defined last.

Legacy servers with cookies

You may find yourself in a situation where you will need to place multiple legacy applications behind one common endpoint. The legacy applications were written for a case where they were the only servers talking directly with the client. They set cookies from their own domain, and assumed that they would always be reachable via the / URI. In placing a new endpoint in front of these servers, these assumptions no longer hold true. The following configuration will rewrite the cookie domain and path to match that of the new application endpoint:

```
server {

  server_name app.example.com;

  location /legacy1 {

    proxy_cookie_domain legacy1.example.com app.example.com;

    proxy_cookie_path $uri /legacy1$uri;

    proxy_redirect default;

    proxy_pass http://legacy1.example.com/;
  }
```

 The value of the $uri variable already includes the beginning slash (/), so it is not necessary to duplicate it here.

```
  location /legacy2 {

    proxy_cookie_domain legacy2.example.org app.example.com;

    proxy_cookie_path $uri /legacy2$uri;

    proxy_redirect default;

    proxy_pass http://legacy2.example.org/;
  }

  location / {

    proxy_pass http://localhost:8080;
  }
}
```

The upstream module

Closely paired with the `proxy` module is the `upstream` module. The `upstream` directive starts a new context in which a group of upstream servers is defined. These servers may be given different weights (the higher the weight, the greater the number of connections NGINX will pass to that particular upstream server), may be of different types (TCP versus UNIX domain), and may even be marked as `down` for maintenance reasons.

The following table summarizes the directives valid within the `upstream` context:

The upstream module directives	Explanation
`ip_hash`	This directive ensures the distribution of connecting clients evenly over all servers by hashing the IP address, keying on its class-C network.
`keepalive`	This directive specifies the number of connections to the upstream servers that are cached per worker process. When used with the HTTP connections, `proxy_http_version` should be set to `1.1` and `proxy_set_header` to `Connection ""`.
`least_conn`	This directive activates the load-balancing algorithm where the server with the least number of active connections is chosen for the next new connection.
`server`	This directive defines an address (domain name or IP address with an optional TCP port, or path to a UNIX-domain socket) and optional parameters for an upstream server. The parameters are as follows: • `weight`: This parameter sets the preference for one server over another • `max_fails`: This parameter is the maximum number of unsuccessful communication attempts to a server within `fail_timeout` before the server is marked as `down` • `fail_timeout`: This parameter is the length of time a server has to respond to a request and the length of time a server will be marked as down • `backup`: This parameter will only receive requests once the other servers are down • `down`: This parameter marks a server as not able to process requests

Keepalive connections

The `keepalive` directive deserves special mention. NGINX will keep this number of connections per worker open to an upstream server. This connection cache is useful in situations where NGINX has to constantly maintain a certain number of open connections to an upstream server. If the upstream server speaks HTTP, NGINX can use the HTTP/1.1 persistent connections mechanism to maintain these open connections.

An example of such a configuration follows:

```
upstream apache {

  server 127.0.0.1:8080;

  keepalive 32;

}

location / {

  proxy_http_version 1.1;

  proxy_set_header Connection "";

  proxy_pass http://apache;

}
```

Here, we've indicated that we'd like to hold open 32 connections to Apache running on port 8080 of the localhost. NGINX need only negotiate the TCP handshake for the initial 32 connections per worker, and will then keep these connections open by not sending a `Connection` header with the close token. With `proxy_http_version`, we specify that we'd like to speak HTTP/1.1 with the upstream server. We also clear the contents of the `Connection` header with `proxy_set_header` so that we are not proxying the client connection properties directly.

If more than 32 connections are needed, NGINX will, of course, open them to satisfy requests. After this peak has passed, NGINX will close the least recently used connections, to bring the number back down to 32, as we indicated in the `keepalive` directive.

This mechanism can also be used to proxy non-HTTP connections, as well. In the following example, we show that NGINX maintains 64 connections to two instances of memcached:

```
upstream memcaches {

    server 10.0.100.10:11211;

    server 10.0.100.20:11211;

    keepalive 64;

}
```

If we were to switch load-balancing algorithms from the default round-robin to either ip_hash or least_conn, we would need to specify this before using the keepalive directive:

```
upstream apaches {

    least_conn;

    server 10.0.200.10:80;

    server 10.0.200.20:80;

    keepalive 32;

}
```

Types of upstream servers

An upstream server is a server to which NGINX proxies a connection. This can be on a different physical or virtual machine, but doesn't have to be. The upstream server may be a daemon listening on a UNIX domain socket for connections on the local machine or could be one of many on a different machine listening over TCP. It may be an Apache server, with multiple modules to handle different kinds of requests, or a Rack middleware server, providing an HTTP interface to Ruby applications. NGINX can be configured to proxy to each of them.

Single upstream server

The Apache web server is used in common hosting scenarios to serve static files as well as multiple types of interpreted files. The extensive documentation and how-to guides found online help users to get up and running quickly with their favorite CMS. Unfortunately, the typical Apache configuration, due to resource limits, is not able to handle many simultaneous requests. NGINX, though, is designed to handle this kind of traffic and performs very well with little resource consumption. Since most CMSs come preconfigured for Apache, integrating the use of the .htaccess files for extended configuration, the easiest way to take advantage of NGINX's strengths is for NGINX to simply proxy connections to an Apache instance:

```
server {

  location / {

    proxy_pass http://localhost:8080;

  }

}
```

This is the most basic proxy configuration possible. NGINX will terminate all client connections and then proxy all requests to the local host on TCP port 8080. We assume here that Apache has been configured to listen on localhost:8080.

A configuration such as this is typically extended so that NGINX will serve any static files directly, and then proxy the remaining requests to Apache:

```
server {

  location / {

    try_files $uri @apache;

  }

  location @apache {

    proxy_pass http://127.0.0.1:8080;

  }

}
```

The `try_files` directive (included in the `http` core module) does just what its name implies—it tries files, in order, until it finds a match. So, in the preceding example, NGINX will deliver any files it finds in its root that match the URI given by the client. If it doesn't find any files, it will proxy the request to Apache for further processing. We use a named location here to proxy the request after an unsuccessful try to locate the file locally.

Multiple upstream servers

It is also possible to configure NGINX to pass the request to more than one upstream server. This is done by declaring an upstream context, defining multiple servers, and referencing the upstream in a `proxy_pass` directive:

```
upstream app {

  server 127.0.0.1:9000;

  server 127.0.0.1:9001;

  server 127.0.0.1:9002;

}
server {

  location / {

    proxy_pass http://app;

  }

}
```

Using this configuration, NGINX will pass consecutive requests in a round-robin fashion to the three upstream servers. This is useful when an application can handle only one request at a time, and you'd like NGINX to handle the client communication so that none of the application servers get overloaded. The configuration is illustrated in the following diagram:

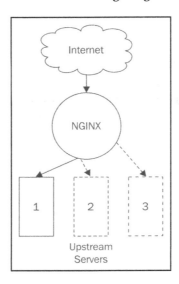

Other load-balancing algorithms are available, as detailed in the *Load-balancing algorithms* section later in this chapter. Which one should be used in a particular configuration depends on the situation.

If a client should always get the same upstream server, to effect a poor-man's session-stickiness, the ip_hash directive should be used. When the distribution of requests leads to widely varying response times per request, the least_conn algorithm should be selected. The default round-robin algorithm is good for a general case where no special consideration of either the client or upstream server is required.

Non-HTTP upstream servers

So far, we've focused on communicating with upstream servers over HTTP. For this, we use the proxy_pass directive. As hinted earlier in this chapter, in the *Keepalive connections* section, NGINX can proxy requests to a number of different kinds of upstream server. Each has its corresponding *_pass directive.

Memcached upstream servers

The memcached NGINX module (enabled by default) is responsible for communicating with a memcached daemon. As such, there is no direct communication between the client and the memcached daemon; that is, NGINX does not act as a reverse proxy in this sense. The memcached module enables NGINX to speak the memcached protocol so that a key lookup can be done before a request is passed to an application server:

```
upstream memcaches {

  server 10.0.100.10:11211;

  server 10.0.100.20:11211;

}

server {

  location / {

    set $memcached_key "$uri?$args";

    memcached_pass memcaches;

    error_page 404 = @appserver;

  }
  location @appserver {

    proxy_pass http://127.0.0.1:8080;

  }

}
```

The memcached_pass directive uses the $memcached_key variable to make the key lookup. If there is no corresponding value (error_page 404), we pass the request on to localhost, where there is presumably a server running that will handle this request and insert a key/value pair into the memcached instance.

FastCGI upstream servers

Using a FastCGI server is a popular way to run the PHP applications behind an NGINX server. The `fastcgi` module is compiled in by default, and is activated with the `fastcgi_pass` directive. This enables NGINX to speak the FastCGI protocol with one or more upstream servers. We define a set of FastCGI upstream servers as follows:

```
upstream fastcgis {

    server 10.0.200.10:9000;

    server 10.0.200.20:9000;

    server 10.0.200.30:9000;
}
```

And we pass connections to them from the root location:

```
location / {

    fastcgi_pass fastcgis;
}
```

This is a very minimalist configuration to illustrate the basics of using FastCGI. The `fastcgi` module contains a number of directives and configuration possibilities, which we will discuss in *Chapter 6, The NGINX HTTP Server*.

SCGI upstream servers

NGINX can also speak the SCGI protocol by using its built-in `scgi` module. The principle is the same as for the `fastcgi` module. NGINX communicates with an upstream server indicated with the `scgi_pass` directive.

The uWSGI upstream servers

The `uWSGI` protocol has been very popular with the Python developers. NGINX provides support for connecting to a Python-based upstream server through its `uwsgi` module. The configuration is similar to the `fastcgi` module, using the `uwsgi_pass` directive instead to indicate an upstream server. An example configuration can be found in *Chapter 6, The NGINX HTTP Server*.

Load-balancing

We've already shown some examples of using load-balancing in our discussion of upstream servers. Besides being a termination point for clients from the Internet as a reverse proxy, NGINX serves the function of a load balancer well. It can protect your upstream servers from overload by spreading out the connections that it proxies. Depending on your use case, you can choose one of three load-balancing algorithms.

Load-balancing algorithms

The upstream module can select which upstream server to connect to in the next step by using one of three load-balancing algorithms—round-robin, IP hash, or least connections. The round-robin algorithm is selected by default, and doesn't need a configuration directive to activate it. This algorithm selects the next server, based on the server that was selected previously, the server that is next in the configuration block, and the weight that each server carries. The round-robin algorithm tries to ensure a fair distribution of traffic, based on the concept of whose turn it is next.

The IP hash algorithm, activated by the ip_hash directive, instead takes the view that certain IP addresses should always be mapped to the same upstream server. NGINX does this by using the first three octets of an IPv4 address or the entire IPv6 address as a hashing key. The same pool of IP addresses are, therefore, always mapped to the same upstream server. So, this mechanism isn't designed to ensure a fair distribution, but rather a consistent mapping between the client and upstream server. This is useful for situations in which you have user sessions tracked locally in an upstream server.

The third load-balancing algorithm supported by the default upstream module, least connections, is activated by the least_conn directive. This algorithm is designed to distribute the load evenly among upstream servers by selecting the one with the fewest active connections. If the upstream servers do not at all have the same processing power, this can be indicated using the weight parameter to the server directive. The algorithm will take into account the differently weighted servers when calculating the number of least connections.

Converting an if-fy configuration to a more modern interpretation

Using the `if` directive within a location is really only considered valid for certain cases. It may be used in combination with a `return` and with a `rewrite` directive with a `last` or `break` flag, but should generally be avoided in other situations. This is due in part to the fact that it can produce some very unexpected results. Consider the following example:

```
location / {

    try_files /img /static @imageserver;

    if ($request_uri ~ "/blog") {

      proxy_pass http://127.0.0.1:9000;

      break;

    }

    if ($request_uri ~ "/tickets") {

      proxy_pass http://tickets.example.com;

      break;
    }

}

location @imageserver {

  proxy_pass http://127.0.0.1:8080;
}
```

Here, we're trying to determine which upstream to pass the request to, based on the value of the `$request_uri` variable. This seems like a very reasonable configuration at first glance, because it works for our simple test cases. But the images will neither be served from the `/img` filesystem location, the `/static` filesystem location, nor from the `@imageserver` named location. The `try_files` directive simply doesn't work when an `if` directive is present in the same location. The `if` directive creates an implicit location with its own content handler; in this case, the `proxy` module. So the outer content handler, where `try_files` is registered, won't ever get invoked. There is a way to write this configuration differently to make it do what we want.

Let's think about our request as NGINX processes it. After having found a matching IP and port, it first selects a virtual host (server) based on the `Host` header. Then, it scans all locations under this server, looking for a matching URI. So, we see that the better way to configure a selector based on the URI is in fact by defining multiple locations, as shown in the following example:

```
location /blog {

  proxy_pass http://127.0.0.1:9000;

}

location /tickets {

  proxy_pass http://tickets.example.com;

}

location /img {

  try_files /static @imageserver;

}

location / {

  root /static;

}

location @imageserver {
  proxy_pass http://127.0.0.1:8080;
}
```

This configuration can be illustrated by the following diagram:

```
/... static files
|
/blog
| ↳ http://127.0.0.1:9000
/tickets
| ↳ http://tickets.example.com
/img
  ↳ ...static files
  ↳ http://127.0.0.1:8080
```

Another example of an `if`-fy configuration is the following code:

```
server {

    server_name marketing.example.com communication.example.com
      marketing.example.org communication.example.org
        marketing.example.
          net communication.example.net;

    if ($host ~* (marketing\.example\.com|marketing\.example\.
      org|marketing\.example\.net)) {

      rewrite ^/$ http://www.example.com/marketing/application.do
        redirect;

    }

    if ($host ~*
      (communication\.example\.com|communication\.example\.
        org|communication\.example\.net)) {

      rewrite ^/$ http://www.example.com/comms/index.cgi redirect;

    }

    if ($host ~* (www\.example\.org|www\.example\.net)) {

      rewrite ^/(.*)$ http://www.example.com/$1 redirect;

    }

}
```

Here, we have a number of `if` directives matching the `Host` header (or, if not present, `server_name`). After each `if`, the URI is rewritten to lead directly to the correct application component. Besides being terribly inefficient due to the processing required to match each regular expression for every URI, it breaks our "no `if` directives within a location" rule.

This type of configuration is better rewritten as a series of separate server contexts, in which the URL is rewritten to the application component:

```
server {

  server_name marketing.example.com marketing.example.org
    marketing.
      example.net;

  rewrite ^ http://www.example.com/marketing/application.do
    permanent;

}

server {

  server_name communication.example.com communication.example.org
    communication.example.net;

  rewrite ^ http://www.example.com/comms/index.cgi permanent;

}

server {

  server_name www.example.org www.example.net;

  rewrite ^ http://www.example.com$request_uri permanent;
}
```

In each block, we placed only those `server_name` instances that are relevant to the respective rewrite, so that no `if` is needed. In each `rewrite` rule, we have replaced the `redirect` flag with the `permanent` flag to indicate that this is a full URL that the browser should remember and automatically use the next time the domain is requested. In the preceding `rewrite` rule, we also replaced the match (`^/(.*)$`) with a readily-available variable, `$request_uri`, which contains the same information but saves the trouble of matching the regular expression and saving the capture variable.

Using error documents to handle upstream problems

There are situations in which the upstream server cannot respond to a request. In these cases, NGINX can be configured to supply a document from its local disk:

```
server {

  error_page 500 502 503 504 /50x.html;

  location = /50x.html {

    root share/examples/nginx/html;

  }

}
```

Or it can also be configured from an external site:

```
server {

  error_page 500 http://www.example.com/maintenance.html;

}
```

When proxying to a set of upstream servers, you may want to define an extra upstream as being a `fallback` server, to handle requests when the others cannot. This is useful in scenarios when the `fallback` server is able to deliver a customized response based on the requested URI:

```
upstream app {

  server 127.0.0.1:9000;

  server 127.0.0.1:9001;

  server 127.0.0.1:9002;

}

server {
```

```
location / {

  error_page 500 502 503 504 = @fallback;

  proxy_pass http://app;
}

location @fallback {

  proxy_pass http://127.0.0.1:8080;

}
}
```

The = notation shown in the preceding `error_page` line is used to indicate that we want to return the status code resulting from the preceding parameter; in this case, the `@fallback` location.

These examples cover cases in which the error code was `500` or greater. NGINX can also supply an `error_page` for error codes `400` or greater, when the `proxy_intercept_errors` directive is set to `on`, as in the following example:

```
server {

  proxy_intercept_errors on;

  error_page 400 403 404 /40x.html;

  location = /40x.html {

    root share/examples/nginx/html;

  }
}
```

 When HTTP error code `401` is configured to be served from an `error_page`, the authentication will not complete. You may want to do this in situations when the authentication backend is offline, for maintenance or other reasons, but you should otherwise avoid them.

Determining the client's real IP address

When using a proxy server, the clients don't have a direct connection to the upstream servers. The upstream servers, therefore, aren't able to get information directly from those clients. Any information, such as the client's IP address, would need to be passed via headers. NGINX provides this with the `proxy_set_header` directive:

```
proxy_set_header X-Real-IP $remote_addr;
proxy_set_header X-Forwarded-For $proxy_add_x_forwarded_for;
```

The client's IP address will then be available in both the X-Real-IP and X-Forwarded-For headers. The second form takes a client request header into account. If present, the IP address of the request will be added to the X-Forwarded-For header from the client, separated by a comma. Depending on your upstream server configuration, you will need one or the other of these. Configuring Apache, for example, to use the X-Forwarded-For header for the client's IP address in its logs is done using the %{<header-name>}i formatting option.

The following example shows how to change the default combined Apache log format:

```
LogFormat "%{X-Forwarded-For}i %l %u %t \"%r\" %>s %b
    \"%{Referer}i\" \"%{User-Agent}i\"" combined
```

If your upstream server, on the other hand, requires a nonstandard header such as Client-IP, this can easily be configured with the following code:

```
proxy_set_header Client-IP $remote_addr;
```

Other information, such as the Host header, can be passed to the upstream servers in the same manner:

```
proxy_set_header Host $host;
```

Summary

We saw how NGINX can be used as a reverse proxy. Its efficient connection-handling model is ideal for interfacing directly with clients. After having terminated requests, NGINX can then open new ones to upstream servers, taking into account the strengths and weaknesses of each upstream server. Using if inside a location is only considered valid under certain situations. By thinking about how NGINX actually handles a request, we can develop a configuration that is more suited to what we want to achieve. If NGINX cannot reach an upstream server for any reason, it can serve another page instead. As NGINX terminates the clients' requests, the upstream servers can obtain information about the client only via headers passed in NGINX's proxied request. These concepts will help you design an ideal NGINX configuration to match your needs.

In the next chapter, we will explore more advanced reverse-proxy techniques.

5

Reverse Proxy
Advanced Topics

As we saw in the previous chapter, a reverse proxy makes connections to the upstream servers on behalf of clients. These upstream servers, therefore, have no direct connection to the client. This is for several different reasons, such as security, scalability, and performance.

Security is enhanced via the dual-layer nature of such a setup. If an attacker were to try to get onto the upstream server directly, he would first have to find a way to get onto the reverse proxy. Connections to the client can be encrypted by running them over HTTPS. These SSL connections may be terminated on the reverse proxy, when the upstream server cannot or should not provide this functionality itself. NGINX can act as an SSL terminator as well as provide additional access lists and restrictions based on various client attributes.

Scalability can be achieved by utilizing a reverse proxy to make parallel connections to multiple upstream servers, enabling them to act as if they were one. If the application requires more processing power, additional upstream servers can be added to the pool served by a single reverse proxy.

Performance of an application may be enhanced through the use of a reverse proxy in several ways. The reverse proxy can cache and compress content before delivering it out to the client. NGINX as a reverse proxy can handle more concurrent client connections than a typical application server. Certain architectures configure NGINX to serve static content from a local disk cache, passing only dynamic requests to the upstream server to handle. Clients can keep their connections to NGINX alive, while NGINX terminates the ones to the upstream servers immediately, thus freeing resources on those upstream servers.

We will discuss these topics, as well as the remaining proxy module directives, in the following sections:

- Security through separation
- Isolating application components for scalability
- Reverse proxy performance tuning

Security through separation

We can achieve a measure of security by separating out the point to which clients connect to an application. This is one of the main reasons for using reverse proxy architecture. The client directly connects only to the machine running the reverse proxy. This machine should, therefore, be secured well enough that an attacker cannot find a point of entry.

Security is such a large topic that we will touch only briefly on the main points to observe:

- Set up a firewall in front of the reverse proxy that only allows public access to port 80 (and 443, if HTTPS connections should also be made)
- Ensure that NGINX is running as an unprivileged user (typically www, webservd, or www-data, depending on the operating system)
- Encrypt traffic where you can to prevent eavesdropping

We will spend some time on this last point in the next section.

Encrypting traffic with SSL

NGINX is often used to terminate SSL connections, either because the upstream server is not capable of using SSL or to offload the processing requirements of SSL connections. This requires that your nginx binary was compiled with SSL support (--with_http_ssl_module) and that you install an SSL certificate and key.

 For details about how to generate your own SSL certificate, see the *Using OpenSSL to generate an SSL certificate* tip in *Chapter 3, Using the mail Module.*

The following code is an example configuration for enabling the HTTPS connections to www.example.com:

```
server {

  listen 443 default ssl;

  server_name www.example.com;


  ssl_prefer_server_ciphers on;

  ssl_protocols TLSv1 SSLv3;

  ssl_ciphers RC4:HIGH:!aNULL:!MD5:@STRENGTH;

  ssl_session_cache shared:WEB:10m;

  ssl_certificate /usr/local/etc/nginx/www.example.com.crt;

  ssl_certificate_key /usr/local/etc/nginx/www.example.com.key;

  location / {

    proxy_set_header X-FORWARDED-PROTO https;

    proxy_pass http://upstream;

  }

}
```

In the preceding example, we first activate the ssl module by using the ssl parameter to the listen directive. Then, we specify that we wish the server's ciphers to be chosen over the client's list, as we can configure the server to use the ciphers that have proven to be most secure. This prevents clients from negotiating a cipher that has been deprecated. The ssl_session_cache directive is set to shared so that all worker processes can benefit from the expensive SSL negotiation that has already been done once per client. Multiple virtual servers can use the same ssl_session_cache directive if they are all configured with the same name, or if this directive is specified in the http context. The second and third parts of the value are the name of the cache and its size, respectively. Then, it is just a matter of specifying the certificate and key for this host. Note that the permissions of this key file should be set so that only the master process may read it. We set the header, X-FORWARDED-PROTO, to the value https, so that the application running on the upstream server can recognize the fact that the original request used HTTPS.

SSL ciphers

The preceding ciphers were chosen based on NGINX's default, which excludes those that offer no authentication (aNULL) as well as those using MD5. The RC4 is placed at the beginning so that ciphers not susceptible to the BEAST attack described in CVE-2011-3389 are preferred. The @STRENGTH string at the end is present to sort the list of ciphers in order of the encryption algorithm key length.

We just encrypted the traffic passing between the client and the reverse proxy. It is also possible to encrypt the traffic between the reverse proxy and the upstream server:

```
server {

...

  proxy_pass https://upstream;

}
```

This is usually only reserved for those architectures in which even the internal network over which such a connection flows is considered insecure.

Authenticating clients using SSL

Some applications use information from the SSL certificate the client presents to authenticate that client, but this information is not directly available in reverse proxy architecture. To pass this information along to the application, you can instruct NGINX to set an additional header:

```
location /ssl {

  proxy_set_header ssl_client_cert $ssl_client_cert;

  proxy_pass http://upstream;

}
```

The $ssl_client_cert variable contains the client's SSL certificate in the PEM format. We pass this on to the upstream server in a header of the same name. The application itself is then responsible for using this information in whatever way is appropriate.

Instead of passing the whole client certificate to the upstream server, NGINX can do some work ahead of time to see if the client is even valid. A valid client SSL certificate is one which has been signed by a recognized **Certificate Authority**, has a validity date in the future, and has not been revoked:

```
server {
...

  ssl_client_certificate /usr/local/etc/nginx/ClientCertCAs.pem;

  ssl_crl /usr/local/etc/nginx/ClientCertCRLs.crl;

  ssl_verify_client on;

  ssl_verify_depth 3;

  error_page 495 = @noverify;

  error_page 496 = @nocert;

  location @noverify {

    proxy_pass http://insecure?status=notverified;

  }

  location @nocert {

    proxy_pass http://insecure?status=nocert;

  }

  location / {

    if ($ssl_client_verify = FAILED) {

      return 495;

    }

    proxy_pass http://secured;

  }

}
```

The preceding configuration is constructed out of the following parts to achieve the objective of having NGINX validate the client SSL certificates before passing the request on to the upstream server:

- The argument to the `ssl_client_certificate` directive specifies the path to the PEM-encoded list of root CA certificates that will be considered valid signers of client certificates.

- The `ssl_crl` argument indicates the path to a certificate revocation list, issued by the CA responsible for signing client certificates. This CRL needs to be downloaded separately and periodically refreshed.

- The `ssl_verify_client` directive states that we want NGINX to check the validity of SSL certificates presented by clients.

- The `ssl_verify_depth` directive is responsible for how many signers will be checked before declaring the certificate invalid. The SSL certificates may be signed by one or more intermediate CAs. Either an intermediate CA certificate or the root CA that signed it needs to be in our `ssl_client_certificate` path for NGINX to consider the client certificate valid.

- If some sort of error occurred during client certificate validation, NGINX will return the nonstandard error code `495`. We defined an `error_page` that matches this code and redirects the request to a named location, to be handled by a separate proxied server. We also include a check for the value of `$ssl_client_verify` within the `proxy_pass` location so that an invalid certificate will also return this code.

- If a certificate is not valid, NGINX will return the nonstandard error code `496`, which we capture as well with an `error_page` directive. The `error_page` directive that we define points to a named location, which proxies the request to a separate error handler.

Only when the client has presented a valid SSL certificate will NGINX pass the request on to the upstream server, `secured`. By doing so, we ensured that only authenticated users actually get to place requests to the upstream server. This is an important security feature of a reverse proxy.

NGINX from version 1.3.7 on provides the capability to use the OCSP responders to verify the client SSL certificates. See the `ssl_stapling*` and `ssl_trusted_certificate` directives in *Appendix A, Directive Reference*, for a description of how to activate this functionality.

If the application still needs some information present in the certificate, for example, to authorize a user, NGINX can deliver this information in a header:

```
location / {

  proxy_set_header X-HTTP-AUTH $ssl_client_s_dn;

  proxy_pass http://secured;

}
```

Now, our application running on the upstream server, secured, can use the value of the X-HTTP-AUTH header to authorize the client for access to different areas. The $ssl_client_s_dn variable contains the subject, DN, of the client certificate. The application can use this information to match the user against a database or make a look-up in a directory.

Blocking traffic based on originating IP address

As the client connections terminate on the reverse proxy, it is possible to limit clients based on the IP address. This is useful in cases of abuse where a number of invalid connections originate from a certain set of IP addresses. As in Perl, there is more than one way to do it. We will discuss the GeoIP module here as a possible solution.

Your nginx binary will need to have been compiled with the GeoIP module activated (--with-http_geoip_module) and the MaxMind GeoIP library installed on your system. Specify the location of the precompiled database file with the geoip_country directive in the http context. This provides the most efficient way to block/allow the IP addresses by country code:

```
geoip_country /usr/local/etc/geo/GeoIP.dat;
```

If a client's connection comes from an IP address listed in this database, the value of the $geoip_country_code variable will be set to the ISO two-letter code for the originating country.

We will use the data provided by the GeoIP module together with the closely-named geo module, as well. The geo module provides a very basic interface for setting variables based on the IP address of a client connection. It sets up a named context within which the first parameter is the IP address to match and the second is the value that match should obtain. By combining these two modules, we can block the IP addresses based on the country of origin, while allowing access from a set of specific IP addresses.

In our scenario, we are providing a service to Swiss banks. We want the public parts of the site to be indexed by Google, but are for now still restricting access to Swiss IPs. We also want a local watchdog service to be able to access the site to ensure it is still responding properly. We define a $exclusions variable, which will have the value 0 by default. If any of our criteria are matched, the value will be set to 1, which we will use to control access to the site:

```
http {

    # the path to the GeoIP database

    geoip_country /usr/local/etc/geo/GeoIP.dat;

    # we define the variable $exclusions and list all IP addresses
      # allowed
    # access by setting the value to "1"

    geo $exclusions {

      default 0;
      127.0.0.1 1;
      216.239.32.0/19 1;
      64.233.160.0/19 1;
      66.249.80.0/20 1;
      72.14.192.0/18 1;
      209.85.128.0/17 1;
      66.102.0.0/20 1;
      74.125.0.0/16 1;
      64.18.0.0/20 1;
      207.126.144.0/20 1;
      173.194.0.0/16 1;

    }

    server {

      # the country code we want to allow is "CH", for Switzerland
      if ($geoip_country_code = "CH") {

        set $exclusions 1;

      }
      location / {
```

```
# any IP's not from Switzerland or in our list above
  # receive the
# default value of "0" and are given the Forbidden HTTP
  # code
if ($exclusions = "0" ) {

    return 403;

}


    # anybody else has made it this far and is allowed access
      # to the
    # upstream server
    proxy_pass http://upstream;

  }

 }

}
```

This is just one way of solving the problem of blocking access to a site based on the client's IP address. Other solutions involve saving the IP address of the client in a key-value store, updating a counter for each request, and blocking access if there have been too many requests within a certain time period.

Isolating application components for scalability

Scaling applications can be described by moving in two dimensions, up and out. Scaling up refers to adding more resources to a machine, growing its pool of available resources to meet client demand. Scaling out means adding more machines to a pool of available responders so that no machine gets tied up handling the majority of clients. Whether these machines are virtualized instances running in the cloud or physical machines sitting in a datacenter, it is often more cost-effective to scale out rather than up. This is where NGINX fits in handily as a reverse proxy.

Due to its very low resource usage, NGINX acts ideally as the broker in a client-application relationship. NGINX handles the connection to the client, able to process multiple requests simultaneously. Depending on the configuration, NGINX will either deliver a file from its local cache or pass the request on to an upstream server for further processing. The upstream server can be any type of server that speaks the HTTP protocol. More client connections can be handled than if an upstream server were to respond directly:

```
upstream app {

    server 10.0.40.10;

    server 10.0.40.20;

    server 10.0.40.30;

}
```

Over time, the initial set of upstream servers may need to be expanded. The traffic to the site has increased so much that the current set can't respond in a timely enough manner. By using NGINX as the reverse proxy, this situation can easily be remedied by adding more upstream servers.

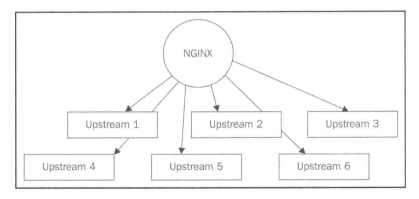

Adding more upstream servers can be done as follows:

```
upstream app {

    server 10.0.40.10;

    server 10.0.40.20;
    server 10.0.40.30;
```

```
server 10.0.40.40;

server 10.0.40.50;

server 10.0.40.60;

}
```

Perhaps the time has come for the application to be rewritten, or to be migrated onto a server with a different application stack. Before moving the whole application over, one server can be brought into the active pool for testing under real load with real clients. This server could be given fewer requests to help minimize any negative reactions should problems arise.

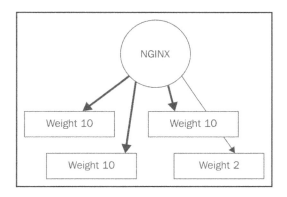

This is done with the following configuration:

```
upstream app {

    server 10.0.40.10 weight 10;

    server 10.0.40.20 weight 10;

    server 10.0.40.30 weight 10;

    server 10.0.40.100 weight 2;

}
```

Alternatively, perhaps it is time for scheduled maintenance on a particular upstream server, so it should not receive any new requests. By marking that server as down in the configuration, we can proceed with that maintenance work:

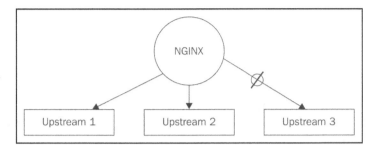

The following configuration describes how to mark the server down:

```
upstream app {

    server 10.0.40.10;

    server 10.0.40.20;

    server 10.0.40.30 down;

}
```

The unresponsive upstream servers should be handled quickly. Depending on the application, the timeout directives can be set aggressively low:

```
location / {

    proxy_connect_timeout 5;

    proxy_read_timeout 10;

    proxy_send_timeout 10;

}
```

Be careful, though, that the upstream servers can usually respond within the time set by the timeout directive, or NGINX may deliver 504 Gateway Timeout Error when no upstream servers respond within this time.

Reverse proxy performance tuning

NGINX can be tuned in a number of ways to get the most out of the application for which it is acting as a reverse proxy. By buffering, caching, and compressing, NGINX can be configured to make the client's experience as snappy as possible.

Buffering data

Buffering can be described with the help of the following diagram:

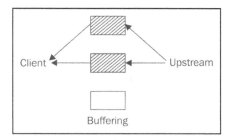

The most important factor to consider performance-wise when acting as a reverse proxy is buffering. NGINX, by default, will try to read as much as possible from the upstream server as fast as possible before returning that response to the client. It will buffer the response locally so that it can deliver it to the client all at once. If any part of the request from the client or the response from the upstream server is written to disk, performance might drop. This is a trade-off between RAM and disk. So, it is very important to consider the following directives when configuring NGINX to act as a reverse proxy:

Proxy module buffering directives	Explanation
`proxy_buffer_size`	This directive specifies the size of the buffer used for the first part of the response from the upstream server, in which the response headers are found.
`proxy_buffering`	This directive activates the buffering of proxied content; when switched off, responses are sent synchronously to the client as soon as they are received, provided the `proxy_max_temp_file_size` parameter is set to 0. Setting this parameter to 0 and turning `proxy_buffering` to on ensures that there is no disk usage during proxying, while still enabling buffering.
`proxy_buffers`	This directive specifies the number and size of buffers used for responses from the upstream servers.

Proxy module buffering directives	Explanation
`proxy_busy_buffers_size`	This directive specifies the total size of buffer space allocated to sending the response to the client while still being read from the upstream server. This is typically set to two `proxy_buffers`.

In addition to the preceding directives, the upstream server may influence buffering by setting the `X-Accel-Buffering` header. The default value of this header is `yes`, meaning that responses will be buffered. Setting the value to `no` is useful for Comet and HTTP streaming applications, where it is important to not buffer the response.

By measuring the average request and response sizes going through the reverse proxy, the proxy buffer sizes can be tuned optimally. Each `buffer` directive counts per connection, in addition to an OS-dependent per-connection overhead, so we can calculate how many simultaneous client connections we can support with the amount of memory on a system.

The default values for the `proxy_buffers` directive (`8 4k` or `8 8k`, depending on the operating system) enable a large number of simultaneous connections. Let's figure out just how many connections that is. On a 1 GB machine, where only NGINX runs, most of the memory can be dedicated to its use. Some will be used by the operating system for the filesystem cache and other needs, so let's be conservative and estimate that NGINX would have up to 768 MB.

Eight 4 KB buffers is 32,768 bytes (8 * 4 * 1024) per active connection.

The 768 MB we allocated to NGINX is 805,306,368 bytes (768 * 1024 * 1024).

Dividing the two, we come up with 805,306,368 / 32,768 = 24,576 active connections.

So, NGINX would be able to handle just under 25,000 simultaneous, active connections in its default configuration, assuming that these buffers will be constantly filled. There are a number of other factors that come into play, such as cached content and idle connections, but this gives us a good ballpark estimate to work with.

Now, if we take the following numbers as our average request and response sizes, we see that eight 4 KB buffers just aren't enough to process a typical request. We want NGINX to buffer as much of the response as possible so that the user receives it all at once, provided the user is on a fast link.

- **Average request size**: 800 bytes
- **Average response size**: 900 KB

The tuning examples in the rest of this section will use more memory at the expense of concurrent, active connections. They are optimizations, and shouldn't be understood as recommendations for a general configuration. NGINX is already optimally tuned to provide for many, slow clients and a few, fast upstream servers. As the trend in computing is more towards mobile users, the client connection is considerably slower than a broadband user's connection. So, it's important to know your users and how they will be connecting before embarking on any optimizations.

We should adjust our buffer sizes accordingly so that the whole response fits in the buffers:

```
http {

  proxy_buffers 240 4k;

}
```

This means, of course, that we will be able to handle far fewer concurrent users.

240 4 KB buffers is 983,040 bytes (240 * 4 * 1024) per connection.

The 768 MB we allocated to NGINX is 805,306,368 bytes (768 * 1024 * 1024).

Dividing the two, we come up with 805,306,368 / 983,040 = 819.2 active connections.

That isn't too many concurrent connections at all. Let's adjust the number of buffers down, and ensure that NGINX will start transferring something to the client while the rest of the response is read into the remaining `proxy_buffers` space:

```
http {

  proxy_buffers 32 4k;

  proxy_busy_buffers_size 64k;

}
```

32 4 KB buffers is 131,072 bytes (32* 4 * 1024) per connection.

The 768 MB we allocated to NGINX is 805,306,368 bytes (768 * 1024 * 1024).

Dividing the two, we come up with 805,306,368 / 131,072 = 6,144 active connections.

For a reverse proxy machine, we may, therefore, want to scale up by adding more memory (6 GB RAM will yield us approximately 37,000 connections) or scale out by adding more 1 GB machines behind a load balancer, up to the number of concurrent, active users we can expect.

Caching data

Caching can be described with the following diagram:

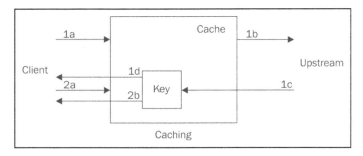

NGINX is also capable of caching the response from the upstream server so that the same request asked again doesn't have to go back to the upstream server to be served. The preceding diagram illustrates this as follows:

- **1a**: A client makes a request
- **1b**: The request's cache key is not currently found in the cache, so NGINX requests it from the upstream server
- **1c**: The upstream server responds and NGINX places the response corresponding to that request's cache key into the cache
- **1d**: The response is delivered to the client
- **2a**: Another client makes a request that has a matching cache key
- **2b**: NGINX is able to serve the response directly from the cache without needing to first get the response from the upstream server

Proxy module caching directives	Explanation
`proxy_cache`	This directive defines a shared memory zone to be used for caching.
`proxy_cache_bypass`	This directive specifies one or more string variables, which when nonempty or nonzero, will cause the response to be taken from the upstream server instead of the cache.

Proxy module caching directives	Explanation
proxy_cache_key	This directive specifies a string used as the key for storing and retrieving the cache values. Variables may be used, but care should be taken to avoid caching multiple copies of the same content.
proxy_cache_lock	Enabling this directive will prevent multiple requests to the upstream server(s) during a cache miss. The requests will wait for the first to return and make an entry into the cache key. This lock is per worker.
proxy_cache_lock_timeout	This directive specifies the length of time a request will wait for an entry to appear in the cache or for the proxy_cache_lock directive to be released.
proxy_cache_min_uses	This directive specifies the number of requests for a certain key needed before a response is cached.
proxy_cache_path	This directive specifies a directory in which to place the cached responses and a shared memory zone (keys_zone=name:size) to store the active keys and response metadata. Optional parameters are as follows: • levels: This parameter specifies the colon-separated length of subdirectory name at each level (1 or 2), a maximum of three levels deep • inactive: This parameter specifies the maximum length of time an inactive response stays in the cache before being ejected • max_size: This parameter specifies the maximum size of the cache; when the size exceeds this value, a cache manager process removes the least recently used items • loader_files: This parameter specifies the maximum number of cached files whose metadata is loaded per iteration of the cache loader process • loader_sleep: This parameter specifies the number of milliseconds paused between each iteration of the cache loader process • loader_threshold: This parameter specifies the maximum length of time a cache loader iteration may take

Proxy module caching directives	Explanation
proxy_cache_use_stale	This directive specifies the cases under which it is acceptable to serve stale cached data when an error occurs while accessing the upstream server. The updating parameter indicates the case when fresh data is being loaded.
proxy_cache_valid	This directive indicates the length of time for which a cached response with response code 200, 301, or 302 is valid. If an optional response code is given before the time parameter, this time is only for that response code. The special parameter, any, indicates that any response code should be cached for that length of time.

The following configuration is designed to cache all responses for six hours, up to a total cache size of 1 GB. Any items that stay fresh, that is, are called within the six hour timeout, are valid for up to one day. After this time, the upstream server will be called again to provide the response. If the upstream server isn't able to respond due to an error, timeout, invalid header, or if the cached item is being updated, a stale cache element may be used. The shared memory zone, CACHE, is defined to be 10 MB large and is referenced within the location where the cache keys need to be set and looked up:

```
http {

    # we set this to be on the same filesystem as proxy_cache_path
    proxy_temp_path /var/spool/nginx;

    # good security practice dictates that this directory is owned
      by the
    # same user as the user directive (under which the workers run)
    proxy_cache_path /var/spool/nginx keys_zone=CACHE:10m levels=1:2
        inactive=6h max_size=1g;

    server {

      location / {

        # using include to bring in a file with commonly-used
          settings
        include proxy.conf;
```

```
        # referencing the shared memory zone defined above
        proxy_cache CACHE;

        proxy_cache_valid any 1d;

        proxy_cache_use_stale error timeout invalid_header updating
          http_500 http_502 http_503 http_504;

        proxy_pass http://upstream;

    }

  }

}
```

Using this configuration, NGINX will set up a series of directories under /var/
spool/nginx that will first differentiate by the last character of the MD5 hash of the
URI, followed by the next two characters from the last. For example, the response for
/this-is-a-typical-url will be stored as follows:

`/var/spool/nginx/3/f1/614c16873c96c9db2090134be91cbf13`

In addition to the proxy_cache_valid directive, a number of headers control how
NGINX caches responses. The header values take precedence over the directive:

- The X-Accel-Expires header can be set by the upstream server to control
  cache behavior:
    - An integer value indicates the time in seconds for which a response
      may be cached
    - If the value of this header is 0, caching for that response is
      disabled completely

- A value beginning with @ indicates the time in seconds since the epoch.
  The response is valid only up to this absolute time.

- The Expires and Cache-Control headers have the same precedence level.

- If the value of the Expires header is in the future, the response will be
  cached until then.

- The Cache-Control header can have multiple values:
    - no-cache
    - no-store
    - private
    - max-age

- The only value for which the response is actually cached is a `max-age` value, which is numeric and nonzero, that is, *max-age=x*, where x is greater than zero.

- If the `Set-Cookie` header is present, the response is not cached.

  This may be overridden, though, by using the `proxy_ignore_headers` directive:

  ```
  proxy_ignore_headers Set-Cookie;
  ```

- However, if doing so, be sure to make the `cookie` value part of the `proxy_cache_key` directive:

  ```
  proxy_cache_key "$host$request_uri $cookie_user";
  ```

Care should be taken when doing this, though, to prevent multiple response bodies from being cached for the same URI. This can happen when public content inadvertently has the `Set-Cookie` header set for it, and this then becomes part of the key used to access this data. Separating public content out to a different location is one way to ensure that the cache is being used effectively. For example, serving images from an `/img` location where a different `proxy_cache_key` directive is defined:

```
server {

  proxy_ignore_headers Set-Cookie;

  location /img {

    proxy_cache_key "$host$request_uri";

    proxy_pass http://upstream;

  }

  location / {

    proxy_cache_key "$host$request_uri $cookie_user";

    proxy_pass http://upstream;

  }

}
```

Storing data

Related to the concept of a cache is a store. If you are serving large, static files that will never change, that is, there is no reason to expire the entries, NGINX offers something called a store to help serve these files faster. NGINX will store a local copy of any files that you configure it to fetch. These files will remain on disk and the upstream server will not be asked for them again. If any of these files should change upstream, they need to be deleted by some external process, or NGINX will continue serving them, so for smaller, static files, using the cache is more appropriate.

The following configuration summarizes the directives used to store these files:

```
http {

  proxy_temp_path /var/www/tmp;

  server {

    root /var/www/data

    location /img {

      error_page 404 = @store;

    }

    location @store {

      internal;

      proxy_store on;

      proxy_store_access group:r all:r;

      proxy_pass http://upstream;

    }

  }

}
```

In this configuration, we define `server` with `root` under the same filesystem as `proxy_temp_path`. The `location` directive, `/img`, will inherit this `root` instance, serving files of the same name as the URI path under `/var/www/data`. If a file is not found (error code `404`), the named `location` directive, `@store`, is called to fetch the file from the upstream server. The `proxy_store` directive indicates that we want to store files under the inherited `root` path with permissions, `0644` (`user:rw` is understood, while `group` or `all` are specified in `proxy_store_access`). That's all it takes for NGINX to store a local copy of static files served by the upstream server.

Compressing data

Compressing can be described with the following diagram:

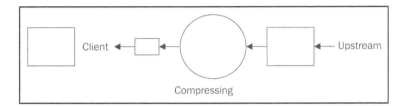

Optimizing for bandwidth can help reduce a response's transfer time. NGINX can compress the response it receives from an upstream server before passing it on to the client. The `gzip` module, enabled by default, is often used on a reverse proxy to compress content where it makes sense. Some file types do not compress well. Some clients do not respond well to compressed content. We can take both cases into account in our configuration:

```
http {

    gzip on;

    gzip_http_version 1.0;

    gzip_comp_level 2;
```

```
gzip_types text/plain text/css application/x-javascript text/xml
    application/xml application/xml+rss text/javascript
        application/javascript application/json;

gzip_disable msie6;
```

```
}
```

Here, we've specified that we want files of the preceding MIME types to be compressed at a `gzip` compression level of 2 if the request has come over at least HTTP/1.0, except if the user agent reports being an older version of Internet Explorer. We've placed this configuration in the `http` context so that it will be valid for all servers we define.

The following table lists the directives available with the `gzip` module:

Gzip module directives	Explanation
gzip	This directive enables or disables the compression of responses.
gzip_buffers	This directive specifies the number and size of buffers used for compressing a response.
gzip_comp_level	This directive specifies the `gzip` compression level (1-9).
gzip_disable	This directive specifies a regular expression of `User-Agents` that shouldn't receive a compressed response. The special value, `msie6`, is a shortcut for `MSIE [4-6]\.` excluding `MSIE 6.0; ... SV1`.
gzip_min_length	This directive specifies the minimum length of a response before compression is considered, determined by the `Content-Length` header.
gzip_http_version	This directive specifies the minimum HTTP version of a request before compression is considered.

Gzip module directives	Explanation
gzip_proxied	This directive enables or disables compression if the request has already come through a proxy. This directive takes one or more of the following parameters: • off: This parameter disables compression • expired: This parameter enables compression if the response should not be cached, as determined by the Expires header • no-cache: This parameter enables compression if the Cache-Control header is equal to no-cache • no-store: This parameter enables compression if the Cache-Control header is equal to no-store • private: This parameter enables compression if the Cache-Control header is equal to private • no_last_modified: This parameter enables compression if the response doesn't have a Last-Modified header • no_etag: This parameter enables compression if the response doesn't have an ETag header • auth: This parameter enables compression if the request contains an Authorization header • any: This parameter enables compression for any response whose request includes the Via header
gzip_types	This directive specifies the MIME types that should be compressed, in addition to the default value, text/html.
gzip_vary	This directive enables or disables the response header, Vary: Accept-Encoding, if gzip is active.

When the gzip compression is enabled and you find large files being truncated, the likely culprit is gzip_buffers. The default value of 32 4k or 16 8k buffers (depending on the platform) leads to a total buffer size of 128 KB. This means that the file NGINX is to compress cannot be larger than 128 KB. If you're using an unzipped large JavaScript library, you may find yourself over this limit. If that is the case, just increase the number of buffers so that the total buffer size is large enough to fit the whole file:

```
http {

    gzip on;
```

```
    gzip_min_length 1024;

    gzip_buffers 40 4k;

    gzip_comp_level 5;

    gzip_types text/plain application/x-javascript application/json;

}
```

For example, the preceding configuration will enable compression of any file up to 40 * 4 * 1024 = 163,840 bytes (or 160 KB) large. We also use the `gzip_min_length` directive to tell NGINX to only compress a file if it is larger than 1 KB. A `gzip_comp_level` directive of `4` or `5` is usually a good trade-off between speed and compressed file size. Measuring on your hardware is the best way to find the right value for your configuration.

Besides on-the-fly compression of responses, NGINX is capable of delivering precompressed files, using the `gzip_static` module. This module is not compiled by default, but can be enabled with the `--with-http_gzip_static_module` compile-time switch. The module itself has one directive, `gzip_static`, but also uses the following directives of the `gzip` module in order to determine when to check for precompressed files:

- `gzip_http_version`
- `gzip_proxied`
- `gzip_disable`
- `gzip_vary`

In the following configuration, we enable delivery of precompressed files if the request contains an `Authorization` header and if the response contains one of the `Expires` or `Cache-Control` headers disabling caching:

```
http {

  gzip_static on;

  gzip_proxied expired no-cache no-store private auth;

}
```

Summary

In this chapter, we saw how NGINX can be used effectively as a reverse proxy. It can act in three roles, either individually or in some combination, which is to enhance security, to enable scalability, and/or to enhance performance. Security is achieved through separation of the application from the end user. NGINX can be combined with multiple upstream servers to achieve scalability. The performance of an application relates directly to how responsive it is to a user's request. We explored different mechanisms to achieve a more responsive application. Faster response times mean happier users.

Up next is an exploration of NGINX as an HTTP server. We have so far only discussed how NGINX can act as a reverse proxy, but there is so much more that NGINX is capable of.

6
The NGINX HTTP Server

An HTTP server is primarily a piece of software that will deliver web pages to clients when requested. These web pages can be anything from a simple HTML file on disk to a multicomponent framework delivering user-specific content, dynamically updated through AJAX or WebSocket. NGINX is modular, and is designed to handle any kind of HTTP serving necessary.

In this chapter, we will investigate the various modules that work together to make NGINX such a scalable HTTP server. The following topics are included in this chapter:

* NGINX's architecture
* The HTTP core module
* Using limits to prevent abuse
* Restricting access
* Streaming media files
* Predefined variables
* SPDY and HTTP/2
* Using NGINX with PHP-FPM
* Wiring NGINX and uWSGI together

NGINX's architecture

NGINX consists of a single master process and multiple worker processes. Each of these processes is single-threaded and designed to handle thousands of connections simultaneously. The worker process is where most of the action takes place, as this is the component that handles client requests. NGINX makes use of the operating system's event mechanism to respond quickly to these requests.

The NGINX **master process** is responsible for reading the configuration, handling sockets, spawning workers, opening log files, and compiling embedded Perl scripts. The master process is the one that responds to administrative requests via signals.

The NGINX **worker process** runs in a tight event loop to handle incoming connections. Each NGINX module is built into the worker, so that any request processing, filtering, handling of proxy connections, and much more is done within the worker process. Due to this worker model, the operating system can handle each process separately and schedule the processes to run optimally on each processor core. If there are any processes that would block a worker, such as disk I/O, more workers than cores can be configured to handle the load.

There are also a small number of helper processes that the NGINX master process spawns to handle dedicated tasks. Among these are the **cache loader** and **cache manager** processes. The cache loader process is responsible for preparing the metadata for worker processes to use the cache. The cache manager process is responsible for checking cache items and expiring the invalid ones.

NGINX is built in a modular fashion. The master process provides the foundation upon which each module may perform its function. Each protocol and handler is implemented as its own module. The individual modules are chained together into a pipeline to handle connections and process requests. After a request is handled, it is then passed on to a series of filters in which the response is processed. One of these filters is responsible for processing subrequests, one of NGINX's most powerful features.

Subrequests are how NGINX can return the results of a request that differs from the URI that the client sent. Depending on the configuration, they may be multiply nested and call other subrequests. Filters can collect the responses from multiple subrequests and combine them into one response to the client. The response is then finalized and sent to the client. Along the way, multiple modules come into play. Visit http://www.aosabook.org/en/nginx.html for a detailed explanation of NGINX internals.

We will be exploring the http module and a few helper modules in the remainder of this chapter.

The HTTP core module

The http module is NGINX's central module; it handles all interactions with clients over HTTP. We already discussed the following aspects of this module in *Chapter 2, A Configuration Guide*:

- Client directives
- File I/O directives
- Hash directives
- Socket directives
- The listen directive
- Matching a request to a server_name and location directive

We will have a look at the remaining directives in the rest of this section, again divided by type.

The server directive

The server directive starts a new context. We have already seen examples of its usage throughout the book so far. One aspect that has not yet been examined in-depth is the concept of a **default server**.

A default server in NGINX means that it is the first server defined in a particular configuration with the same listen IP address and port as another server. A default server may also be denoted by the default_server parameter to the listen directive.

The default server is useful to define a set of common directives that will then be reused for subsequent servers listening on the same IP address and port:

```
server {

  listen 127.0.0.1:80;

  server_name default.example.com;

  server_name_in_redirect on;
```

```
    }

    server {

        listen 127.0.0.1:80;

        server_name www.example.com;

    }
```

In this example, the www.example.com server will have the server_name_in_ redirect directive set to on as well as the default.example.com server. Note that this would also work if both servers had no listen directive, since they would still both match the same IP address and port number (that of the default value for listen, which is *:80). Inheritance, though, is not guaranteed. There are only a few directives that are inherited, and which ones are changes over time.

A better use for the default server is to handle any request that comes in on that IP address and port, and does not have a Host header. If you do not want the default server to handle requests without a Host header, it is possible to define an empty server_name directive. This server will then match those requests:

```
    server {

        server_name "";

    }
```

The following table summarizes the directives relating to server:

HTTP server directives	Explanation
port_in_redirect	This directive determines whether or not the port will be specified in a redirect issued by NGINX.
server	This directive creates a new configuration context, defining a virtual host. The listen directive specifies the IP address(es) and port(s); the server_name directive lists the Host header values that this context matches.
server_name	This directive configures the names that a virtual host may respond to.
server_name_in_redirect	This directive activates using the first value of the server_name directive in any redirect issued by NGINX within this context.

HTTP server directives	Explanation
server_tokens	This directive disables sending the NGINX version string in error messages and the Server response header (the default value is on).

Logging in NGINX

NGINX has a very flexible logging model. Each level of configuration may have an access log. In addition, more than one access log may be specified per level, each with a different log_format directive. The log_format directive allows you to specify exactly what will be logged, and needs to be defined within the http section.

The path to the log file itself may contain variables so that you can build a dynamic configuration. The following example describes how this can be put into practice:

```
http {

  log_format vhost '$host $remote_addr - $remote_user
    [$time_local] '
'"$request" $status $body_bytes_sent '
'"$http_referer" "$http_user_agent"';

  log_format downloads '$time_iso8601 $host $remote_addr '
'"$request" $status $body_bytes_sent $request_
    time';

  open_log_file_cache max=1000 inactive=60s;

  access_log logs/access.log;

  server {

    server_name ~^(www\.)?(.+)$;

    access_log logs/combined.log vhost;

    access_log logs/$2/access.log;

    location /downloads {

      access_log logs/downloads.log downloads;

    }

  }

}
```

The following table describes the directives used in the preceding configuration snippet:

HTTP logging directives	Explanation
access_log	This directive describes where and how access logs are to be written. The first parameter is a path to the file where the logs are to be stored. Variables may be used in constructing the path. The special value, off, disables the access log. An optional second parameter indicates the log_format directive that will be used to write the logs. If no second parameter is configured, the predefined combined format is used. An optional third parameter indicates the size of the buffer if write buffering should be used to record the logs. If write buffering is used, this size cannot exceed the size of an atomic disk write for that filesystem. If this third parameter is gzip, the buffered logs will be compressed on-the-fly, provided that the nginx binary was built with the zlib library. A final flush parameter indicates the maximum length of time buffered log data may remain in memory before being flushed to disk.
log_format	This directive specifies which fields should appear in the log file and what format they should take. See the next table for a description of the log-specific variables.
log_not_found	This directive disables reporting of the 404 errors in the error log (the default value is on).
log_subrequest	This directive enables the logging of subrequests in the access log (the default value is off).

HTTP logging directives	Explanation
open_log_file_cache	This directive stores a cache of open file descriptors used in the access_log directives with a variable in the path. The parameters used are as follows: • max: This parameter specifies the maximum number of file descriptors present in the cache • inactive: With this parameter, NGINX will wait this amount of time for something to be written to this log before its file descriptor is closed • min_uses: With this parameter, the file descriptor has to be used this amount of times within the inactive period in order to remain open • valid: With this parameter, NGINX will check this often to see if the file descriptor still matches a file with the same name • off: This parameter disables the cache

In the following example, log entries will be compressed at a gzip level of 4. The buffer size is 64 KB by default and will be flushed to disk at least every minute:

```
access_log /var/log/nginx/access.log.gz combined gzip=4 flush=1m;
```

Note that when specifying gzip, the log_format parameter is not optional.

The default value combined log_format is constructed like this:

```
log_format combined '$remote_addr - $remote_user [$time_local] '
'"$request" $status $body_bytes_sent '
'"$http_referer" "$http_user_agent"';
```

As you can see, line breaks may be used to improve readability. They do not affect the `log_format` directive itself. Any variables may be used in the `log_format` directive. The variables in the following table that are marked with an asterisk (*) are specific to logging and may only be used in the `log_format` directive. The others may be used elsewhere in the configuration, as well.

Log format variable names	Value
$body_bytes_sent	This variable specifies the number of bytes sent to the client, excluding the response header.
$bytes_sent	This variable specifies the number of bytes sent to the client.
$connection	This variable specifies a serial number, used to identify unique connections.
$connection_requests	This variable specifies the number of requests made through a particular connection.
$msec	This variable specifies the time in seconds, with millisecond resolution.
$pipe *	This variable indicates whether the request was pipelined (p) or not (.).
$request_length *	This variable specifies the length of the request, including the HTTP method, URI, HTTP protocol, header, and request body.
$request_time	This variable specifies the request processing time, with millisecond resolution, from the first byte received from the client to the last byte sent to the client.
$status	This variable specifies the response status.
$time_iso8601 *	This variable specifies the local time in the ISO8601 format.
$time_local *	This variable specifies the local time in the common log format (%d/%b/%Y:%H:%M:%S %z).

In this section, we focused solely on `access_log` and how this directive can be configured. You can also configure NGINX to log errors. The `error_log` directive is described in *Chapter 9, Troubleshooting Techniques*.

Finding files

In order for NGINX to respond to a request, it passes it to a content handler, determined by the configuration of the location directive. The unconditional content handlers are tried first: perl, proxy_pass, flv, mp4, and so on. If none of these handlers is a match, the request is passed to one of the following, in order: random index, index, autoindex, gzip_static, and static. Requests with a trailing slash are handled by one of the index handlers. If gzip is not activated, the static module handles the request. How these modules find the appropriate file or directory on the filesystem is determined by a combination of certain directives. The root directive is best defined in a default server directive, or at least outside of a specific location directive so that it will be valid for the whole server:

```
server {

  root /home/customer/html;

  location / {

    index index.html index.htm;

  }
  location /downloads {

    autoindex on;

  }

}
```

In the preceding example, any files to be served are found under the root directive, /home/customer/html. If the client entered just the domain name, NGINX will try to serve index.html. If that file does not exist, NGINX will serve index.htm. When a user enters the /downloads URI in their browser, they will be presented with a directory listing in the HTML format. This makes it easy for users to access sites hosting software that they would like to download. NGINX will automatically rewrite the URI of a directory so that the trailing slash is present, and then issue an HTTP redirect. NGINX appends the URI to the root directive to find the file to deliver to the client.

If this file does not exist, the client receives a `404 Not Found` error message. If you don't want the error message to be returned to the client, one alternative is to try to deliver a file from different filesystem locations, falling back to a generic page, if none of those options are available. The `try_files` directive can be used as follows:

```
location / {

  try_files $uri $uri/ backups$uri /generic-not-found.html;

}
```

As a security precaution, NGINX can check the path to a file it's about to deliver, and if part of the path to the file contains a symbolic link, it returns an error message to the client:

```
server {

  root /home/customer/html;

  disable_symlinks if_not_owner from=$document_root;

}
```

In the preceding example, NGINX will return a `Permission Denied` error if `symlink` is found after `/home/customer/html`, and that `symlink` instance and the file it points to do not both belong to the same user ID.

The following table summarizes these directives:

HTTP file-path directives	Explanation
`disable_symlinks`	This directive determines whether NGINX should perform a symbolic link check on the path to a file before delivering it to the client. The following parameters are recognized: • `off`: This parameter disables checking for `symlinks` (default) • `on`: In this parameter, if any part of a path is `symlink`, access is denied • `if_not_owner`: In this parameter, if any part of a path contains `symlink` in which the link and the referent have different owners, access to the file is denied • `from=part`: When this parameter is specified, the path up to part is not checked for `symlinks`, everything afterward is according to either the `on` or `if_not_owner` parameter

HTTP file-path directives	Explanation
`root`	This directive sets the path to the document root. Files are found by appending the URI to the value of this directive.
`try_files`	This directive tests the existence of files given as parameters. If none of the previous files are found, the last entry is used as a fallback, so ensure that this path or named `location` exists, or is set to return a status code indicated by `=<status code>`.

Name resolution

If logical names instead of IP addresses are used in an `upstream` or `*_pass` directive, NGINX will, by default, use the operating system's resolver to get the IP address, which is what it really needs to connect to that server. This will happen only once, the first time `upstream` is requested, and won't work at all if a variable is used in the `*_pass` directive. It is possible, though, to configure a separate resolver for NGINX to use. By doing this, you can override the TTL returned by DNS, as well as use variables in the `*_pass` directives:

```
server {

  resolver 192.168.100.2 valid=300s;

}
```

The following table summarizes the name resolution directive:

Name resolution directive	Explanation
`resolver`	This directive configures one or more name servers to be used to resolve the upstream server names into the IP addresses. An optional `valid` parameter overrides the TTL of the domain name record.

In order to get NGINX to resolve an IP address anew, place the logical name into a variable. When NGINX resolves that variable, it implicitly makes a DNS look-up to find the IP address. For this to work, a `resolver` directive must be configured:

```
server {

  resolver 192.168.100.2;

  location / {

    set $backend upstream.example.com;
```

```
        proxy_pass http://$backend;

    }

}
```

Of course, by relying on DNS to find an upstream, you are dependent on the resolver always being available. When the resolver is not reachable, a gateway error occurs. In order to make the client wait time as short as possible, the `resolver_timeout` parameter should be set low. The gateway error can then be handled by an `error_page` designed for that purpose:

```
server {

    resolver 192.168.100.2;

    resolver_timeout 3s;

    error_page 504 /gateway-timeout.html;
    location / {

        proxy_pass http://upstream.example.com;

    }

}
```

 `resolver_timeout` is now only available with a commercial subscription.

Interacting with the client

There are a number of ways in which NGINX can interact with clients. This can range from attributes of the connection itself (IP address, timeouts, keepalive, and so on) to content negotiation headers. The directives listed in the following table describe how to set various headers and response codes to get the clients to request the correct page or serve up that page from its own cache:

HTTP client interaction directives	Explanation
default_type	This directive sets the default MIME type of a response. This directive comes into play if the MIME type of the file cannot be matched to one of those specified by the types directive.

HTTP client interaction directives	Explanation
error_page	This directive defines a URI to be served when an error level response code is encountered. Adding an = parameter allows the response code to be changed. If the argument to this parameter is left empty, the response code will be taken from the URI, which must in this case be served by an upstream server of some sort.
etag	This directive disables automatically generating the ETag response header for static resources (the default value is on).
if_modified_since	This directive controls how the modification time of a response is compared to the value of the If-Modified-Since request header: • off: With this parameter, the If-Modified-Since header is ignored • exact: With this parameter, an exact match is made (default) • before: With this parameter, the modification time of the response is less than or equal to the value of the If-Modified-Since header
ignore_invalid_headers	This directive disables ignoring headers with invalid names (the default value is on). A valid name is composed of ASCII letters, numbers, a hyphen, and possibly an underscore (controlled by the underscores_in_headers directive).
merge_slashes	This directive disables the removal of multiple slashes. The default value of on means that NGINX will compress two or more / characters into one.
recursive_error_pages	This directive enables doing more than one redirect using the error_page directive (the default value is off).
types	This directive sets up a map of MIME types to file name extensions. NGINX ships with a conf/mime.types file that contains most MIME type mappings. Using include to load this file should be sufficient for most purposes.
underscores_in_headers	This directive enables the use of the underscore character in client request headers. If left at the default value off, evaluation of such headers is subject to the value of the ignore_invalid_headers directive.

The `error_page` directive is one of NGINX's most flexible. Using this directive, we may serve any page when an error condition presents. This page could be on the local machine, but could also be a dynamic page produced by an application server, and could even be a page on a completely different site.

```
http {

  # a generic error page to handle any server-level errors
  error_page 500 501 502 503 504 share/examples/nginx/50x.html;

  server {

    server_name www.example.com;

    root /home/customer/html;

    # for any files not found, the page located at
    # /home/customer/html/404.html will be delivered
    error_page 404 /404.html;
    location / {

      # any server-level errors for this host will be directed
      # to a custom application handler
      error_page 500 501 502 503 504 = @error_handler;

    }

    location /microsite {

      # for any non-existent files under the /microsite URI,
      # the client will be shown a foreign page
      error_page 404 http://microsite.example.com/404.html;

    }

    # the named location containing the custom error handler
    location @error_handler {

      # we set the default type here to ensure the browser
      # displays the error page correctly
      default_type text/html;
```

```
        proxy_pass http://127.0.0.1:8080;

    }

    }

}
```

Using limits to prevent abuse

We build and host websites because we want users to visit them. We want our
websites to always be available for legitimate access. This means that we may have
to take measures to limit access to abusive users. We may define *abusive* to mean
anything from one request per second to a number of connections from the same
IP address. Abuse can also take the form of a **distributed denial-of-service (DDoS)**
attack, where bots running on multiple machines around the world all try to access
the site as many times as possible at the same time. In this section, we will explore
methods to counter each type of abuse to ensure that our websites are available.

First, let's take a look at the different configuration directives that will help us
achieve our goal:

HTTP limits directives	Explanation
limit_conn	This directive specifies a shared memory zone (configured with limit_conn_zone) and the maximum number of connections that are allowed per key value.
limit_conn_log_level	When NGINX limits a connection due to the limit_conn directive, this directive specifies at which log level that limitation is reported.
limit_conn_zone	This directive specifies the key to be limited in limit_conn as the first parameter. The second parameter, zone, indicates the name of the shared memory zone used to store the key, current number of connections per key, and the size of that zone (name:size).
limit_rate	This directive limits the rate (in bytes per second) at which clients can download content. The rate limit works on a connection level, meaning that a single client could increase their throughput by opening multiple connections.
limit_rate_after	This directive starts the limit_rate directive after these numbers of bytes have been transferred.

HTTP limits directives	Explanation
limit_req	This directive sets a limit with bursting capability on the number of requests for a specific key in a shared memory store (configured with limit_req_zone). The burst can be specified with the second parameter. If there shouldn't be a delay in between requests up to the burst, a third parameter, nodelay, needs to be configured.
limit_req_log_level	When NGINX limits the number of requests due to the limit_req directive, this directive specifies at which log level that limitation is reported. A delay is logged at a level one less than the one indicated here.
limit_req_zone	This directive specifies the key to be limited in limit_req as the first parameter. The second parameter, zone, indicates the name of the shared memory zone used to store the key, the current number of requests per key, and the size of that zone (name:size). The third parameter, rate, configures the number of requests per second (r/s) or per minute (r/m) before the limit is imposed.
max_ranges	This directive sets the maximum number of ranges allowed in a byte-range request. Specifying 0 disables byte-range support.

Here we limit access to 10 connections per unique IP address. This should be enough for normal browsing, as modern browsers open two to three connections per host. Keep in mind, though, that any users behind a proxy will appear to come from the same address. So observe the logs for the error code 503 (Service Unavailable), meaning that this limit has come into effect:

```
http {

    limit_conn_zone $binary_remote_addr zone=connections:10m;

    limit_conn_log_level notice;

    server {

        limit_conn connections 10;

    }

}
```

Limiting access based on a rate looks almost the same, but works a bit differently. When limiting how many pages per unit of time a user may request, NGINX will insert a delay after the first page request, up to a burst. This may or may not be what you want, so NGINX offers the possibility to remove this delay with the `nodelay` parameter:

```
http {

  limit_req_zone $binary_remote_addr zone=requests:10m rate=1r/s;

  limit_req_log_level warn;

  server {

    limit_req zone=requests burst=10 nodelay;

  }
}
```

We can also limit the bandwidth per client. In this way, we can ensure that a few clients don't take up all the available bandwidth. One caveat, though: the `limit_rate` directive works on a connection basis. A single client that is allowed to open multiple connections will still be able to get around this limit:

```
location /downloads {

  limit_rate 500k;

}
```

Alternatively, we can allow a kind of bursting to freely download smaller files, but make sure that larger ones are limited:

```
location /downloads {

  limit_rate_after 1m;

  limit_rate 500k;

}
```

Combining these different rate limitations enables us to create a configuration that is very flexible as to how and where clients are limited:

```
http {

    limit_conn_zone $binary_remote_addr zone=ips:10m;

    limit_conn_zone $server_name zone=servers:10m;

    limit_req_zone $binary_remote_addr zone=requests:10m rate=1r/s;

    limit_conn_log_level notice;

    limit_req_log_level warn;

    # immediately release socket buffer memory on timeout
    reset_timedout_connection on;

    server {

        # these limits apply to the whole virtual server
        limit_conn ips 10;
        # only 1000 simultaneous connections to the same server_name
        limit_conn servers 1000;

        location /search {

            # here we want only the /search URL to be rate-limited
            limit_req zone=requests burst=3 nodelay;

        }

        location /downloads {

            # using limit_conn to ensure that each client is
              # bandwidth-limited
            # with no getting around it
            limit_conn connections 1;

            limit_rate_after 1m;

            limit_rate 500k;

        }

    }

}
```

Restricting access

In the previous section, we explored ways to limit abusive access to websites running under NGINX. Now, we will take a look at ways to restrict access to a whole website or certain parts of it. Access restriction can take two forms here: restricting a certain set of IP addresses, or restricting a certain set of users. These two methods can also be combined to satisfy requirements that some users can access the website either from a certain set of IP addresses or if they are able to authenticate with a valid username and password.

The following directives will help us achieve these goals:

HTTP access module directives	Explanation
allow	This directive allows access from this IP address, network, or the all value.
auth_basic	This directive enables authentication using HTTP Basic Authentication. The string parameter is used as the realm name. If the special value, off, is used, this indicates that the auth_basic value of the parent configuration level is negated.
auth_basic_user_file	This directive indicates the location of a file of username:password:comment tuples used to authenticate users. The password field needs to be encrypted with the crypt algorithm. The comment field is optional.
deny	This directive denies access from this IP address, network, or the all value.
satisfy	This directive allows access if all or any of the preceding directives grant access. The default value, all, indicates that a user must come from a specific network address and enter the correct password.

To restrict access to clients coming from a certain set of IP addresses, the allow and deny directives can be used as follows:

```
location /stats {

    allow 127.0.0.1;
    deny all;

}
```

This configuration will allow access to the /stats URI only from localhost.

To restrict access to authenticated users, the auth_basic and auth_basic_user_file directives are used as follows:

```
server {

  server_name restricted.example.com;

  auth_basic "restricted";

  auth_basic_user_file conf/htpasswd;

}
```

Any user wanting to access restricted.example.com would need to provide credentials matching those in the htpasswd file located in the conf directory of NGINX's root. The entries in the htpasswd file can be generated using any available tool that uses the standard UNIX crypt() function. For example, the following Ruby script will generate a file of the appropriate format:

```ruby
#!/usr/bin/env ruby

# setup the command-line options
require 'optparse'

OptionParser.new do |o|

o.on('-f FILE') { |file| $file = file }

o.on('-u', "--username USER") { |u| $user = u }

o.on('-p', "--password PASS") { |p| $pass = p }

o.on('-c', "--comment COMM (optional)") { |c| $comm = c }

o.on('-h') { puts o; exit }

o.parse!

if $user.nil? or $pass.nil?
puts o; exit

end
```

```
end

# initialize an array of ASCII characters to be used for the salt
ascii = ('a'..'z').to_a + ('A'..'Z').to_a + ('0'..'9').to_a + [
  ".", "/" ]

$lines = []

begin

# read in the current http auth file
File.open($file) do |f|

f.lines.each { |l| $lines << l }

end

rescue Errno::ENOENT

# if the file doesn't exist (first use), initialize the array
$lines = ["#{$user}:#{$pass}\n"]

end

# remove the user from the current list, since this is the one
  we're editing
$lines.map! do |line|

unless line =~ /#{$user}:/

line

end

end

# generate a crypt()ed password
pass = $pass.crypt(ascii[rand(64)] + ascii[rand(64)])
# if there's a comment, insert it
if $comm

$lines << "#{$user}:#{$pass}:#{$comm}\n"
```

```
else

$lines << "#{$user}:#{pass}\n"

end

# write out the new file, creating it if necessary

File.open($file, File::RDWR|File::CREAT) do |f|

$lines.each { |l| f << l}

end
```

Save this file as http_auth_basic.rb and give it a filename (-f), a user (-u),
and a password (-p), and it will generate entries appropriate to use in the
auth_basic_user_file directive of NGINX:

$ ./http_auth_basic.rb -f htpasswd -u testuser -p 123456

To handle scenarios where a username and password should only be entered if not
coming from a certain set of IP addresses, NGINX has the satisfy directive. The any
parameter is used here for this either/or scenario:

```
server {

  server_name intranet.example.com;

  location / {

    auth_basic "intranet: please login";

    # select a user/password combo from this file
    auth_basic_user_file conf/htpasswd-intranet;

    # unless coming from one of these networks
    allow 192.168.40.0/24;

    allow 192.168.50.0/24;

    # deny access if these conditions aren't met
    deny all;

    # if either condition is met, allow access
    satisfy any;
  }
}
```

If, instead, the requirements are for a configuration in which the user must come from a certain IP address and provide authentication, the `all` parameter is the default. So, we omit the `satisfy` directive itself and include only `allow`, `deny`, `auth_basic`, and `auth_basic_user_file`:

```
server {

  server_name stage.example.com;

  location / {

    auth_basic "staging server";

    auth_basic_user_file conf/htpasswd-stage;

    allow 192.168.40.0/24;

    allow 192.168.50.0/24;

    deny all;
  }
}
```

Streaming media files

NGINX is capable of serving certain video media types. The `flv` and `mp4` modules, included in the base distribution, can perform what is called pseudo-streaming. This means that NGINX will seek a certain location in the video file, as indicated by the `start` request parameter.

In order to use the pseudo-streaming capabilities, the corresponding module needs to be included at compile time: `--with-http_flv_module` for **Flash Video** (**FLV**) files and/or `--with-http_mp4_module` for H.264/AAC files. The following directives will then become available for configuration:

HTTP streaming directives	Explanation
flv	This directive activates the `flv` module for this location.
mp4	This directive activates the `mp4` module for this location.
mp4_buffer_ size	This directive sets the initial buffer size for delivering the MP4 files.
mp4_max_ buffer_size	This directive sets the maximum size of the buffer used to process MP4 metadata.

Activating FLV pseudo-streaming for a location is as simple as just including the `flv` keyword:

```
location /videos {

    flv;

}
```

There are more options for MP4 pseudo-streaming, as the H.264 format includes metadata that needs to be parsed. Seeking is available once `moov atom` has been parsed by the player. So, to optimize performance, ensure that the metadata is at the beginning of the file. If an error message, such as the following line, shows up in the logs, the `mp4_max_buffer_size` directive value needs to be increased:

mp4 moov atom is too large

The `mp4_max_buffer_size` value can be increased as follows:

```
location /videos {

    mp4;

    mp4_buffer_size 1m;

    mp4_max_buffer_size 20m;

}
```

Predefined variables

NGINX makes constructing configurations based on the values of variables easy. Not only can you instantiate your own variables by using the `set` or `map` directives, but there are also predefined variables used within NGINX. They are optimized for quick evaluation and the values are cached for the lifetime of a request. You can use any of them as a key in an `if` statement, or pass them on to a proxy. A number of them may prove useful if you define your own log file format. If you try to redefine any of them, though, you will get an error message, as follows:

```
<timestamp> [emerg] <master pid>#0: the duplicate "<variable_name>"
variable in <path-to-configuration-file>:<line-number>
```

They are also not made for macro expansion in the configuration—they are mostly used at runtime.

The following table lists the variables and their values defined in the `http` module:

HTTP variable names	Value
$arg_name	This variable specifies the name argument present in the request parameters.
$args	This variable specifies all of the request parameters.
$binary_remote_addr	This variable specifies the client's IP address in binary form (always 4 bytes long).
$content_length	This variable specifies the value of the Content-Length request header.
$content_type	This variable specifies the value of the Content-Type request header.
$cookie_name	This variable specifies the cookie labeled name.
$document_root	This variable specifies the value of the root or alias directive for the current request.
$document_uri	This variable specifies an alias for $uri.
$host	This variable specifies the value of the Host request header, if present. If this header is not present, the value is equal to the server_name directive matching the request.
$hostname	This variable specifies the name of the host where NGINX is running.
$http_name	This variable specifies the value of the name request header. If this header has dashes, they are converted to underscores, capital letters to lowercase.
$https	If the connection was made over SSL, the value of this variable is on. Otherwise, it's an empty string.
$is_args	If the request has arguments, the value of this variable is ?. Otherwise, it's an empty string.
$limit_rate	This variable specifies the value of the limit_rate directive. If the value is not set, it allows rate limitation to be set using this variable.
$nginx_version	This variable specifies the version of the running nginx binary.
$pid	This variable specifies the process ID of the worker process.
$query_string	This variable specifies an alias for $args.
$realpath_root	This variable specifies the value of the root or alias directive for the current request, with all symbolic links resolved.
$remote_addr	This variable specifies the client's IP address.
$remote_port	This variable specifies the client's port.

HTTP variable names	Value
`$remote_user`	When using HTTP basic authentication, this variable is set to the username.
`$request`	This variable specifies the complete request, as received from the client, including the HTTP method, URI, HTTP protocol, header, and request body.
`$request_body`	This variable specifies the body of the request, for use in locations processed by a `*_pass` directive.
`$request_body_file`	This variable specifies the path to the temporary file where the request's body is saved. For this file to be saved, the `client_body_in_file_only` directive needs to be set to `on`.
`$request_completion`	If the request has completed, the value of this variable is `OK`. Otherwise, it's an empty string.
`$request_filename`	This variable specifies the path to the file for the current request, based on the value of the `root` or `alias` directive plus the URI.
`$request_method`	This variable specifies the HTTP method used in the current request.
`$request_uri`	This variable specifies the complete request URI, as received from the client, including arguments.
`$scheme`	This variable specifies the scheme for the current request, either HTTP or HTTPS.
`$sent_http_name`	This variable specifies the value of the `name` response header. If this header has dashes, they are converted to underscores; capital letters are converted to lowercase.
`$server_addr`	This variable specifies the value of the server's address that accepted the request.
`$server_name`	This variable specifies the `server_name` value of the virtual host that accepted the request.
`$server_port`	This variable specifies the value of the server's port that accepted the request.
`$server_protocol`	This variable specifies the HTTP protocol used in the current request.
`$status`	This variable specifies the status of response.
`$tcpinfo_rtt`, `$tcpinfo_rttvar`, `$tcpinfo_snd_cwnd`, and `$tcpinfo_rcv_space`	If a system supports the `TCP_INFO` socket option, these variables will be filled with the relevant information.
`$uri`	This variable specifies the normalized URI of the current request.

SPDY and HTTP/2

The SPDY protocol was developed by Google to accelerate the web browsing experience. There are currently four drafts; the final one supported in NGINX labeled Draft 3.1. NGINX supported this draft as of version 1.5.10.

The protocol developers also had a hand in the ratification of HTTP/2. SPDY has since been deprecated; all support for it will end in 2016. It is superseded by HTTP version 2 (HTTP/2), which NGINX has supported since version 1.9.5.

Support for HTTP/2 can be activated by including the compile-time flag, `--with-http_v2_module`. This will make the following directives available for configuration:

HTTP/2 directives	Explanation
http2_chunk_size	This directive sets the maximum chunk size for the response body.
http2_idle_timeout	This directive specifies the amount of time with no activity after which the connection is closed.
http2_max_concurrent_streams	This directive sets the number of HTTP/2 streams that may be active in a single connection.
http2_max_field_size	This directive sets the maximum size of the compressed request header field.
http2_max_header_size	This directive sets the maximum size of the uncompressed request headers.
http2_recv_buffer_size	This directive specifies the size of the input buffer for each worker.
http2_recv_timeout	This directive specifies the amount of time a client has to send data before the connection is closed.

The HTTP/2 module is considered experimental, so users should be cautious when activating it. Since most browsers only support HTTP/2 under encrypted connections, best practice dictates activating it via the `http2` keyword of the `listen` directive:

```
server {

  listen 443 ssl http2;

  ssl_certificate www.example.com.crt;

  ssl_certificate_key www.example.com.key;

}
```

HTTP/2 over TLS requires OpenSSL 1.0.2 due to the **Application-Layer Protocol Negotiation (ALPN)** support. Be sure your nginx binary is compiled with at least this version of OpenSSL.

Using NGINX with PHP-FPM

Apache has long been considered the only option for serving the PHP websites because the mod_php Apache module makes integrating PHP directly into the web server an easy task. With **PHP-FPM** being accepted into PHP's core, there is now an alternative bundled with the PHP distribution. PHP-FPM is a way of running PHP under a FastCGI server. The PHP-FPM master process takes care of spawning workers, adapting to site usage, and restarting sub-processes when necessary. It communicates with other services using the FastCGI protocol. You can learn more about PHP-FPM itself at http://php.net/manual/en/install.fpm.php.

NGINX has a fastcgi module, which is capable of communicating not only with PHP-FPM, but also with any FastCGI-compliant server. It is enabled by default, so no special consideration needs to be made to start using NGINX with FastCGI servers. The following table lists the FastCGI directives:

FastCGI Directive	Explanation
fastcgi_buffer_size	This directive specifies the size of the buffer used for the first part of the response from the FastCGI server, in which the response headers are found.
fastcgi_buffers	This directive specifies the number and size of buffers used for the response from a FastCGI server, for a single connection.
fastcgi_busy_buffers_size	This directive specifies the total size of buffer space allocated to sending the response to the client while still being read from the FastCGI server. This is typically set to two fastcgi_buffers.
fastcgi_cache	This directive defines a shared memory zone to be used for caching.
fastcgi_cache_bypass	This directive specifies one or more string variables, which, when non-empty or non-zero, will cause the response to be taken from the FastCGI server instead of the cache.
fastcgi_cache_key	This directive specifies a string used as the key for storing and retrieving cache values.
fastcgi_cache_lock	Enabling this directive will prevent multiple requests from making an entry into the same cache key.

FastCGI Directive	Explanation
fastcgi_cache_lock_timeout	This directive specifies the length of time a request will wait for an entry to appear in the cache or for the fastcgi_cache_lock directive to be released.
fastcgi_cache_min_uses	This directive specifies the number of requests for a certain key needed before a response is cached.
fastcgi_cache_path	This directive specifies a directory that places the cached responses and a shared memory zone (keys_zone = name:size) to store active keys and response metadata. The optional parameters are as follows: • levels: This parameter specifies the colon-separated length of the subdirectory name at each level (one or two); a maximum of three levels deep • inactive: This parameter specifies the maximum length of time an inactive response stays in the cache before being ejected • max_size: This parameter specifies the maximum size of the cache; when the size exceeds this value, a cache manager process removes the least recently used items • loader_files: This parameter specifies the maximum number of cached files whose metadata are loaded per iteration of the cache loader process • loader_sleep: This parameter specifies the number of milliseconds paused between each iteration of the cache loader process • loader_threshold: This parameter specifies the maximum length of time a cache loader iteration may take
fastcgi_cache_use_stale	This directive specifies the cases under which it is acceptable to serve stale cached data if an error occurs when accessing the FastCGI server. The updating parameter indicates the case when fresh data is being loaded.

FastCGI Directive	Explanation
`fastcgi_cache_valid`	This directive indicates the length of time for which a cached response with response code `200`, `301`, or `302` is valid. If an optional response code is given before the `time` parameter, that time is only for that response code. The special parameter, `any`, indicates that any response code should be cached for that length of time.
`fastcgi_connect_timeout`	This directive specifies the maximum amount of time NGINX will wait for its connection to be accepted when making a request to a FastCGI server.
`fastcgi_hide_header`	This directive specifies a list of header fields that should not be passed on to the client.
`fastcgi_ignore_client_abort`	If this directive is set to `on`, NGINX will not abort the connection to a FastCGI server if the client aborts the connection.
`fastcgi_ignore_headers`	This directive sets the headers that may be disregarded when processing the response from the FastCGI server.
`fastcgi_index`	This directive sets the name of a file to be appended to `$fastcgi_script_name` that ends with a slash.
`fastcgi_intercept_errors`	If this directive is enabled, NGINX will display a configured `error_page` directive instead of the response directly from the FastCGI server.
`fastcgi_keep_conn`	This directive enables the `keepalive` connections to the FastCGI servers by instructing the server not to immediately close the connection.
`fastcgi_max_temp_file_size`	This directive specifies the maximum size of the overflow file; this directive is written when the response doesn't fit into memory buffers.

FastCGI Directive	Explanation
fastcgi_next_upstream	This directive indicates the conditions under which the next FastCGI server will be selected for the response. This won't be used if the client has already been sent something. The conditions are specified using the following parameters: • error: This parameter specifies an error occurred while communicating with the FastCGI server • timeout: This parameter specifies a timeout occurred while communicating with the FastCGI server • invalid_header: This parameter specifies the FastCGI server returned an empty or otherwise invalid response • http_500: This parameter specifies the FastCGI server responded with a 500 error code • http_503: This parameter specifies the FastCGI server responded with a 503 error code • http_404: This parameter specifies the FastCGI server responded with a 404 error code • off: This parameter specifies disables passing the request to the next FastCGI server when an error occurs
fastcgi_no_cache	This directive specifies one or more string variables, which, when non-empty or non-zero, will instruct NGINX to not save the response from the FastCGI server in the cache.
fastcgi_param	This directive sets a parameter and its value to be passed to the FastCGI server. If the parameter should only be passed when the value is non-empty, the if_not_empty additional parameter should be set.
fastcgi_pass	This directive specifies the FastCGI server to which the request is passed, either as an address:port combination or as unix:path for a UNIX-domain socket.

FastCGI Directive	Explanation
`fastcgi_pass_header`	This directive overrides the disabled headers set in `fastcgi_hide_header`, allowing them to be sent to the client.
`fastcgi_read_timeout`	This directive specifies the length of time that needs to elapse between two successive read operations from a FastCGI server before the connection is closed.
`fastcgi_send_timeout`	This directive specifies the length of time that needs to elapse between two successive `write` operations to a FastCGI server before the connection is closed.
`fastcgi_split_path_info`	This directive defines a regular expression with two captures. The first capture will be the value of the `$fastcgi_script_name` variable. The second capture becomes the value of the `$fastcgi_path_info` variable. This directive is only necessary for applications that rely upon `PATH_INFO`.
`fastcgi_store`	This directive enables storing responses retrieved from a FastCGI server as files on disk. The `on` parameter will use the `alias` or `root` directive as the base path under which to store the file. A string may instead be given to indicate an alternative location to store the files.
`fastcgi_store_access`	This directive sets file access permissions for the newly-created `fastcgi_store` files.
`fastcgi_temp_file_write_size`	This directive limits the amount of data buffered to a temporary file at one time so that NGINX will not block for too long on a single request.
`fastcgi_temp_path`	This directive specifies a directory where temporary files may be buffered as they are proxied from the FastCGI server, optionally multilevel deep.

An example Drupal configuration

Drupal (`http://drupal.org`) is a popular open source content management platform. There is a large installed user base, and many popular websites are run on Drupal. As with most PHP web frameworks, Drupal is typically run under Apache using `mod_php`. We are going to explore how to configure NGINX to run Drupal.

There is a very comprehensive Drupal configuration guide for NGINX found at `https://github.com/perusio/drupal-with-nginx`. It goes more in-depth than we are able to do here, but we will point out some features mentioned, and go through some of the differences between Drupal 6 and Drupal 7:

```
## Defines the $no_slash_uri variable for drupal 6.
map $uri $no_slash_uri {

    ~^/(?<no_slash>.*)$ $no_slash;
}

server {

  server_name www.example.com;

  root /home/customer/html;
  index index.php;

  # keep alive to the FastCGI upstream (used in conjunction with
  # the "keepalive" directive in the upstream section)
  fastcgi_keep_conn on;

  # The 'default' location.
  location / {
    ## (Drupal 6) Use index.html whenever there's no index.php.
    location = / {
      error_page 404 =200 /index.html;
    }
    # Regular private file serving (i.e. handled by Drupal).
    location ^~ /system/files/ {

      include fastcgi_private_files.conf;

      fastcgi_pass 127.0.0.1:9000;
      # For not signaling a 404 in the error log whenever the
      # system/files directory is accessed add the line below.
      # Note that the 404 is the intended behavior.
      log_not_found off;

    }
```

```
# Trying to access private files directly returns a 404.
location ^~ /sites/default/files/private/ {
  internal;
}

## (Drupal 6) If accessing an image generated by imagecache,
## serve it directly if available, if not relay the request to
  # Drupal
## to (re)generate the image.
location ~* /imagecache/ {

  access_log off;

  expires 30d;

  try_files $uri /index.php?q=$no_slash_uri&$args;

}

# Drupal 7 image handling, i.e., imagecache in core
location ~* /files/styles/ {

  access_log off;

  expires 30d;

  try_files $uri @drupal;

}
```

The Advanced Aggregation module configuration coming up next differs only in the location path used. The Advanced Aggregation module configuration for CSS is as follows:

```
# Advanced Aggregation module CSS support.
location ^~ /sites/default/files/advagg_css/ {
  location ~*
    /sites/default/files/advagg_css/css_[[:alnum:]]+\.css$ {
```

And for JavaScript, is as follows:

```
# Advanced Aggregation module JS
location ^~ /sites/default/files/advagg_js/ {
  location ~*
    /sites/default/files/advagg_js/js_[[:alnum:]]+\.js$ {
```

The common lines to both sections are as follows:

```
access_log off;

add_header Pragma '';

add_header Cache-Control 'public, max-age=946080000';

add_header Accept-Ranges '';

# This is for Drupal 7
try_files $uri @drupal;

## This is for Drupal 6 (use only one)
try_files $uri /index.php?q=$no_slash_uri&$args;

    }

}


# All static files will be served directly.
location ~* ^.+\.(?:css|cur|js|jpe?g|gif|htc|ico|png|html|x
  ml)$ {

  access_log off;

  expires 30d;

  # Send everything all at once.
  tcp_nodelay off;

  # Set the OS file cache.
  open_file_cache max=3000 inactive=120s;
  open_file_cache_valid 45s;

  open_file_cache_min_uses 2;

  open_file_cache_errors off;

}
```

```
# PDFs and powerpoint files handling.
location ~* ^.+\.(?:pdf|pptx?)$ {

  expires 30d;

  # Send everything all at once.
  tcp_nodelay off;

}
```

Serving audio files exemplifies the use of AIO. The MP3 location is as follows:

```
# MP3 files are served using AIO where supported by the OS.
location ^~ /sites/default/files/audio/mp3 {

  location ~* ^/sites/default/files/audio/mp3/.*\.mp3$ {
```

And the Ogg/Vorbis location is as follows:

```
# Ogg/Vorbis files are served using AIO where supported by the
OS.
location ^~ /sites/default/files/audio/ogg {

  location ~* ^/sites/default/files/audio/ogg/.*\.ogg$ {
```

These have the following lines in common:

```
      directio 4k; # for XFS

      tcp_nopush off;
      aio on;
      output_buffers 1 2M;
    }

}
# Pseudo-streaming of FLV files
location ^~ /sites/default/files/video/flv {

  location ~* ^/sites/default/files/video/flv/.*\.flv$ {

    flv;

  }

}
```

The next two pseudo-streaming sections are also similar. The Pseudo-streaming for H264 files is specified as follows:

```
# Pseudo-streaming of H264 files.
location ^~ /sites/default/files/video/mp4 {

    location ~* ^/sites/default/files/video/mp4/.*\.(?:mp4|mov)$ {
```

And pseudo-streaming for AAC files is specified as follows:

```
# Pseudo-streaming of AAC files.
location ^~ /sites/default/files/video/m4a {

    location ~* ^/sites/default/files/video/m4a/.*\.m4a$ {
```

These have the following lines in common between them:

```
        mp4;

        mp4_buffer_size 1M;

        mp4_max_buffer_size 5M;

    }

}

# Advanced Help module makes each module-provided
# README available.
location ^~ /help/ {

    location ~* ^/help/[^/]*/README\.txt$ {
        include fastcgi_private_files.conf;

        fastcgi_pass 127.0.0.1:9000;

    }
}

    # Replicate the Apache <FilesMatch> directive of Drupal
    # standard
    # .htaccess. Disable access to any code files. Return a 404 to
    # curtail
    # information disclosure. Also hide the text files.
```

```
location ~* ^(?:.+\.(?:htaccess|make|txt|engine|inc|info|inst
  all|module|profile|po|sh|.*sql|test|theme|tpl(?:\.
    php)?|xtmpl)|code-style\.pl|/Entries.*|/Repository|/Root|/
      Tag|/Template)$ {

  return 404;

}


  #First we try the URI and relay to the /index.php?q=$uri&$args
    if not found.
  try_files $uri @drupal;

  ## (Drupal 6) First we try the URI and relay to the /index.
    php?q=$no_slash_uri&$args if not found. (use only one)
  try_files $uri /index.php?q=$no_slash_uri&$args;

} # default location ends here

# Restrict access to the strictly necessary PHP files. Reducing
  the
# scope for exploits. Handling of PHP code and the Drupal event
  loop.
location @drupal {

  # Include the FastCGI config.
  include fastcgi_drupal.conf;

  fastcgi_pass 127.0.0.1:9000;

}

location @drupal-no-args {
  include fastcgi_private_files.conf;

  fastcgi_pass 127.0.0.1:9000;

}

## (Drupal 6)
## Restrict access to the strictly necessary PHP files. Reducing
  # the
## scope for exploits. Handling of PHP code and the Drupal event
  # loop.
## (use only one)
```

```
location = /index.php {

  # This is marked internal as a pro-active security practice.
  # No direct access to index.php is allowed; all accesses are
    # made
  # by NGINX from other locations or internal redirects.
  internal;

  fastcgi_pass 127.0.0.1:9000;

}
```

The following `location` instances all have `return 404` in order to deny access:

```
# Disallow access to .git directory: return 404 as not to disclose
# information.
location ^~ /.git { return 404; }
# Disallow access to patches directory.
location ^~ /patches { return 404; }
# Disallow access to drush backup directory.
location ^~ /backup { return 404; }
# Disable access logs for robots.txt.
location = /robots.txt {

  access_log off;

}

# RSS feed support.
location = /rss.xml {

  try_files $uri @drupal-no-args;
  ## (Drupal 6: use only one)
  try_files $uri /index.php?q=$uri;

}

# XML Sitemap support.
location = /sitemap.xml {
  try_files $uri @drupal-no-args;

  ## (Drupal 6: use only one)
  try_files $uri /index.php?q=$uri;
  }
```

```
# Support for favicon. Return an 1x1 transparent GIF if it
  doesn't
# exist.
location = /favicon.ico {

  expires 30d;

  try_files /favicon.ico @empty;

}

# Return an in-memory 1x1 transparent GIF.
location @empty {

  expires 30d;

  empty_gif;

}

# Any other attempt to access PHP files returns a 404.
location ~* ^.+\.php$ {

  return 404;

}

} # server context ends here
```

The include files mentioned in the above are not reproduced here, for brevity's sake. They can be found in perusio's GitHub repository mentioned at the beginning of this section.

Wiring NGINX and uWSGI together

The Python **Web Server Gateway Interface (WSGI)** is an interface specification formalized as PEP-3333 (http://www.python.org/dev/peps/pep-3333/). Its purpose is to provide a standard interface between web servers and Python web applications or frameworks to promote web application portability across a variety of web servers. Due to its popularity in the Python community, a number of other languages have implementations that conform to the WSGI specification. The uWSGI server, although not written exclusively for Python, provides a way of running applications that conform to this specification. The native protocol used to communicate with the uWSGI server is called uwsgi.

More details about the uWSGI server, including installation instructions, example configurations, and other supported languages, can be found at http://projects.unbit.it/ uwsgi/ and https://github.com/unbit/uwsgi-docs.

The uwsgi module of NGINX can be configured to talk to this server using directives similar to the fastcgi_* directives discussed in the previous section. Most directives have the same meaning as their FastCGI counterparts, with the obvious difference being that they begin with uwsgi_ instead of fastcgi_. There are a few exceptions, however—uwsgi_modifier1 and uwsgi_modifier2, as well as uwsgi_string. The first two directives set either the first or second modifier, respectively, of the uwsgi packet header. uwsgi_string enables NGINX to pass an arbitrary string to uWSGI, or any other uwsgi server that supports the eval modifier. These modifiers are specific to the uwsgi protocol. A table of valid values and their meanings can be found at http://uwsgi-docs.readthedocs.org/en/latest/Protocol.html.

An example Django configuration

Django (https://www.djangoproject.com/) is a Python web framework in which developers can quickly create high-performing web applications. It has become a popular framework in which many different kinds of web application are written.

The following configuration is an example of how to connect NGINX to multiple Django applications running under an emperor mode uWSGI server with fastrouter activated. See the URLs embedded in the comments in the following code for more information about running uWSGI like this:

```
http {
  # spawn a uWSGI server to connect to
  # uwsgi --master --emperor /etc/djangoapps --fastrouter
    127.0.0.1:3017 --fastrouter-subscription-server 127.0.0.1:3032
  # see http://uwsgi-docs.readthedocs.org/en/latest/Emperor.html
  # and http://projects.unbit.it/uwsgi/wiki/Example
  upstream emperor {
    server 127.0.0.1:3017;
  }

  server {
    # the document root is set with a variable so that multiple
    # sites
    # may be served - note that all static application files are
    # expected to be found under a subdirectory "static" and all
    # user
```

```
# uploaded files under a subdirectory "media"
# see https://docs.djangoproject.com/en/dev/howto/static-
  files/
root /home/www/sites/$host;

location / {
  # CSS files are found under the "styles" subdirectory
  location ~* ^.+\.$ {
    root /home/www/sites/$host/static/styles;
    expires 30d;
  }
  # any paths not found under the document root get passed
    # to
  # the Django running under uWSGI
  try_files $uri @django;
}

location @django {
  # $document_root needs to point to the application code
  root /home/www/apps/$host;
  # the uwsgi_params file from the nginx distribution
  include uwsgi_params;
  # referencing the upstream we defined earlier, a uWSGI
    # server
  # running in Emperor mode with FastRouter
  uwsgi_param UWSGI_FASTROUTER_KEY $host;
  uwsgi_pass emperor;
}

# the robots.txt file is found under the "static" subdirectory
# an exact match speeds up the processing

location = /robots.txt {
  root /home/www/sites/$host/static;
  access_log off;
}

# again an exact match
location = /favicon.ico {
  error_page 404 = @empty;
  root /home/www/sites/$host/static;
  access_log off;
  expires 30d;
}
```

```
    # generates the empty image referenced above
    location @empty {
      empty_gif;
    }

    # if anyone tries to access a '.py' file directly,
    # return a File Not Found code
    location ~* ^.+\.py$ {
      return 404;
    }
  }
}
```

This code enables multiple sites to be dynamically hosted without changing the NGINX configuration.

Summary

In this chapter, we explored a number of directives used to make NGINX serve files over HTTP. Not only does the http module provide this functionality, but there are also a number of helper modules that are essential to the normal operation of NGINX. These helper modules are enabled by default. Combining the directives of these various modules enables us to build a configuration that meets our needs. We explored how NGINX finds files based on the URI requested. We examined how different directives control how the HTTP server interacts with the client, and how the error_page directive can be used to serve a number of needs. Limiting access based on bandwidth usage, request rate, and number of connections is all possible.

We saw, too, how we can restrict access based on either IP address or through requiring authentication. We explored how to use NGINX's logging capabilities to capture just the information we want. Pseudo-streaming was examined briefly, as well. NGINX provides us with a number of variables that we can use to construct our configurations. We also explored the possibility of using the fastcgi module to connect to the PHP-FPM applications and the uwsgi module to communicate with a uWSGI server. The example configurations combined the directives discussed in this chapter, as well as some discussed in other chapters.

The next chapter will introduce some modules that will help you as a developer integrate NGINX into your application.

7
NGINX for the Application Developer

Throughout the book so far, we saw how to configure NGINX for a number of different scenarios. What we have not yet done is look at the possibilities that NGINX offers to the application developer. There are a number of ways that NGINX can be integrated directly into your application. We will explore those possibilities in the following sections:

- Caching integration
- Changing content on-the-fly
- Using Server Side Includes
- Decision-making in NGINX
- Creating a secure link
- Generating images
- Tracking website visitors
- Preventing inadvertent code execution

Caching integration

NGINX is superb at serving static content. It is designed to support over 100,000 simultaneous connections while using only minimal system resources. Integrating a dynamic web application into such a well-architected server may mean a performance hit for the server. We may not be able to support as many simultaneous connections, but that does not mean that we cannot still give our users a snappy web experience.

Caching was introduced in *Chapter 5*, *Reverse Proxy Advanced Topics*. In this section, we will take an in-depth look at integrating NGINX's caching mechanisms into a web application. Your web application may already cache to a certain extent. Perhaps it writes prerendered pages into a database so that an expensive rendering task does not have to be repeated at each page view. Or, even better, your application may write prerendered pages into the filesystem so that they can simply be served by NGINX's stellar static file performance. No matter the caching mechanism your application already has (even if it has none), NGINX offers a way to integrate it into the server.

No application caching

When your application does no caching at all, NGINX can still help speed up response times to your users. Both the `proxy` and the `fastcgi` modules are able to make use of this caching feature. You will, therefore, either be using the `proxy_cache_*` or `fastcgi_cache_*` directives to configure caching for your application. The `proxy_cache_*` directives were described in the *Caching* section in *Chapter 5*, *Reverse Proxy Advanced Topics*; the `fastcgi_cache_*` directives were summarized in *Chapter 6*, *The NGINX HTTP Server*.

Here we will describe how to extend your application to instruct NGINX how to cache individual pages. This is done by using headers sent to NGINX. You can use either the standard `Expires` and `Cache-Control` headers or the special `X-Accel-Expires` header, which NGINX interprets for caching and does not pass on to the client. This header allows the application to completely control how long NGINX caches a file. This normally makes it very easy to expire long-lived objects.

Let's say that you have a news application that's suffering from slow page load times. This can happen for different reasons, but after analysis, you have determined that each page is rendered in real time from the content stored in a database. When a user visits the site, this causes a new database connection to be opened, multiple SQL queries to be made, and the result to be parsed, before a fully-rendered page can be delivered to that user. Due to multiple connections in the application's backend system, the architecture cannot easily be restructured to make use of a more reasonable rendering strategy.

Given these restrictions, you decide on the following caching strategy:

- The front page is to be cached for 1 minute, as this contains links to articles and the list is frequently updated
- Each article will be cached for 1 day because once they are written they don't change, but we don't want the cache to be filled with older entries that need to be removed due to lack of space

- Any image will be cached for as long as possible, due to the images also being stored in the database, making it a truly expensive operation to retrieve them

We will configure NGINX to support this strategy as follows:

```
http {

    # here we configure two separate shared memory zones for the
    keys/metadata
    # and filesystem paths for the cached objects themselves
    proxy_cache_path /var/spool/nginx/articles
        keys_zone=ARTICLES:16m levels=1:2 inactive=1d;

    proxy_cache_path /var/spool/nginx/images keys_zone=IMAGES:128m
        levels=1:2 inactive=30d;

    # but both paths still lie on the same filesystem as proxy_temp_
    path
    proxy_temp_path /var/spool/nginx;

    server {

        location / {

            # this is where the list of articles is found
            proxy_cache_valid 1m;

        }

        location /articles {

            # each article has a URI beginning with "/articles"
            proxy_cache_valid 1d;

        }

        location /img {

            # every image is referenced with a URI under "/img"
            proxy_cache_valid 10y;

        }

    }
}
```

That takes care of our requirements. We have now activated caching for a legacy application that has no caching support.

Caching in the database

If your application currently caches prerendered pages in a database, it should be possible without too much additional effort to place those pages into a memcached instance instead. NGINX is capable of answering requests directly from what is stored in memcached. The logic is shown in the following diagram:

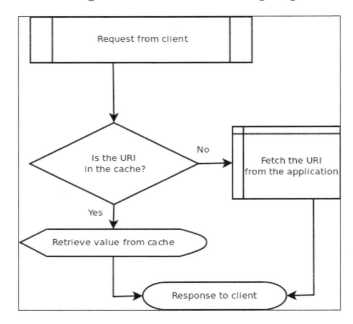

The interface is very simple, allowing it to be as flexible as possible. NGINX looks up a key in the store. If it is found, the value is returned to the client. Constructing the proper key is a configuration task, which we will discuss next. Storing the value at that key is outside the scope of what NGINX was designed to do. That job belongs to the application.

Determining which key to use is a fairly simple task. For resources that are not personalized, the best key to use is the URI itself. This is set in the $memcached_key variable:

```
location / {

  set $memcached_key $uri;

  memcached_pass 127.0.0.1:11211;

}
```

If your application reads request arguments to construct a page, the `$memcached_key` variable will include these arguments as well:

```
location / {

  set $memcached_key "$uri?$args";

  memcached_pass 127.0.0.1:11211;

}
```

If the key is not present, NGINX will need a means of requesting the page from the application. Hopefully, the application will then write the key/value pair into `memcached` so that the next request can be directly served from memory. NGINX will report a `Not Found` error if the key couldn't be found in `memcached`, so the best way to then pass the request to the application is to use the `error_page` and `location` directive to handle the request. We should also include the error codes for a `Bad Gateway` error and a `Gateway Timeout` error, in case `memcached` does not respond to our key lookup:

```
server {

  location / {

    set $memcached_key "$uri?$args";

    memcached_pass 127.0.0.1:11211;

    error_page 404 502 504 = @app;

  }

  location @app {

    proxy_pass http://127.0.0.1:8080;

  }

}
```

Remember that by using the equals sign (=) in the arguments to `error_page`, NGINX will substitute in the return code from the last argument. This enables us to turn an error condition into a normal response.

The following table describes the directives available with the memcached module, which is compiled into an nginx binary by default:

memcached module directives	Explanation
memcached_buffer_size	This directive specifies the size of the buffer for the response from memcached. This response is then sent synchronously to the client.
memcached_connect_timeout	This directive specifies the maximum length of time NGINX will wait for its connection to be accepted when making a request to a memcached server.
memcached_next_upstream	This directive specifies the conditions under which a request will be passed to the next memcached server, as specified by one or more of the following parameters: • error: This parameter indicates that an error occurred when communicating with the memcached server • timeout: This parameter indicates that a timeout was reached when communicating with the memcached server • invalid_response: This parameter indicates that the memcached server returned an empty or otherwise invalid response • not_found: This parameter indicates that the key was not found on this memcached instance • off: This parameter disables passing a request to the next memcached server
memcached_pass	This directive specifies the name or address of a memcached server and its port. It may also be a server group, as declared in an upstream context.
memcached_read_timeout	This directive specifies the length of time that needs to pass between two successive read operations from a memcached server before the connection is closed.
memcached_send_timeout	This directive specifies the length of time that needs to pass between two successive write operations to a memcached server before the connection is closed.

Caching in the filesystem

Suppose your application writes prerendered pages as files. You know how long each file should be valid. You can configure NGINX to deliver certain headers with each file that instructs the client, and any proxy in between, how long the file should be cached. In this way, you enabled a local cache for your users without having to change a single line of code.

You can do this by setting the Expires and Cache-Control headers. These are the standard HTTP headers understood by clients and HTTP proxies alike. No change is required in your application; you merely need to set these headers in the NGINX configuration block for the corresponding locations. NGINX makes it convenient by providing the expires and add_header directives.

Header modifying directives	Explanation
add_header	This directive adds fields to a header present in the responses with the HTTP codes 200, 204, 206, 301, 302, 303, 304, or 307.
expires	This directive adds or modifies the Expires and Cache-Control headers. The parameters can be an optional modified parameter, followed by time, or one of epoch, max, or off. If time alone is present, the Expires header will be set to the current time plus the time specified in the time parameter. The Cache-Control header will be set to max-age=t, where t is the time specified as an argument in seconds. If the modified parameter precedes a time value, the Expires header is set to the file's modification time plus the time specified in the time parameter. If the time parameter contains an @ symbol, the time specified will be interpreted as the time of day, for example, @12h is 12 noon. The epoch parameter is defined to be the exact date and time, for instance, Thu, 01 Jan 1970 00:00:01 GMT. The max parameter sets Expires to Thu, 31 Dec 2037 23:55:55 GMT and Cache-Control to 10 years. Any negative time will set Cache-Control to no-cache.

Knowing what you do about the files your application generates, you can set these headers appropriately. Let's take an example application where the main page should be cached for 5 minutes, all the JavaScript and CSS files for 24 hours, each HTML page for 3 days, and each image for as long as possible:

```
server {

    root /home/www;

    location / {
```

```
        # match the index.html page explicitly so the *.html below
        # won't match the main page
        location = /index.html {

            expires 5m;

        }

        # match any file ending in .js or .css (Javascript or CSS
          files)
        location ~* /.*\.(js|css)$ {

            expires 24h;

        }

        # match any page ending in .html
        location ~* /.*\.html$ {

            expires 3d;

        }

    }

    # all of our images are under a separate location (/img)
    location /img {

        expires max;

    }

}
```

To see how this configuration sets the headers, let's take a look at what each location looks like in the browser. Each modern browser has a tool either built-in or available as a plugin that enables you to view the headers of both the request and the response. The following series of screenshots show how Chrome displays the response headers for these locations:

- **The main page**: In this page (index.html), the Expires header is set to 5 minutes later than the Date header. The Cache-Control header has a max-age parameter set to 300 seconds.

```
▼ Response Headers        view parsed
  HTTP/1.1 200 OK
  Server: nginx/1.2.2
  Date: Sat, 15 Dec 2012 19:01:33 GMT
  Content-Type: text/html
  Content-Length: 170
  Last-Modified: Sat, 15 Dec 2012 18:31:41 GMT
  Connection: keep-alive
  Expires: Sat, 15 Dec 2012 19:06:33 GMT
  Cache-Control: max-age=300
  Accept-Ranges: bytes
```

- **A CSS file**: The `Expires` header is set to 24 hours later than the `Date` header. The `Cache-Control` header has a `max-age` parameter of 86400 seconds.

```
▼ Response Headers        view parsed
  HTTP/1.1 200 OK
  Server: nginx/1.2.2
  Date: Sat, 15 Dec 2012 19:07:43 GMT
  Content-Type: text/plain
  Content-Length: 69
  Last-Modified: Sat, 15 Dec 2012 18:31:33 GMT
  Connection: keep-alive
  Expires: Sun, 16 Dec 2012 19:07:43 GMT
  Cache-Control: max-age=86400
  Accept-Ranges: bytes
```

- **An HTML file**: The `Expires` header is set to 3 days later than the `Date` header. The `Cache-Control` header has a `max-age` parameter set to 259200 seconds.

```
▼ Response Headers        view parsed
  HTTP/1.1 200 OK
  Server: nginx/1.2.2
  Date: Sat, 15 Dec 2012 19:10:16 GMT
  Content-Type: text/html
  Content-Length: 170
  Last-Modified: Sat, 15 Dec 2012 18:39:12 GMT
  Connection: keep-alive
  Expires: Tue, 18 Dec 2012 19:10:16 GMT
  Cache-Control: max-age=259200
  Accept-Ranges: bytes
```

- **An image**: The Expires header is set to Thu, 31 Dec 2037 23:55:55 GMT. The Cache-Control header has a max-age parameter set to 315360000 seconds.

```
▼ Response Headers        view parsed
    HTTP/1.1 200 OK
    Server: nginx/1.2.2
    Date: Sat, 15 Dec 2012 19:07:43 GMT
    Content-Type: image/jpeg
    Content-Length: 26246
    Last-Modified: Sat, 15 Dec 2012 18:28:41 GMT
    Connection: keep-alive
    Expires: Thu, 31 Dec 2037 23:55:55 GMT
    Cache-Control: max-age=315360000
    Accept-Ranges: bytes
```

Just by setting one directive, expires, in the appropriate location, we can ensure that our prerendered files are cached locally for as long as they should be.

Changing content on-the-fly

Sometimes, it may be helpful to postprocess what comes from your application. Maybe you would like to add a string at a certain point in your page to show which frontend server delivered that page to the client. Or maybe you would like to perform a transformation on the rendered HTML page. NGINX provides three modules that could be useful here: the addition module, the sub module, and the xslt module.

Using the addition module

The addition module works as a filter to add text before and/or after a response. It is not compiled by default, so if you want to make use of this feature, you must enable it at configure time by adding --with-http_addition_module.

This filter works by referencing a subrequest, which is then either appended to a request, or placed at the beginning of one:

```
server {

    root /home/www;

    location / {
```

```
    add_before_body /header;

    add_after_body /footer;

}

location /header {

    proxy_pass http://127.0.0.1:8080/header;

}

location /footer {

    proxy_pass http://127.0.0.1:8080/footer;

}

}
```

The `addition` module directives are summarized in the following table:

HTTP addition module directives	Explanation
`add_before_body`	This directive adds the result of processing a subrequest before the `response` body.
`add_after_body`	This directive adds the result of processing a subrequest after the `response` body.
`addition_types`	This directive lists the MIME types of a response in addition to `text/html`, in which an addition will be made. It may be `*` to enable all MIME types.

The sub module

The `sub` module works as a filter to replace (substitute) one text for another. It is not compiled by default, so if you want to make use of this feature, you must enable it at configure time by adding `--with-http_sub_module`.

It is fairly easy to work with. You use the `sub_filter` directive to specify a string to be replaced and its replacement, and the filter makes a case-insensitive match for your string, and substitutes in the replacement:

```
location / {

  sub_filter </head> '<meta name="frontend"
    content="web3"></head>';

}
```

In the preceding example, we added a new `meta` tag to the header of the page as it passed through NGINX.

It's also possible to make the match more than once. To do this, you set the `sub_filter_once` directive to `off`. This can be useful to replace all relative links in a page with absolute ones; for example, refer to this:

```
location / {

  sub_filter_once off;

  sub_filter '<img src="img/' '<img src="/img/';

}
```

If there are any spaces or embedded quotes in the string to be matched, they must be enclosed in quotes in order for NGINX to recognize them as the first parameter.

NGINX will automatically use the `sub_filter` directive on any HTML file. If you want to use substitution on other types of files, such as JavaScript or CSS, just add the corresponding MIME type to the `sub_filter_types` directive:

```
location / {

  sub_filter_types text/css;

  sub_filter url(img/ 'url(/img/';

}
```

 Since `text/html` is the default value, this type doesn't need to be added — it won't be overwritten by adding additional MIME types to be transformed. This principle applies to all MIME type specification directives in NGINX.

The following table summarizes these directives:

HTTP sub module directives	Explanation
sub_filter	This directive sets the string to be matched without regard to case and the string to be substituted into that match. The substitution string may contain variables.
sub_filter_once	Setting this directive to off will cause the match in sub_filter to be made as many times as the string is found.
sub_filter_types	This directive lists the MIME types of a response in addition to text/html in which a substitution will be made. It may be * to enable all MIME types.

The xslt module

The xslt module works as a filter to transform XML using XSLT stylesheets. It is not compiled by default; so if you would like to make use of it, you will need to install the libxml2 and libxslt libraries and enable compilation of the module by passing --with-http_xslt_module to NGINX's configure script.

To use the xslt module, you define a DTD in which the character entities are declared. You then specify one or more XSLT stylesheets and their corresponding parameters to process the XML document:

```
location / {

  xml_entities /usr/local/share/dtd/entities.dtd;

  xsl_stylesheet /usr/local/share/xslt/style1.xslt;

  xsl_stylesheet /usr/local/share/xslt/style2.xslt theme=blue;

}
```

The directives included in the `xslt` module are summarized in the following table:

HTTP XSLT module directives	Explanation
`xml_entities`	This directive specifies the path to the DTD that declares the character entities referenced in the XML to be processed.
`xslt_param`	This directive specifies the parameters passed to the stylesheets, whose values are the XPath expressions.
`xslt_string_param`	This directive specifies the parameters passed to the stylesheets, whose values are strings.
`xslt_stylesheet`	This directive specifies the path to an XSLT stylesheet used to transform an XML response. Parameters may be passed as a series of key/value pairs.
`xslt_types`	This directive lists the MIME types of a response in addition to `text/xml` in which a substitution will be made. It may be * to enable all MIME types. If the transformation results in an HTML response, the MIME type will be changed to `text/html`.

Using Server Side Includes

The `ssi` module is also a filter, and one of NGINX's most flexible. It enables the use of **Server Side Includes (SSI)** for processing logic embedded in a webpage. It supports a series of commands that are controlled by the following directives:

SSI directives	Explanation
`ssi`	This directive enables the processing of SSI files.
`ssi_silent_errors`	This directive suppresses the error message normally output when an error occurs during SSI processing.
`ssi_types`	This directive lists the MIME types of a response in addition to `text/html` in which the SSI commands are processed. It may be * to enable all MIME types.

The SSI commands and arguments supported by NGINX are shown in the following table:

The SSI commands	Arguments	Explanation
block		This command defines a section that can be referenced in the `include` command. This command ends with `<!--# endblock -->`.
	name	This argument defines the name of the block.
config		This command sets global parameters used during SSI processing.
	errmsg	This argument configures the string used as the error message if something goes wrong during SSI processing. The default message is `[an error occurred while processing the directive]`.
	timefmt	This argument specifies a string passed to `strftime()` to format a timestamp used in other commands. The default value is `%A, %d-%b-%Y %H:%M:%S %Z`.
echo		This command writes out the value of a variable.
	var	This argument specifies the name of the variable whose value is written out.
	encoding	This argument specifies the encoding method used for the variable. The value it can take is one of `none`, `url`, and `entity`. The default value is `entity`.
	default	This argument specifies a value to write out if the variable is undefined. If unset, `none` is the default value.
if		This command evaluates a condition. If `true`, the block enclosed will be included. The sequence `if`, `elsif`, `else`, and `endif` is supported one level deep.

The SSI commands	Arguments	Explanation
	expr	This argument specifies the expression to be evaluated for truth: • **Variable existence**: `expr="$var"` • **Text comparison**: `expr="$var = text"` or `expr="$var != text"` • **Regular expression match**: `expr="$var = /regexp/"` or `expr="$var != /regexp/"`
include		This command writes the result of a subrequest.
	file	This argument specifies the name of a file to `include`.
	virtual	This argument specifies the URI of a subrequest to `include`.
	stub	This argument specifies the block to be included instead of an empty body, or if there was an error in processing.
	wait	If there are multiple `include` commands on the same page, they will be processed serially if this parameter is present.
	set	If the subrequest made in virtual is to a `proxy_pass` or `memcached_pass` location, the result can be stored in the variable named as the argument to `set`.
set		This argument creates a variable and sets the value to it.
	var	This argument specifies the name of the variable to be set.
	value	This argument specifies the value of the variable to set.

They all adhere to the following pattern:

```
<!--# command parameter1=value1 parameter2=value2 … -->
```

An SSI file is nothing more than an HTML file with these commands embedded within comments. That way, if ssi isn't enabled for a particular location that contains such a file, the HTML portion will still render, albeit incompletely.

The following is an example of an SSI file, which uses calls to a subrequest to render the header, footer, and menu of a page:

```
<html>
  <head>
    <title>*** SSI test page ***</title>
    <link rel="stylesheet" href="/css/layout.css"
      type="text/css"/>
    <!--# block name="boilerplate" -->
    <p>...</p>
    <!--# endblock -->
  </head>
  <body>
    <div id="header">
      <!--# include virtual="/render/header?page=$uri"
        stub="boilerplate" -->
    </div>
    <div id="menu">
      <!--# include virtual="/render/menu?page=$uri"
        stub="boilerplate" -->
    </div>
    <div id="content">
      <p>This is the content of the page.</p>
    </div>
    <div id="footer">
      <!--# include virtual="/render/footer?page=$uri"
        stub="boilerplate" -->
    </div>
  </body>
</html>
```

The `stub` method is used to render some default content in case of an error in processing the subrequest.

If these primitives don't offer enough flexibility in processing logic, you can use the embedded `perl` module to solve just about any other processing or configuration need you may have.

Decision-making in NGINX

You may find yourself trying to bend NGINX's configuration directives in ways that were not meant to be used. This is frequently seen in configurations where there are a lot of `if` checks to try to emulate some sort of logic chain. A better option would be to use NGINX's embedded `perl` module. With this module, you will be able to use the flexibility of Perl to achieve your configuration goals.

The **perl** module is not built by default, so it needs to be enabled with the `--with-http_perl_module` configure switch. A minimum of Perl 5.6.1 is required. Ensure as well that your Perl was built with `-Dusemultiplicity=yes` (or `-Dusethreads=yes`) and `-Dusemymalloc=no`. NGINX configuration reloads will cause the `perl` module to leak memory over time, so this last parameter is included to help mitigate that problem.

After having built NGINX with embedded Perl, the following directives are available:

Perl module directives	Explanation
`perl`	This directive activates a Perl handler for this location. The argument is the name of the handler or a string describing a full subroutine.
`perl_modules`	This directive specifies an additional search path for the Perl modules.
`perl_require`	This directive indicates a Perl module that will be loaded at each NGINX reconfiguration. This directive may be specified multiple times for separate modules.
`perl_set`	This directive installs a Perl handler to set the value of a variable. The argument is the name of the handler or a string describing a full subroutine.

When writing Perl scripts to be used in an NGINX configuration, the $r object represents the current request. The methods on this object are as follows:

- `$r->args`: This method specifies the request arguments.
- `$r->filename`: This method specifies the name of the file referenced by the URI.
- `$r->has_request_body(handler)`: If there is a request body, the handler will be called.
- `$r->allow_ranges`: This method enables the use of byte ranges in a response.
- `$r->discard_request_body`: This method discards the body of the request.
- `$r->header_in(header)`: This method specifies the value of the specified request header.
- `$r->header_only`: This method instructs NGINX to return only the header to the client.

- `$r->header_out(header, value)`: This method sets the specified response header to this value.

- `$r->internal_redirect(uri)`: This method makes an internal redirect to the specified URI once the Perl handler has completed execution.

- `$r->print(text)`: This method prints the specified text out to the client.

- `$r->request_body`: This method specifies the body of the request, if it fits in memory.

- `$r->request_body_file`: This method specifies the body of the request, if written out to a temporary file.

- `$r->request_method`: This method specifies the HTTP method of the request.

- `$r->remote_addr`: This method specifies the client's IP address.

- `$r->flush`: This method immediately sends data to the client.

- `$r->sendfile(name[, offset[, length]])`: This method sends the specified file to the client, with an optional offset and length, once the Perl handler has completed execution.

- `$r->send_http_header([type])`: This method sends the response headers to the client, with an optional content type.

- `$r->status(code)`: This method sets the HTTP status of the response.

- `$r->sleep(milliseconds, handler)`: This method sets a timer to execute the handler after having waited the specified number of milliseconds. NGINX will continue processing other requests while the timer is running.

- `$r->unescape(text)`: This method decodes the URI-encoded text.

- `$r->uri`: This method specifies the URI in the request.

- `$r->variable(name[, value])`: This method either returns a named, request-local variable, or sets one to the specified value.

The `perl` module may also be used within SSI. An SSI command using Perl has the following format:

```
<!--# perl sub="module::function" arg="parameter1"
  arg="parameter2" ... -->
```

Let's take a look at an example of using the `perl` module. Our goal is to pass requests to a different upstream server, as determined by the first letter of the request URI. We could implement this as a series of locations in NGINX, but it will be more concise expressed as a Perl handler.

The first step is to define the processing actions in a Perl handler:

```perl
# upstreammapper.pm

# name our package
package upstreammapper;

# include the nginx request methods and return code definitions
use nginx;

# this subroutine will be called from nginx
sub handler {

  my $r = shift;

  my @alpha = ("a".."z");

  my %upstreams = ();

  # simplistically create a mapping between letter and
  # an IP which is between 10 and 35 of that network
  foreach my $idx (0..$#alpha) {

    $upstreams{ $alpha[$idx] } = $idx + 10;

  }

  # get the URI into an array
  my @uri = split(//,$r->uri);

  # so that we can use the first letter as a key
  my $ip = "10.100.0." . $upstreams{ $uri[1] };

  return $ip;

}

1;

__END__
```

Then, we set up NGINX to use this module to do the mapping:

```
http {

    # this path is relative to the main configuration file
    perl_modules perl/lib;

    perl_require upstreammapper.pm;

    # we'll store the result of the handler in the $upstream
      variable
    perl_set $upstream upstreammapper::handler;
```

Then, we pass the request along to the correct upstream server:

```
location / {

    include proxy.conf;

    proxy_pass http://$upstream;

  }

}
```

We saw a very simple example of implementing some configuration logic in a Perl handler. Just about any kind of special requirement can be done in a similar way.

 Request processing in a Perl handler should be as well-defined as possible. Whenever NGINX has to wait on a Perl handler finishing, the whole worker responsible for handling that request will block. So, any I/O or DNS-related tasks should be done outside of a Perl handler.

Creating a secure link

You may have cause to protect certain content on your site, but do not want to integrate full user authentication to allow access to that content. One way of enabling this is to use the secure_link module of NGINX. By passing the --with-http_secure_link_module switch at compile time, you get access to the secure_link_secret directive, and its corresponding variable, $secure_link.

The secure_link module works by computing the MD5 hash of a link concatenated with a secret word. If the hash matches that value found in the URI, the $secure_link variable is set to the portion of the URI after the hash. If there is no match, $secure_link is set to the empty string.

One possible scenario is to generate a page of download links using a secret word. This word is then placed in the NGINX configuration to enable access to these links. The word and page are replaced periodically to prevent saved links from being called again at a later time. The following example illustrates this scenario.

We first decide on a secret word, supersecret. Then, we generate the MD5 hash of the links we want to enable:

```
$ echo -n "alphabet_soup.pdfsupersecret" |md5sum
8082202b04066a49a1ae8da9ec4feba1 -
$ echo -n "time_again.pdfsupersecret" |md5sum
5b77faadb4f5886c2ffb81900a6b3a43 -
```

Now, we can create the HTML for our links:

```
<a
  href="/downloads/8082202b04066a49a1ae8da9ec4feba1/
    alphabet_soup.pdf">alphabet soup</a>
<a
  href="/downloads/5b77faadb4f5886c2ffb81900a6b3a43/
    time_again.pdf">time again</a>
```

These links will only be valid if we use the same `secure_link_secret` directive in our configuration that we used to generate these hashes:

```
# any access to URIs beginning with /downloads/ will be protected
location /downloads/ {

  # this is the string we used to generate the hashes above
  secure_link_secret supersecret;

  # deny access with a Forbidden if the hash doesn't match
  if ($secure_link = "") {

    return 403;

  }

  try_files /downloads/$secure_link =404;

}
```

To ensure that links without a hash will not work, we can add an additional link to our HTML code:

```
<a href="/downloads/bare_link.pdf">bare link</a>
```

Calling this link reports a `403 Forbidden` error, as it should.

> The technique for generating a `secure_link` module described before is just one possible way of solving this type of problem. NGINX itself even offers an alternative way described at `http://nginx.org/en/docs/http/ngx_http_secure_link_module.html`.

Generating images

Instead of writing an image manipulation module for your application, you can configure NGINX to handle some simple transformations. If your image-manipulation needs are as simple as rotating an image, resizing it, or cropping it, NGINX is capable of doing this for you.

To make use of this functionality, you need to have installed the `libgd` library, and enabled the `image_filter` module at compile time (`--with-http_image_filter_module`). If that is the case, you now have use of the directives in the following table:

Image filter directives	Explanation
`empty_gif`	This directive causes a 1x1 pixel transparent GIF to be emitted for that `location` directive.
`image_filter`	This directive transforms an image, according to one of the following parameters: • `off`: This parameter turns off image transformation. • `test`: This parameter ensures that responses are either GIF, JPEG, or PNG images. If not, an error `415` (`Unsupported Media Type`) is returned. • `size`: This parameter emits information about an image in the JSON format. • `rotate`: This parameter rotates an image counter-clockwise by either 90, 180, or 270 degrees. • `resize`: This parameter reduces an image proportionally by the width and height given. One dimension may be - in order to reduce by only the other dimension. If combined with `rotate`, rotation happens after reduction. An error will result, returning `415` (`Unsupported Media Type`). • `crop`: This parameter reduces an image by the size of the largest side, as specified by the width and height given. Any extraneous space along the other edges will be cut. One dimension may be - in order to reduce by only the other dimension. If combined with `rotate`, rotation happens before reduction. An error will result, returning `415` (`Unsupported Media Type`).
`image_filter_buffer`	This directive specifies the size of the buffer used to process images. If more memory is needed, the server will return a `415` error (`Unsupported Media Type`).
`image_filter_jpeg_quality`	This directive specifies the quality of the resulting JPEG image, after processing. Exceeding `95` is not recommended.

Image filter directives	Explanation
image_filter_sharpen	This directive increases the sharpness of a processed image by this percentage.
image_filter_transparency	This directive disables preserving the transparency of transformed GIF and PNG images. The default value, on, preserves transparency.

Note that the empty_gif directive is not part of the image_filter module, but is included in a default installation of NGINX.

 The GD library (libgd) is an image generation library written in C. It is often used in combination with a programming language, such as PHP or Perl to generate images for websites. The image_filter module of NGINX uses libgd to provide the capability of creating a simple image resizing proxy, which we will discuss in the following example.

Using these directives, we can construct an image resizing module as follows:

```
location /img {

  try_files $uri /resize/$uri;

}

location ~*
  /resize/(?.<name>.*)_(?<width>[[:digit:]]*)x
    (?<height>[[:digit:]]*)\.(?<extension>gif|jpe?g|png)$ {

  error_page 404 =
    /resizer/$name.$extension?width=$width&height=$
      height;

}

location /resizer {

  image_filter resize $arg_width $arg_height;

}
```

This little snippet will first try to serve an image as requested in the URI. If it cannot find an appropriately-named image, it will then move on to the /resize location. The /resize location is defined as a regular expression so that we can capture the size we'd like the image to be. Note that we use named capture groups to create meaningful variable names. We then pass these on to the /resizer location so that we have the name of the original file as the URI and the width and height as named arguments.

We can now combine this functionality with the proxy_store or proxy_cache capability of NGINX to save the resized images so that another request for the same URI won't need to hit the image_filter module:

```
server {

  root /home/www;

  location /img {

    try_files $uri /resize/$uri;

  }

  location /resize {

    error_page 404 = @resizer;
  }

  location @resizer {

    internal;

    proxy_pass http://localhost:8080$uri;

    proxy_store /home/www/img$request_uri;

    proxy_temp_path /home/www/tmp/proxy_temp;

  }

}
```

```
server {

  listen 8080;

  root /home/www/img;

  location ~* /resize/(?.<name>.*)_(?<width>[[:digit:]]*)
    x(?<height>[[:digit:]]*)\.(?<extension>gif|jpe?g|png)$ {

    error_page 404 = /resizer/$name.$extension?width=$width&heigh
      t=$height;

  }

  location /resizer {

    image_filter resize $arg_width $arg_height;

  }

}
```

As you can see, in the table of directives for the image_filter module, any error returned by this module has the code 415. We can catch this error to replace it with an empty GIF so that the end user will still get an image instead of an error message:

```
location /thumbnail {

  image_filter resize 90 90;

  error_page 415 = @empty;

}
location = @empty {

  access_log off;

  empty_gif;

}
```

The `size` parameter of `image_filter` deserves special mention. When this parameter is configured for a location, information about the image is delivered instead of the image itself. This could be useful in your application for discovering metadata about an image before calling a resize or crop URI:

```
location /img {

    image_filter size;

}
```

The result is a JSON object, as in the following example:

```
{ "img" : { "width": 150, "height": 200, "type": "png" } }
```

Tracking website visitors

A fairly unobtrusive way to track unique website visitors is to use the `userid` module. This module sets cookies that are used to identify unique clients. The value of these cookies is referenced by the `$uid_set` variable. When that same user returns to the site and the cookie is still valid, the value is available in the `$uid_got` variable. An example of how to use these cookies is as follows:

```
http {

    log_format useridcomb '$remote_addr - $uid_got [$time_local] '
    '"$request" $status $body_bytes_sent '
    '"$http_referer" "$http_user_agent"';

    server {

        server_name .example.com;

        access_log logs/example.com-access.log useridcomb;

        userid on;
        userid_name uid;

        userid_domain example.com;

        userid_path /;

        userid_expires 365d;
```

```
userid_p3p 'policyref="/w3c/p3p.xml", CP="CUR ADM OUR NOR
    STA NID"';

    }

}
```

These directives are summarized in the following table:

Userid module directives	Explanation
userid	This directive activates the module according to the following parameters: • on: This parameter sets version 2 cookies and logs those are received • v1: This parameter sets version 1 cookies and logs those are received • log: This parameter disables setting of cookies, but enables logging them • off: This parameter disables both the setting of cookies and the logging of them
userid_domain	This directive configures a domain to be set in the cookie.
userid_expires	This directive sets the age of the cookie. If the max keyword is used, this translates to 31 Dec 2037 23:55:55 GMT.
userid_name	This directive sets the name of the cookie (the default value is uid).
userid_p3p	This directive configures the P3P header; for sites that declare their privacy policy using the protocol of the **Platform for Privacy Preferences Project**.
userid_path	This directive defines the path set in the cookie.
userid_service	This directive specifies the identity of the service that set the cookie. For example, the default value for the version 2 cookies is the IP address of the server that set the cookie.

Preventing inadvertent code execution

When trying to construct a configuration that does what you expect it to do, you may inadvertently enable something that you did not expect. Take the following configuration block, for example:

```
location ~* \.php {

    include fastcgi_params;

    fastcgi_pass 127.0.0.1:9000;

}
```

Here we seem to be passing all requests for the PHP files to the FastCGI server responsible for processing them. This would be OK if PHP only processed the file it was given, but due to differences in how PHP is compiled and configured this may not always be the case. This can become a problem if user uploads are made into the same directory structure that PHP files are in.

Users may be prevented from uploading files with a .php extension but are allowed to upload .jpg, .png, and .gif files. A malicious user could upload an image file with embedded PHP code, and cause the FastCGI server to execute this code by passing a URI with the uploaded filename in it.

To prevent this from happening, either set the PHP parameter, cgi.fix_pathinfo, to 0 or use something similar to the following in your NGINX configuration:

```
location ~* \.php {

    try_files $uri =404;

    include fastcgi_params;

    fastcgi_pass 127.0.0.1:9000;

}
```

We used try_files to ensure that the file actually exists before passing the request on to the FastCGI server for PHP processing.

Keep in mind that you should evaluate your configuration to see if it matches your goals. If you have only a few files, you would be better served by explicitly specifying which PHP files may be executed instead of the regular expression, `location`, and corresponding `try_files` expression.

Summary

NGINX provides a number of ways to support developers wishing to integrate a high-performance web server into their application. We looked at various possibilities of integrating both legacy and new applications. Caching plays a key role in the modern web application. NGINX offers both passive and active ways of using caching to help deliver a web page more quickly.

We also explored how NGINX can help manipulate a response by adding or replacing text. SSI are also possible with NGINX. We saw a way of integrating these commands into normal text. We then examined the powerful embedded Perl capabilities in NGINX. Image transformation is also possible using just core NGINX. We examined how to set a unique cookie to track website visitors. We wound up the chapter with a word of caution about how to prevent code from inadvertently being executed. On the whole, there are quite a few tools at the developer's disposal when working with NGINX as a web server.

We will touch upon integrating Lua in the next chapter. Lua goes beyond the capabilities we explored in this chapter to provide even more flexibility to the application developer.

8

Integrating Lua with NGINX

NGINX is extensible to handle varying use cases. In this chapter, we'll be exploring some possibilities of extending NGINX with Lua, an embedded scripting language designed for just such a purpose. The topics we'll be covering include the following:

- The `ngx_lua` module
- Integrating with Lua
- Logging with Lua

The ngx_lua module

Similar in intent to the included `perl` module, the third-party `ngx_lua` module was made to cover use cases that couldn't be solved with configuration alone. Due to its embeddable design and coroutine (green threading) implementation, Lua serves this purpose well because it doesn't block an entire worker as the `perl` module can.

The `OpenResty` project (`https://openresty.org/`) is the official source of `ngx_lua` and provides a bundle of NGINX, `ngx_lua`, a Lua interpreter, plus a number of third-party modules that are useful for turning NGINX into an application server. This is an alternative to the installation instructions detailed in *Chapter 1*, *Installing NGINX and Third-Party Modules*. After downloading the source, it can be unpacked and installed with the standard `./configure; make; make install` command. Here is an example session disabling a number of extra modules, and placing the whole installation under `/opt/resty`:

```
$ ./configure \
      --prefix=/opt/resty \
      --user=www \
      --group=www \
      --conf-path=/opt/resty/nginx.conf \
      --with-cc-opt="-I/usr/local/include" \
```

```
--with-ld-opt="-L/usr/local/lib" \
--with-pcre-jit \
--with-ipv6 \
--with-http_gunzip_module \
--with-http_secure_link_module \
--with-http_gzip_static_module \
--without-http_redis_module \
--without-http_xss_module \
--without-http_memc_module \
--without-http_rds_json_module \
--without-http_rds_csv_module \
--without-lua_resty_memcached \
--without-lua_resty_mysql \
--without-http_ssi_module \
--without-http_autoindex_module \
--without-http_fastcgi_module \
--without-http_uwsgi_module \
--without-http_scgi_module \
--without-http_memcached_module \
--without-http_empty_gif_module
```

Note that we disabled the ssi module. Processing a request with both the ssi and ngx_lua modules isn't supported.

When using ngx_lua, keep in mind that global variables are loaded once per worker, when the module itself is read in. Good practice dictates declaring all variables local for this reason.

Integrating with Lua

Using NGINX with ngx_lua can help you write more performant applications. Instead of passing logic to an upstream server, Lua can handle this processing. The ngx_lua module can be invoked at different phases of NGINX request processing.

Many of the ngx_lua configuration directives directly reference the phase of the request that they affect. For instance, there will be init_by_lua, init_worker_by_lua, content_by_lua, rewrite_by_lua, access_by_lua, header_filter_by_lua, body_filter_by_lua, and log_by_lua to do something with Lua at that phase of the request. Depending on where in the request processing chain you want to use Lua, you use the corresponding directive.

Loading a Lua script to handle a request involves using the `lua_package_path` directive to specify the location in which to find the script, and then using the appropriate `_by_lua` directive to execute the script:

```
lua_package_path     "$prefixlib/?.lua;;";
server {
    location / {
        content_by_lua_block {
            local logging = require("logging")
            ngx.say("Hello world")
        }
    }
}
```

Aside from directives, `ngx_lua` makes certain functions available to interact with NGINX. These functions make up the NGINX API for Lua. The following table is an excerpt of the complete API available at `https://github.com/openresty/lua-nginx-module#nginx-api-for-lua`:

Selected NGINX directives that serve as API for Lua	Explanation
`ngx.cookie_time`	Given the time in seconds since the epoch, this directive returns a string that may be used as a cookie expiration timestamp.
`ngx.ctx`	Specifies a Lua table used to hold context data for the current request.
`ngx.decode_args`	Outputs a Lua table of URI arguments, parsed as key/value pairs from the URI query-string given as an argument.
`ngx.encode_args`	Takes a Lua table of URI arguments and encodes them as a string suitable to use in a URI.
`ngx.eof`	Specifies the end of the output stream.
`ngx.escape_uri`	Formats the string given as an argument using URI escaping.
`ngx.exec`	Initiates an internal redirect to another NGINX location, with optional arguments passed as a second string or a Lua table.
`ngx.exit`	Exits the current request, returning either the status code given as an argument or that set with a previous call to `ngx.status`.

Selected NGINX directives that serve as API for Lua	Explanation
ngx.flush	This directive, when called with `true`, will cause the previous `ngx.print` or `ngx.say` call to run in synchronous mode, not returning until all output is written to the send buffer.
ngx.get_phase	Returns the current phase of NGINX request processing; one of `init`, `init_worker`, `ssl_cert`, `set`, `rewrite`, `balancer`, `access`, `content`, `header_filter`, `body_filter`, `log`, or `timer`.
ngx.http_time	Given the time in seconds since the epoch, this directive returns a string that may be used as a header timestamp.
ngx.is_subrequest	Returns `true` if the current request is an NGINX subrequest.
ngx.localtime	Returns the local time in `yyyy-mm-dd hh:mm:ss` format from NGINX's cache.
ngx.location.capture	Issues a subrequest to another NGINX location. This directive returns a table with four keys: `status`, `header`, `body`, and `truncated` (a Boolean to represent if the body is truncated).
ngx.log	Takes as the first parameter a logging level (one of `ngx.STDERR`, `ngx.EMERG`, `ngx.ALERT`, `ngx.CRIT`, `ngx.ERR`, `ngx.WARN`, `ngx.NOTICE`, `ngx.INFO`, and `ngx.DEBUG`), and then the line to be emitted into the error log.
ngx.now	Returns the epoch time in seconds and milliseconds from NGINX's cache.
ngx.parse_http_time	Takes a timestamp string and returns the seconds since the epoch or nil (if badly formatted).
ngx.print	Sends output into the response body.
ngx.say	Sends output into the response body, with a trailing newline.
ngx.status	Retrieves or sets the value of the request's response status. If setting, ensure doing so before the response header is sent.
ngx.time	Returns the epoch time in seconds from NGINX's cache.
ngx.today	Returns the current, local time and date in `yyyy-mm-dd` format from NGINX's cache.
ngx.unescape_uri	Takes a string and reverses the URI escaping of it.

Selected NGINX directives that serve as API for Lua	Explanation
`ngx.update_time`	Updates NGINX's time cache using a syscall.
`ngx.utctime`	Returns the UTC time in `yyyy-mm-dd hh:mm:ss` format from NGINX's cache.

Any variable set in NGINX is available to access within a Lua script via `ngx.var.VARIABLE_NAME`. These variables can be set within the Lua script as well. Headers are available similarly via `ngx.header.HEADER`.

Array and hash table (dictionary) variables are stored as `tables` in Lua. When nesting tables, the one including the other is called a **metatable**. Inheritance can be implemented through metatables, as well as generally describing how entries in the table should be acted upon. (Visit `https://www.lua.org/pil/13.html` for more details.) A shared table created with the `lua_shared_dict` directive is referenced within a Lua script via the `ngx.shared.DICT` variable.

When writing scripts with Lua, place the NGINX variables in local variables if they are to be reused. This helps prevent memory bloat because each of these variables is allocated to the per-request memory pool, which will only be freed at the end of the request.

Logging with Lua

To give what we learned in this chapter a practical application, let's add some request logging with Lua. Lua works well for this as we're able to keep track of each request in a shared table. The data stored in this table can be represented in any way we choose. The code is available at `https://github.com/mtourne/nginx_log_by_lua`.

Summary

As you saw, there is quite a lot to be gained from learning to work with Lua. The `ngx_lua` module increases the possibilities of working with NGINX, turning the humble web server and reverse proxy into a full-fledged application server. We have only scratched the surface here. A full treatment of this topic would be a book in itself.

In the next chapter, we will explore troubleshooting techniques to try to get at the root of the problem when something doesn't work as expected.

Troubleshooting Techniques

9

We live in an imperfect world. Despite our best intentions and planning, sometimes things don't turn out the way we had expected. We need to be able to step back and take a look at what went wrong. When we cannot immediately see what is causing the error, we need to be able to reach into a toolbox of techniques to help us discover the problem. This process of figuring out what went wrong and how to fix it is what we call troubleshooting.

In this chapter, we will explore different techniques for troubleshooting NGINX:

- Analyzing log files
- Configuring advanced logging
- Common configuration errors
- Operating system limits
- Performance problems
- Using the Stub Status module

Analyzing log files

Before going into a prolonged debugging session trying to track down the cause of a problem, it is usually helpful to first look at the log files. They will often provide the clue we need to track down the error and correct it. The messages that appear in `error_log` can sometimes be a bit cryptic, however, so we will discuss the format of the log entries, and then take a look at a few examples to show you how to interpret what they mean.

The formats of the error_log file

NGINX uses a couple of different logging functions that produce the `error_log` entries. The formats used with these functions take on the following patterns:

```
<timestamp> [log-level] <master/worker pid>#0: message
```

Consider the following example:

```
2012/10/14 18:56:41 [notice] 2761#0: using inherited sockets from "6;"
```

This is an example of informational messages (log level `notice`). In this case, an `nginx` binary has replaced a previously-running one, and was able to successfully inherit the old binary's sockets.

The error-level logger produces a message like the following:

```
2012/10/14 18:50:34 [error] 2632#0: *1 open() "/opt/nginx/html/blog"
failed (2: No such file or directory), client: 127.0.0.1, server: www.
example.com, request: "GET /blog HTTP/1.0", host: "www.example.com"
```

Depending on the error, you will see messages from the operating system (such as in this case), or just from NGINX itself. In this case, we see the following components:

*   Timestamp (`2012/10/14 18:50:34`)
*   Log level (`error`)
*   Worker PID (`2632`)
*   Connection number (`1`)
*   System call (`open`)
*   Argument to the system call (`/opt/nginx/html/blog`)
*   Error message resulting from the system call (`2: No such file or directory`)
*   The client that made the request resulting in the error (`127.0.0.1`)
*   The server context that was responsible for handling the request (`www.example.com`)
*   The request itself (`GET /blog HTTP/1.0`)
*   The `Host` header sent in the request (`www.example.com`)

Here is an example of a critical-level log entry:

```
2012/10/14 19:11:50 [crit] 3142#0: the changing binary signal is ignored:
you should shutdown or terminate before either old or new binary's
process
```

A critical-level message means that NGINX cannot perform the requested action. If it was not already running, this means that NGINX would not start.

Here is an example of an emergency message:

```
2012/10/14 19:12:05 [emerg] 3195#0: bind() to 0.0.0.0:80 failed (98:
Address already in use)
```

An emergency message also means that NGINX could not do what was requested. It also means that NGINX won't start, or if it was already running when asked to read the configuration, it won't perform the requested change.

 If you are wondering why your configuration change is not taking effect, check the error log. NGINX has most likely encountered an error in the configuration and has not applied the change.

Error log file entry examples

Some examples of error messages found in real log files are shown here. After each example, a short explanation of what it could mean follows. Please note that the exact text may be different from what you see in your log files, due to improvements made in newer releases of NGINX.

Look at the following log file entry example:

```
2012/11/29 21:31:34 [error] 6338#0: *1 upstream prematurely
closed connection while reading response header from upstream,
client: 127.0.0.1, server: , request: "GET / HTTP/1.1", upstream:
"fastcgi://127.0.0.1:8080", host: "www.example.com"
```

Here we have a message that could be interpreted in a couple of ways. It might mean that the server we are talking to has an error in its implementation, and does not speak the FastCGI protocol properly. It could also mean that we have mistakenly directed traffic to an HTTP server, instead of a FastCGI server. If that is the case, a simple configuration change (using proxy_pass instead of fastcgi_pass, or using the correct address for the FastCGI server) could fix the problem.

This type of message could also simply mean that the upstream server takes too long to generate a response. The reason could be due to a number of factors, but the solution, as far as NGINX is concerned, is fairly simple: increase the timeouts. Depending on the module that was responsible for making this connection, the proxy_read_timeout or fastcgi_read_timeout (or other *_read_timeout) directive would need to be increased from the default value of 60s.

Look at the following log file entry example:

```
2012/11/29 06:31:42 [error] 2589#0: *6437 client intended to send too
large body: 13106010 bytes, client: 127.0.0.1, server: , request: "POST
/upload_file.php HTTP/1.1", host: "www.example.com", referrer: "http://
www.example.com/file_upload.html"
```

This one is fairly straightforward. NGINX reports that the file could not be uploaded because it is too large. To fix this problem, raise the value of `client_body_size`. Keep in mind that due to encoding, the uploaded size will be about 30 percent greater than the file size itself (for example, if you want to allow your users to upload files up to 12 MB, set this directive to `16m`).

Look at the following log file entry example:

```
2012/10/14 19:51:22 [emerg] 3969#0: "proxy_pass" cannot have URI part in
location given by regular expression, or inside named location, or inside
"if" statement, or inside "limit_except" block in /opt/nginx/conf/nginx.
conf:16
```

In this example, we see that NGINX won't start due to a configuration error. The error message is very informative as to why NGINX won't start. We see that there is a URI in the argument to the `proxy_pass` directive in a place where it should not have one. NGINX even tells us on which line (here 16) of which file (here `/opt/nginx/conf/nginx.conf`) the error occurred:

```
2012/10/14 18:46:26 [emerg] 2584#0: mkdir() "/home/www/tmp/proxy_temp"
failed (2: No such file or directory)
```

This is an example of a case where NGINX won't start because it can't perform what was asked of it. The `proxy_temp_path` directive specifies a location for NGINX to store temporary files when proxying. If NGINX cannot create this directory, it won't start, so ensure that the path leading up to this directory exists.

Look at the following log file entry example:

```
2012/10/14 18:46:54 [emerg] 2593#0: unknown directive "client_body_temp_
path" in /opt/nginx/conf/nginx.conf:6
```

We see what may appear to be a puzzling message. We know that `client_body_temp_path` is a valid directive, but NGINX does not accept it and gives an `unknown directive` message. When we think about how NGINX processes its configuration file, we realize that this does make sense after all. NGINX is built in a modular fashion. Each module is responsible for processing its own configuration context. We, therefore, conclude that this directive appeared in a part of the configuration file outside the context of the module that parses this directive:

```
2012/10/16 20:56:31 [emerg] 3039#0: "try_files" directive is not allowed
here in /opt/nginx/conf/nginx.conf:16
```

Sometimes, NGINX will give us a hint as to what is wrong. In the preceding example, NGINX has understood the `try_files` directive, but tells us that it is used in the wrong place. It very conveniently gives us the location in the configuration file where the error occurred, so that we can find it more easily.

```
2012/10/16 20:56:42 [emerg] 3043#0: host not found in upstream "tickets.
example.com" in /opt/nginx/conf/nginx.conf:22
```

This emergency-level message shows us how dependent NGINX is on DNS if hostnames are used in the configuration. If NGINX can't resolve the hostnames used in the `upstream`, `proxy_pass`, `fastcgi_pass`, or other `*_pass` directives, it won't start. This will have implications on the order in which NGINX is started after a fresh boot. Ensure that name resolution works at the time when NGINX starts:

```
2012/10/29 18:59:26 [emerg] 2287#0: unexpected "}" in /opt/nginx/conf/
nginx.conf:40
```

This type of message is indicative of a configuration error in which NGINX can't close the context. Something leading up to the line given has prevented NGINX from forming a complete context with the { and } characters. This usually means that the previous line is missing a semicolon, so NGINX reads the } character as a part of that unfinished line:

```
2012/10/28 21:38:34 [emerg] 2318#0: unexpected end of file, expecting "}"
in /opt/nginx/conf/nginx.conf:21
```

Related to the previous error, this one means that NGINX reached the end of the configuration file before finding a matching closing brace. This kind of error occurs when there are unbalanced { and } characters. Using a text editor that matches sets of braces is helpful in locating exactly where one is missing. Depending on where that missing brace is inserted, the configuration can end up meaning something completely different from what was intended:

```
2012/10/29 18:50:11 [emerg] 2116#0: unknown "exclusion" variable
```

Here we see an example of using a variable without first declaring it. This means that `$exclusion` appeared in the configuration before a `set`, `map`, or `geo` directive defined what the value was to be. This type of error could also be indicative of a typo. We may have defined the `$exclusions` variable, but mistakenly later referenced it as `$exclusion`:

```
2012/11/29 21:26:51 [error] 3446#0: *2849 SSL3_GET_FINISHED:digest check
failed
```

This means that you need to disable the SSL session reuse. You can do this by setting the `proxy_ssl_session_reuse` directive to off.

Configuring advanced logging

Under normal circumstances, we want logging to be as minimal as possible. Usually, what's important is which URIs were called by which clients and when, and if there was an error, to show the resulting error message. If we want to see more information, this leads into a debug logging configuration.

Debug logging

To activate debug logging, the nginx binary needs to have been compiled with the --with-debug configure flag. As this flag is not recommended for high performance production systems, we may want to provide two separate nginx binaries for our needs: the one that we use in production, and the one that has all the same compile-time flags (options given to the configure script), with the addition of --with-debug so that we may simply swap out the binary at runtime in order to be able to debug.

Switching binaries at runtime

NGINX provides the capability to switch out binaries at runtime. After having replaced the nginx binary with a different one, either because we're upgrading or we would like to load a new NGINX, which has different modules compiled in, we can begin the procedure for replacing a running nginx binary:

1. Send the running NGINX master process a USR2 signal to tell it to start a new master process. It will rename its PID file .oldbin (for example, /var/run/nginx.pid.oldbin):

   ```
   # kill -USR2 `cat /var/run/nginx.pid`
   ```

   There will now be two NGINX master processes running, each with its own set of workers to handle incoming requests:

   ```
   root 1149 0.0 0.2 20900 11768 ?? Is Fri03PM 0:00.13 nginx: master
   process /usr/local/sbin/nginx

   www 36660 0.0 0.2 20900 11992 ?? S 12:52PM 0:00.19 nginx: worker
   process (nginx)

   www 36661 0.0 0.2 20900 11992 ?? S 12:52PM 0:00.19 nginx: worker
   process (nginx)

   www 36662 0.0 0.2 20900 12032 ?? I 12:52PM 0:00.01 nginx: worker
   process (nginx)

   www 36663 0.0 0.2 20900 11992 ?? S 12:52PM 0:00.18 nginx: worker
   process (nginx)

   root 50725 0.0 0.1 18844 8408 ?? I 3:49PM 0:00.05 nginx: master
   process /usr/local/sbin/nginx
   ```

```
www 50726 0.0 0.1 18844 9240 ?? I 3:49PM 0:00.00 nginx: worker
process (nginx)

www 50727 0.0 0.1 18844 9240 ?? S 3:49PM 0:00.01 nginx: worker
process (nginx)

www 50728 0.0 0.1 18844 9240 ?? S 3:49PM 0:00.01 nginx: worker
process (nginx)

www 50729 0.0 0.1 18844 9240 ?? S 3:49PM 0:00.01 nginx: worker
process (nginx)
```

2. Send the old NGINX master process a WINCH signal to tell it to stop handling new requests, and phase out its worker processes once they are done with their current requests:

```
# kill -WINCH `cat /var/run/nginx.pid.oldbin`
```

You'll get the following response output:

```
root 1149 0.0 0.2 20900 11768 ?? Ss Fri03PM 0:00.14 nginx: master
process /usr/local/sbin/nginx

root 50725 0.0 0.1 18844 8408 ?? I 3:49PM 0:00.05 nginx: master
process /usr/local/sbin/nginx

www 50726 0.0 0.1 18844 9240 ?? I 3:49PM 0:00.00 nginx: worker
process (nginx)

www 50727 0.0 0.1 18844 9240 ?? S 3:49PM 0:00.01 nginx: worker
process (nginx)

www 50728 0.0 0.1 18844 9240 ?? S 3:49PM 0:00.01 nginx: worker
process (nginx)

www 50729 0.0 0.1 18844 9240 ?? S 3:49PM 0:00.01 nginx: worker
process (nginx)
```

3. Send the old NGINX master process a QUIT signal, once all its worker processes have ended, and we will have only the new nginx binary running, responding to requests:

```
# kill -QUIT `cat /var/run/nginx.pid.oldbin`
```

If there is any problem with the new binary, we can roll back to the old one before sending the QUIT signal to the old binary:

```
# kill -HUP `cat /var/run/nginx.pid.oldbin`
# kill -QUIT `cat /var/run/nginx.pid`
```

If the new binary still has a master process running, you can send it a TERM signal to force it to quit:

```
# kill -TERM `cat /var/run/nginx.pid`
```

Likewise, any new worker processes that are still running may first be stopped with a KILL signal.

 Note that some operating systems will automatically perform the binary upgrade procedure for you when the NGINX package is upgraded.

Once we have our debug-enabled NGINX binary running, we can configure debug logging:

```
user www;

events {

  worker_connections 1024;

}

error_log logs/debug.log debug;

http {

  ...

}
```

We have placed the error_log directive in the main context of the NGINX configuration so that it will be valid for each subcontext, if not overwritten within. We can have multiple error_log directives, each with a different logging level, and each pointing to a different file. In addition to debug, error_log can also take on the following values:

- debug_core
- debug_alloc
- debug_mutex
- debug_event
- debug_http
- debug_imap

Each level is to debug a specific module within NGINX.

It also makes sense to configure a separate error log per virtual server. That way, the errors related only to that server are found in a specific log. This concept can be extended to include the core and http modules as well:

```
error_log logs/core_error.log;

events {

  worker_connections 1024;

}

http {

  error_log logs/http_error.log;

  server {

    server_name www.example.com;

    error_log logs/www.example.com_error.log;

  }

  server {

    server_name www.example.org;

    error_log logs/www.example.org_error.log;

  }

}
```

Using this pattern, we are able to debug a particular virtual host, if that is the area we are interested in:

```
server {

  server_name www.example.org;

  error_log logs/www.example.org_debug.log debug_http;

}
```

What follows is an example of the `debug_http` level output from a single request. Some comments as to what is going on at each point are interspersed throughout:

```
<timestamp> [debug] <worker pid>#0: *<connection number>
  http cl:-1 max:1048576
```

The `rewrite` module is activated very early on in the request processing phase:

```
<timestamp> [debug] <worker pid>#0: *<connection number> rewrite phase: 3
```

```
<timestamp> [debug] <worker pid>#0: *<connection number> post rewrite
phase: 4
```

```
<timestamp> [debug] <worker pid>#0: *<connection number> generic phase: 5
```

```
<timestamp> [debug] <worker pid>#0: *<connection number> generic phase: 6
```

```
<timestamp> [debug] <worker pid>#0: *<connection number> generic phase: 7
```

Access restrictions are checked:

```
<timestamp> [debug] <worker pid>#0: *<connection number> access phase: 8
```

```
<timestamp> [debug] <worker pid>#0: *<connection number> access: 0100007F
FFFFFFFF 0100007F
```

The `try_files` directive is parsed next. The path to the file is constructed from any string (`http script copy`) plus the value of any variable (`http script var`) in the parameters to the `try_files` directive:

```
<timestamp> [debug] <worker pid>#0: *<connection number> try files phase:
11
```

```
<timestamp> [debug] <worker pid>#0: *<connection number> http script
copy: "/"
```

```
<timestamp> [debug] <worker pid>#0: *<connection number> http script var:
"ImageFile.jpg"
```

The evaluated parameter is then concatenated with the `alias` or `root` directives for that `location` directive, and the full path to the file is found:

```
<timestamp> [debug] <worker pid>#0: *<connection number> trying to use
file: "/ImageFile.jpg" "/data/images/ImageFile.jpg"
```

```
<timestamp> [debug] <worker pid>#0: *<connection number> try file uri: "/
ImageFile.jpg"
```

Once the file is found, its contents are processed:

```
<timestamp> [debug] <worker pid>#0: *<connection number> content phase:
12
```

```
<timestamp> [debug] <worker pid>#0: *<connection number> content phase:
13
```

```
<timestamp> [debug] <worker pid>#0: *<connection number> content phase:
14
<timestamp> [debug] <worker pid>#0: *<connection number> content phase:
15
<timestamp> [debug] <worker pid>#0: *<connection number> content phase:
16
```

The `http` filename is the full path to the file to be sent:

```
<timestamp> [debug] <worker pid>#0: *<connection number> http filename:
"/data/images/ImageFile.jpg"
```

The `static` module receives the file descriptor for this file:

```
<timestamp> [debug] <worker pid>#0: *<connection number> http static fd:
15
```

Any temporary content in the body of the response is no longer needed:

```
<timestamp> [debug] <worker pid>#0: *<connection number> http set discard
body
```

Once all information about the file is known, NGINX can construct the full response headers:

```
<timestamp> [debug] <worker pid>#0: *<connection number> HTTP/1.1 200 OK
Server: nginx/<version>
Date: <Date header>
Content-Type: <MIME type>
Content-Length: <filesize>
Last-Modified: <Last-Modified header>
Connection: keep-alive
Accept-Ranges: bytes
```

The next phase involves any transformations to be performed on the file due to output filters that may be active:

```
<timestamp> [debug] <worker pid>#0: *<connection number> http write
filter: l:0 f:0 s:219
<timestamp> [debug] <worker pid>#0: *<connection number> http output
filter "/ImageFile.jpg?file=ImageFile.jpg"
<timestamp> [debug] <worker pid>#0: *<connection number> http copy
filter: "/ImageFile.jpg?file=ImageFile.jpg"
<timestamp> [debug] <worker pid>#0: *<connection number> http postpone
filter "/ImageFile.jpg?file=ImageFile.jpg" 00007FFF30383040
```

```
<timestamp> [debug] <worker pid>#0: *<connection number> http write
filter: 1:1 f:0 s:480317

<timestamp> [debug] <worker pid>#0: *<connection number> http write
filter limit 0

<timestamp> [debug] <worker pid>#0: *<connection number> http write
filter 0000000001911050

<timestamp> [debug] <worker pid>#0: *<connection number> http copy
filter: -2 "/ImageFile.jpg?file=ImageFile.jpg"

<timestamp> [debug] <worker pid>#0: *<connection number> http finalize
request: -2, "/ImageFile.jpg?file=ImageFile.jpg" a:1, c:1

<timestamp> [debug] <worker pid>#0: *<connection number> http run
request: "/ImageFile.jpg?file=ImageFile.jpg"

<timestamp> [debug] <worker pid>#0: *<connection number> http writer
handler: "/ImageFile.jpg?file=ImageFile.jpg"

<timestamp> [debug] <worker pid>#0: *<connection number> http output
filter "/ImageFile.jpg?file=ImageFile.jpg"

<timestamp> [debug] <worker pid>#0: *<connection number> http copy
filter: "/ImageFile.jpg?file=ImageFile.jpg"

<timestamp> [debug] <worker pid>#0: *<connection number> http postpone
filter "/ImageFile.jpg?file=ImageFile.jpg" 0000000000000000

<timestamp> [debug] <worker pid>#0: *<connection number> http write
filter: 1:1 f:0 s:234338

<timestamp> [debug] <worker pid>#0: *<connection number> http write
filter limit 0

<timestamp> [debug] <worker pid>#0: *<connection number> http write
filter 0000000000000000

<timestamp> [debug] <worker pid>#0: *<connection number> http copy
filter: 0 "/ImageFile.jpg?file=ImageFile.jpg"

<timestamp> [debug] <worker pid>#0: *<connection number> http writer
output filter: 0, "/ImageFile.jpg?file=ImageFile.jpg"

<timestamp> [debug] <worker pid>#0: *<connection number> http writer
done: "/ImageFile.jpg?file=ImageFile.jpg"
```

Once the output filters have run, the request is finalized:

```
<timestamp> [debug] <worker pid>#0: *<connection number> http finalize
request: 0, "/ImageFile.jpg?file=ImageFile.jpg" a:1, c:1
```

The `keepalive` handler is responsible for determining if the connection should remain open:

```
<timestamp> [debug] <worker pid>#0: *<connection number> set http
keepalive handler

<timestamp> [debug] <worker pid>#0: *<connection number> http close
request
```

After the request has been processed, it can then be logged:

```
<timestamp> [debug] <worker pid>#0: *<connection number> http log handler

<timestamp> [debug] <worker pid>#0: *<connection number> hc free:
0000000000000000 0

<timestamp> [debug] <worker pid>#0: *<connection number> hc busy:
0000000000000000 0

<timestamp> [debug] <worker pid>#0: *<connection number> tcp_nodelay
```

The client has closed the connection, so NGINX will as well:

```
<timestamp> [debug] <worker pid>#0: *<connection number> http keepalive
handler

<timestamp> [info] <worker pid>#0: *<connection number> client <IP
address> closed keepalive connection

<timestamp> [debug] <worker pid>#0: *<connection number> close http
connection: 3
```

As you can see, there is quite a bit of information included here. If you have trouble figuring out why a particular configuration isn't working, going through the output of the debug log can be helpful. You can immediately see in what order the various filters run, as well as what handlers are involved in serving the request.

Using access logs for debugging

When I was learning how to program, and couldn't find the source of a problem, a friend of mine told me to "put printf's everywhere". That was how he was most quickly able to find the source of a problem. What he meant by this was to place a statement that would print a message at each code branch point so that we could see which code path was getting executed and where the logic was breaking down. By doing this, we could visualize what was going on and could more easily see where the problem lies.

This same principle can be applied to configuring NGINX. Instead of `printf()`, we can use the `log_format` and `access_log` directives to visualize request flow and analyze what's going on during request processing. Use the `log_format` directive to see the values of variables at different points in the configuration:

```
http {

  log_format sentlog '[$time_local] "$request" $status
    $body_bytes_sent ';
  log_format imagelog '[$time_local] $image_file $image_type '
  '$body_bytes_sent $status';


  log_format authlog '[$time_local] $remote_addr $remote_user '
  '"$request" $status';


}
```

Use multiple `access_logs` to see which locations are getting called at what times. By configuring a different `access_log` for each location, we can easily see the ones that are not being used. Any change to such a location will have no effect on request processing; the locations higher up in the processing hierarchy need to be examined first:

```
http {

  log_format sentlog '[$time_local] "$request" $status
    $body_bytes_sent ';

  log_format imagelog '[$time_local] $image_file $image_type '
  '$body_bytes_sent $status';

  log_format authlog '[$time_local] $remote_addr $remote_user '
  '"$request" $status';

  server {

    server_name .example.com;

    root /home/www;

    location / {
```

```
    access_log logs/example.com-access.log combined;

    access_log logs/example.com-root_access.log sentlog;

    rewrite ^/(.*)\.(png|jpg|gif)$ /images/$1.$2;

    set $image_file $1;

    set $image_type $2;
  }

  location /images {

    access_log logs/example.com-images_access.log imagelog;

  }

  location /auth {

    auth_basic "authorized area";

    auth_basic_user_file conf/htpasswd;

    deny all;

    access_log logs/example.com-auth_access.log authlog;

  }

 }

}
```

In the preceding example, there is an access_log declaration for each location, as well as a different log_format directive for each access_log declaration. We can determine the requests that made it to each location depending on the entries found in the corresponding access_log directive. If there are no entries in the example. com-images_access.log file, for example, we know that no requests reached the /images location. We can compare the contents of the various log files to see if the variables are being set to the proper values. For example, if the $image_file and $image_type variables are empty, the corresponding placeholders in the imagelog format access_log will be empty.

Common configuration errors

The next step in troubleshooting a problem is to take a look at the configuration to see whether it actually achieves the goal you are trying to accomplish. NGINX configurations have been floating around the Internet for a number of years. Often, they were designed for an older version of NGINX, and to solve a specific problem. Unfortunately, these configurations are copied without really understanding the problem they were designed to solve. There is sometimes a better way to solve the same problem, using a newer configuration.

Using if instead of try_files

One such case is a situation in which a user wants to deliver a static file if it is found on the filesystem, and if not, to pass the request on to a FastCGI server:

```
server {

  root /var/www/html;

  location / {

    if (!-f $request_filename) {

      include fastcgi_params;

      fastcgi_pass 127.0.0.1:9000;

      break;

    }

  }

}
```

This was the way this problem was commonly solved before NGINX had the `try_files` directive, which appeared in version 0.7.27. The reason why this is considered a configuration error is that it involves using `if` within a `location` directive. As detailed in the *Converting an if-fy configuration to a more modern interpretation* section in *Chapter 4, NGINX as a Reverse Proxy*, this can lead to unexpected results or possibly even a crash. The way to correctly solve this problem is as follows:

```
server {

    root /var/www/html;

    location / {

        try_files $uri $uri/ @fastcgi;

    }

    location @fastcgi {
        include fastcgi_params;

        fastcgi_pass 127.0.0.1:9000;

    }

}
```

The `try_files` directive is used to determine whether the file exists on the filesystem, and if not, passes the request on to the FastCGI server without using `if`.

Using if as a hostname switch

There are countless examples of configurations where `if` is used to redirect requests based on the HTTP `Host` header. These types of configuration work as selectors and are evaluated for each request:

```
server {

    server_name .example.com;

    root /var/www/html;
```

```
    if ($host ~* ^example\.com) {

        rewrite ^/(.*)$ http://www.example.com/$1 redirect;

    }

}
```

Instead of incurring the processing costs associated with evaluating `if` for each request, NGINX's normal request-matching routine can route the request to the correct virtual server. The redirect can then be placed where it belongs, and even without a rewrite:

```
server {

    server_name example.com;

    return 301 $scheme://www.example.com;

}
server {

    server_name www.example.com;

    root /var/www/html;

    location / {

        ...

    }

}
```

Not using the server context to best effect

Another place where copied configuration snippets often lead to incorrect configurations is the area of the `server` context. The `server` context describes the whole virtual server (everything that should be addressed under a particular `server_name` instance). It is underutilized in these copied configuration snippets.

Often, we will see root and index specified per location:

```
server {

  server_name www.example.com;

  location / {

    root /var/www/html;

    index index.php index.html index.htm;

  }

  location /ftp{

    root /var/www/html;

    index index.php index.html index.htm;

  }

}
```

This can lead to configuration errors when new locations are added, and the directives are not copied to those new locations or are copied incorrectly. The point of using the root and index directives is to indicate the document root for the virtual server and the files that should be tried when a directory is given in the URI, respectively. These values are then inherited for any location directive within that server context:

```
server {

  server_name www.example.com;

  root /var/www/html;

  index index.php index.html index.htm;

  location / {
```

```
    . . .

  }

  location /ftp{

    . . .

  }

}
```

Here, we specified that all files will be found under `/var/www/html` and that `index.php`, `index.html`, and `index.htm` are to be tried, in order, as `index` files for any location.

Operating system limits

The operating system is often the last place we look to for discovering a problem. We assume that whoever set up the system has tuned the operating system for our workload and tested it under similar scenarios. This is often not the case. We sometimes need to look into the operating system itself to identify a bottleneck.

As with NGINX, there are two major areas where we can initially look for performance problems: **file descriptor limits** and **network limits**.

File descriptor limits

NGINX uses file descriptors in several different ways. The major use is to respond to client connections, each one using a file descriptor. Each outgoing connection (especially prevalent in proxy configurations) requires a unique IP:TCP port pair, which NGINX refers to using a file descriptor. If NGINX is serving any static files or a response from its cache, a file descriptor is used as well. As you can see, the number of file descriptors can climb quickly with the number of concurrent users. The total number of file descriptors that NGINX may use is limited by the operating system.

The typical UNIX-like operating system has a different set of limits for the superuser (`root`) than for a regular user, so make sure to execute the following command as the non-privileged user under which you're running NGINX (specified either by the `--user compile-time` option or the `user` configuration directive):

```
ulimit -n
```

This command will show you the number of open file descriptors allowed for that user. Usually, this number is set conservatively to 1,024 or even lower. Since we know that NGINX will be the major user of file descriptors on the machine, we can set this number much higher. How to do this depends on the specific operating system. This can be done as follows:

- Linux:

```
vi /etc/security/limits.conf

www-run hard nofile 65535
$ ulimit -n 65535
```

- FreeBSD:

```
vi /etc/sysctl.conf

kern.maxfiles=65535
kern.maxfilesperproc=65535
kern.maxvnodes=65535
# /etc/rc.d/sysctl reload
```

- Solaris:

```
# projadd -c "increased file descriptors" -K "process.max-file-descriptor=(basic,65535,deny)" resource.file

# usermod -K project=resource.file www
```

The preceding three commands will increase the maximum number of file descriptors allowed for a new process running as user, www. This will also persist across a reboot.

The following two commands will increase the maximum number of file descriptors allowed for a running NGINX process:

```
# prctl -r -t privileged -n process.max-file-descriptor -v 65535 -i process `pgrep nginx`

# prctl -x -t basic -n process.max-file-descriptor -i process `pgrep nginx`
```

Each of these methods will change the operating system limit itself, but will have no effect on the running NGINX process. To enable NGINX to use the number of file descriptors specified, set the `worker_rlimit_nofile` directive to this new limit:

```
worker_rlimit_nofile 65535;

worker_processes 8;

events {

  worker_connections 8192;

}
```

Now, send the running `nginx` master process the HUP signal:

```
# kill -HUP `cat /var/run/nginx.pid`
```

NGINX will then be able to handle just over 65,000 simultaneous clients, connections to upstream servers, and any local static or cached files. This many `worker_processes` instances only makes sense if you actually have eight CPU cores or are heavily I/O bound. If that is not the case, decrease the number of `worker_processes` to match the number of CPU cores and increase `worker_connections` so that the product of the two approaches 65,000.

You can, of course, increase the number of total file descriptors and `worker_connections` up to a limit that makes sense for your hardware and use case. NGINX is capable of handling millions of simultaneous connections, provided the operating system limits and configuration are set correctly.

Network limits

If you find yourself in a situation in which no network buffers are available, you will most likely only be able to log in at the console, if at all. This can happen when NGINX receives so many client connections that all available network buffers are used up. Increasing the number of network buffers is also specific to a particular operating system and may be done as follows:

- FreeBSD:

  ```
  vi /boot/loader.conf

  kern.ipc.nmbclusters=262144
  ```

- Solaris:

  ```
  # ndd -set /dev/tcp tcp_max_buf 16777216
  ```

When NGINX is acting as either a mail or an HTTP proxy, it will need to open many connections to its upstream servers. To enable as many connections as possible, the ephemeral TCP port range should be adjusted to its maximum:

- Linux:
  ```
  vi /etc/sysctl.conf
  ```

  ```
  net.ipv4.ip_local_port_range = 1024 65535
  # sysctl -p /etc/sysctl.conf
  ```

- FreeBSD:
  ```
  vi /etc/sysctl.conf
  ```

  ```
  net.inet.ip.portrange.first=1024
  net.inet.ip.portrange.last=65535
  # /etc/rc.d/sysctl reload
  ```

- Solaris:
  ```
  # ndd -set /dev/tcp tcp_smallest_anon_port 1024
  # ndd -set /dev/tcp tcp_largest_anon_port 65535
  ```

Having adjusted these basic values, we will now take a look at more specific performance-related parameters in the next section.

Performance problems

When designing an application and configuring NGINX to deliver it, we expect it to perform well. When we experience performance problems, however, we need to take a look at the reasons that could cause them. It may be in the application itself. It may be our NGINX configuration. We will investigate how to discover where the problem lies.

When proxying, NGINX does most of its work over the network. If there are any limitations at the network level, NGINX cannot perform optimally. Network tuning is again specific to the operating system and network on which you are running NGINX, so these tuning parameters should be examined in your particular situation.

One of the most important values relating to network performance is the size of the `listen` queue for new TCP connections. This number should be increased to enable more clients. Exactly how to do this and what value to use depends on the operating system and optimization goal:

- Linux:

```
vi /etc/sysctl.conf


net.core.somaxconn = 3240000
# sysctl -p /etc/sysctl.conf
```

- FreeBSD:

```
vi /etc/sysctl.conf


kern.ipc.somaxconn=4096
# /etc/rc.d/sysctl reload
```

- Solaris:

```
# ndd -set /dev/tcp tcp_conn_req_max_q 1024
# ndd -set /dev/tcp tcp_conn_req_max_q0 4096
```

The next parameter to change is the size of the send and receive buffers. Note that these values are for illustration purposes only— they may lead to excessive memory usage, so be sure to test in your specific scenario:

- Linux:

```
vi /etc/sysctl.conf


net.ipv4.tcp_wmem = 8192 87380 1048576
net.ipv4.tcp_rmem = 8192 87380 1048576
# sysctl -p /etc/sysctl.conf
```

- FreeBSD:

```
vi /etc/sysctl.conf


net.inet.tcp.sendspace=1048576
net.inet.tcp.recvspace=1048576
# /etc/rc.d/sysctl reload
```

- Solaris:

```
# ndd -set /dev/tcp tcp_xmit_hiwat 1048576
# ndd -set /dev/tcp tcp_recv_hiwat 1048576
```

You can also change these buffers in NGINX's configuration directly so that they are only valid for NGINX and not for any other software you are running on the machine. This may be desirable when you have multiple services running, but want to ensure that NGINX gets the most out of your network stack:

```
server {

  listen 80 sndbuf=1m rcvbuf=1m;

}
```

Depending on your network setup, you will note a marked change in performance. You should examine your particular setup, though, and make one change at a time, observing the results after each change. Performance tuning can be done on so many different levels that this small treatment here does not do the subject justice. If you are interested in learning more about performance tuning, there are a number of books and online resources that you should take a look at. Visit `http://www.brendangregg.com/linuxperf.html` for examples.

Making network tuning changes in Solaris persistent

In the previous two sections, we changed several TCP-level parameters on the command line. For Linux and FreeBSD, these changes would be persisted after a reboot due to the changes also being made in system configuration files (for example, `/etc/sysctl.conf`). For Solaris, the situation is different. These changes are not made in `sysctls`, so they cannot be persisted in this file.

The ways to set these changes on Solaris are detailed in *Appendix D, Persisting Solaris Network Tunings*.

Using the Stub Status module

NGINX provides an introspection module that outputs certain statistics about how it is running. This module is called **stub_status** and is enabled with the `--with-http_stub_status_module` configure flag.

To see the statistics produced by this module, the stub_status directive needs to be set to on. A separate location directive should be created for this module so that an ACL may be applied:

```
location /nginx_status {

    stub_status on;

    access_log off;

    allow 127.0.0.1;

    deny all;

}
```

Calling this URI from the localhost (for example, with curl http://localhost/ nginx_status) will show output similar to the following lines:

```
Active connections: 2532
server accepts handled requests
1476737983 1476737983 3553635810
Reading: 93 Writing: 13 Waiting: 2426
```

Here we see that there are 2,532 open connections, of which NGINX is currently reading the request header of 93, and 13 connections are in a state in which NGINX is either reading the request body, processing the request, or writing a response to the client. The remaining 2,426 requests are considered keepalive connections. Since this nginx process was started, it has both accepted and handled 1,476,737,983 connections, meaning that none were closed immediately after having been accepted. There were a total of 3,553,635,810 requests handled through these 1,476,737,983 connections, meaning there were approximately 2.4 requests per connection.

This kind of data can be collected and graphed using your favorite system metrics tool chain. There are plugins for Munin, Nagios, collectd, and others, which use the stub_status module to collect statistics. Over time, you may note certain trends and be able to correlate them to specific factors, but only if the data is collected. Spikes in user traffic as well as changes in the operating system should be visible in these graphs.

Summary

Problems surface on a number of levels when bringing a new piece of software into production. Some errors can be tested for and eradicated in a test environment; others surface only under real load with real users. To discover the reasons for these problems, NGINX provides very detailed logging at a number of levels. Some of the messages may have multiple interpretations, but the overall pattern is understandable. By experimenting with the configuration and seeing what kinds of error message are produced, we can gain a feeling for how to interpret the entries in the error log. The operating system has an influence on how NGINX runs, as it imposes certain limits due to default settings for a multiuser system. Understanding what is going on at the TCP level will help when tuning these parameters to meet the load under real conditions. Rounding off our tour of troubleshooting, we saw what kind of information the `stub_status` module was capable of delivering. This data can be useful for getting an overall idea for how our NGINX is performing.

The appendices are up next. The first is a directive reference, listing all of NGINX's configuration directives in one place, including default values and in which context they may be used.

A
Directive Reference

This appendix lists the configuration directives used throughout the book. There are also some directives that did not appear in the book, but are listed here for completeness. The entries have been expanded to show under which context each directive may be used. If a directive has a default value, it has been listed as well. These directives are current as of NGINX version 1.9.11. The most up-to-date list can be found at `http://nginx.org/en/docs/dirindex.html`.

Directive	Explanation	Context / default value
`accept_mutex`	Serializes the `accept()` method on new connections by worker processes.	Valid context: `events` Default value: `on`
`accept_mutex_delay`	The maximum time a worker process will wait to accept new connections if another worker is already doing this.	Valid context: `events` Default value: `500ms`
`access_log`	Describes where and how are to be written. The first parameter is a path to the file where the logs are to be stored. Variables may be used in constructing the path. The special value, `off`, disables the access log. An optional second parameter indicates the `log_format` directive that will be used to write the logs. If no second parameter is configured, the predefined combined format is used. An optional third parameter indicates the size of the buffer if write buffering should be used to record the logs. If write buffering is used, this size cannot exceed the size of the atomic disk write for that filesystem.	Valid contexts: `http`, `server`, `location`, `if in location`, and `limit_except` Default value: `logs/access.log combined`
`add_after_body`	Adds the result of processing a subrequest after the response body.	Valid contexts: `http`, `server`, and `location` Default value: -

Directive	Explanation	Context / default value
add_before_body	Adds the result of processing a subrequest before the response body.	Valid contexts: http, server, and location Default value: -
add_header	Adds fields to a header present in responses with the HTTP codes 200, 204, 206, 301, 302, 303, 304, or 307.	Valid contexts: http, server, location, and if in location Default value: -
addition_types	Lists the MIME types of a response in addition to text/html, in which an addition will be made. May be * to enable all MIME types.	Valid contexts: http, server, and location Default value: text/html
aio	Enables the use of asynchronous file I/O. It is available on all modern versions of FreeBSD and distributions of Linux. On FreeBSD, aio may be used to preload data for sendfile. Under Linux, directio is required, which automatically disables sendfile.	Valid contexts: http, server, and location Default value: off
alias	Defines another name for the location, as found on the filesystem. If the location is specified with a regular expression, the alias directive should reference captures defined in that regular expression.	Valid context: location Default value: -
allow	Allows access from this IP address, network, or all.	Valid contexts: http, server, location, and limit_except Default value: -
ancient_browser	One or more strings, which if found in the User-Agent header, will indicate that the browser is considered ancient by setting the $ancient_browser variable to the ancient_browser_value directive.	Valid contexts: http, server, and location Default value: -
ancient_browser_value	The value to which the $ancient_browser variable will be set.	Valid contexts: http, server, and location Default value: 1
auth_basic	Enables authentication using HTTP Basic Authentication. The string parameter is used as the realm name. If the special value, off, is used, this indicates that the auth_basic value of the parent configuration level is negated.	Valid contexts: http, server, location, and limit_except Default value: off
auth_basic_user_file	The location of a file of the username:password:comment tuples used to authenticate users. The password needs to be encrypted with the crypt algorithm. The comment is optional.	Valid contexts: http, server, location, and limit_except Default value: -

Directive	Explanation	Context / default value
auth_http	The server used for authenticating the POP3/IMAP user.	Valid contexts: mail and server Default value: -
auth_http_header	Sets an additional header (first parameter) to the specified value (second parameter).	Valid contexts: mail and server Default value: -
auth_http_pass_client_cert	Specifies whether to pass the PEM-encoded client certificate as the Auth-SSL-Cert header.	Valid contexts: mail and server Default value: off
auth_http_timeout	The maximum amount of time NGINX will wait when communicating with an authentication server.	Valid contexts: mail and server Default value: 60s
auth_request	The URI to which an authorization subrequest should be sent.	Valid contexts: http, server, and location Default value: off
auth_request_set	The given variable to the value, which may contain variables from the authorization request.	Valid contexts: http, server, and location Default value: -
autoindex	The automatic generation of a directory listing page.	Valid contexts: http, server, and location Default value: off
autoindex_exact_size	Indicates whether the file sizes in a directory listing page should be listed in bytes or rounded to kilobytes, megabytes, and gigabytes.	Valid contexts: http, server, and location. Default value: on
autoindex_format	The format to be used for the directory listing.	Valid contexts: http, server, and location Default value: html
autoindex_localtime	Sets the file modification time in a directory listing page to either local time (on) or UTC (off).	Valid contexts: http, server, and location Default value: off
break	Ends the processing of the rewrite module directives found within the same context.	Valid contexts: server, location, and if Default value: -
charset	Adds the character set specified to the Content-Type response header. If this is different than the source_charset directive, a conversion is performed.	Valid contexts: http, server, location, and if in location Default value: off

Directive	Explanation	Context / default value
charset_map	Sets up a conversion table from one character set to another. Each character code is specified in hexadecimal. The files conf/koi-win, conf/koi-utf, and conf/win-utf include mappings from koi8-r to windows-1251, from koi8-r to utf-8, and from windows-1251 to utf-8, respectively.	Valid context: http Default value: -
charset_types	Lists the MIME types of a response in addition to text/html, in which a character set conversion will be made. It may be * to enable all MIME types.	Valid contexts: http, server, and location Default values: text/html, text/xml, text/plain, text/vnd.wap.wml, application/x-javascript, and application/rss+xml
chunked_transfer_encoding	Allows disabling the standard HTTP/1.1 chunked transfer encoding in responses to clients.	Valid contexts: http, server, and location Default value: on
client_body_buffer_size	Used to set a buffer size for the client request body larger than the default two memory pages, in order to prevent temporary files from being written to disk.	Valid contexts: http, server, and location Default value: 8k|16k (platform dependent)
client_body_in_file_only	Used for debugging or further processing of the client request body; this directive can be set to on to force saving the client request body to a file. The value, clean, will cause the files to be removed after the request processing has finished.	Valid contexts: http, server, and location Default value: off
client_body_in_single_buffer	This directive will force NGINX to save the entire client request body in a single buffer, to reduce copy operations.	Valid contexts: http, server, and location Default value: off
client_body_temp_path	Defines a directory path for saving the client request body. If a second, third, or fourth parameter is given, these specify a subdirectory hierarchy with the parameter value as the number of characters in the subdirectory name.	Valid contexts: http, server, and location Default value: client_body_temp
client_body_timeout	Specifies the length of time between successive read operations of the client body. If reached, the client receives a 408 error message (Request Timeout).	Valid contexts: http, server, and location Default value: 60s

Directive	Explanation	Context / default value
client_header_buffer_size	Used for specifying a buffer size for the client request header, when this needs to be larger than the default 1 KB.	Valid contexts: http and server Default value: 1k
client_header_timeout	Specifies the length of time for reading the entire client header. If reached, the client receives a 408 error message (Request Timeout).	Valid contexts: http and server Default value: 60s
client_max_body_size	Defines the largest allowable client request body, before a 413 (Request Entity Too Large) error is returned to the browser.	Valid contexts: http, server, and location Default value: 1m
connection_pool_size	Fine tunes per-connection memory allocation.	Valid contexts: http and server Default values: 256 (on 32-bit platforms) and 512 (on 64-bit platforms)
create_full_put_path	Allows recursive directory creation when using WebDAV.	Valid contexts: http, server, and location Default value: off
daemon	Sets whether or not to daemonize the NGINX process.	Valid context: main Default value: on
dav_access	Sets filesystem access permissions for newly-created files and directories. If group or all is specified, user may be omitted.	Valid contexts: http, server, and location Default value: user:rw
dav_methods	Allows the specified HTTP and WebDAV methods. When PUT is used, a temporary file is first created, and then renamed. So, it's recommended to put client_body_temp_path on the same filesystem as the destination. A modification date for such files may be specified in the Date header.	Valid contexts: http, server, and location Default value: off
debug_connection	Enables debug logging for any client matching the value of this directive. It may be specified multiple times. To debug UNIX-domain sockets, use unix:.	Valid context: events Default value: -
debug_points	When debugging, the process will either create a core file (abort) or stop (stop) so that a system debugger may be attached.	Valid context: main Default value: -
default_type	Sets the default MIME type of a response. This comes into play if the MIME type of the file cannot be matched to one of those specified by the types directive.	Valid contexts: http, server, and location Default value: text/plain

Directive	Explanation	Context / default value
deny	Denies access from this IP address, network, or all.	Valid contexts: `http`, `server`, `location`, and `limit_except` Default value: -
directio	Enables the operating system-specific flag or function for serving files larger than the parameter given. This directive is required when using `aio` on Linux.	Valid contexts: `http`, `server`, and `location` Default value: `off`
directio_alignment	Sets the alignment for `directio`. The default value of `512` is usually enough, although it's recommended to increase this to 4K when using XFS on Linux.	Valid contexts: `http`, `server`, and `location` Default value: `512`
disable_symlinks	For more information on this directive, refer to the table (The HTTP file path directives) given in the *Finding files* section in *Chapter 6, The NGINX HTTP Server.*	Valid contexts: `http`, `server`, and `location` Default value: `off`
empty_gif	Causes a 1x1 pixel transparent GIF to be emitted for that location.	Valid context: `location` Default value: -
env	Sets the environment variables for use in the following ways: • Inheritance during a live upgrade • Making use of them in the `perl` module • Making them available to worker processes • Specifying the variable alone will use the value found in the `nginx` environment • Setting a variable may be done in the form, `var=value` • N.B. NGINX is an internal variable and shouldn't be set by the user.	Valid context: `main` Default value: `TZ`

Directive	Explanation	Context / default value
error_log	The error_log file is where all errors will be written. It may be set to a file or stderr. If no other error_log is given in a separate context, this log file will be used for all errors, globally. A second parameter to this directive indicates at which level (debug, info, notice, warn, error, crit, alert, emerg) errors will be written to the log. Note that the debug level errors are only available if the --with-debug configuration switch was given at compile time.	Valid contexts: main, http, server, and location Default value: logs/error.log error
error_page	Defines a URI to be served when an error level response code is encountered. Adding an = parameter allows the response code to be changed. If the argument to this parameter is left empty, the response code will be taken from the URI, which must in this case be served by an upstream server of some sort.	Valid contexts: http, server, location, and if in location Default value: -
etag	Disables automatically generating the ETag response header for static resources.	Valid contexts: http, server, and location Default value: on
events	Defines a new context in which connection-processing directives are specified.	Valid context: main. Default value: -
expires	For more information on this directive, refer to the table (Header modifying directives) given in the *Caching in the filesystem* section in *Chapter 7, NGINX for the Application Developer*.	Valid contexts: http, server, location, and if in location Default value: off
fastcgi_bind	Specifies the address that should be used for outgoing connections to a FastCGI server.	Valid contexts: http, server, and location Default value: -
fastcgi_buffer_size	The size of the buffer used for the first part of the response from the FastCGI server, in which the response headers are found.	Valid contexts: http, server, and location Default value: 4k	8k (platform dependent)
fastcgi_buffering	Whether or not to buffer responses from the FastCGI server.	Valid contexts: http, server, and location Default value: on
fastcgi_buffers	The number and size of buffers used for the response from a FastCGI server, for a single connection.	Valid contexts: http, server, and location Default value: 4k	8k (platform dependent)

Directive	Explanation	Context / default value
fastcgi_busy_buffers_size	The total size of the buffer space allocated to sending the response to the client while still being read from the FastCGI server. This is typically set to two fastcgi_buffers.	Valid contexts: http, server, and location Default value: 4k | 8k (platform dependent)
fastcgi_cache	Defines a shared memory zone to be used for caching.	Valid contexts: http, server, and location Default value: off
fastcgi_cache_bypass	One or more string variables, which when nonempty or nonzero, will cause the response to be taken from the FastCGI server instead of the cache.	Valid contexts: http, server, and location Default value: -
fastcgi_cache_key	A string used as the key for storing and retrieving cache values.	Valid contexts: http, server, and location Default value: -
fastcgi_cache_lock	Enabling this directive will prevent multiple requests from making an entry into the same cache key.	Valid contexts: http, server, and location Default value: off
fastcgi_cache_lock_age	The time for an entry to appear in the cache or one final request will be made.	Valid contexts: http, server, and location Default value: 5s
fastcgi_cache_lock_timeout	The length of time a request will wait for an entry to appear in the cache or for the fastcgi_cache_lock to be released.	Valid contexts: http, server, and location Default value: 5s
fastcgi_cache_methods	This directive specifies the methods that are present in the client request in order for it to be cached.	Valid contexts: http, server, and location Default value: GET HEAD
fastcgi_cache_min_uses	The number of requests for a certain key needed before a response is cached.	Valid contexts: http, server, and location Default value: 1
fastcgi_cache_path	For more information on this directive, refer to the table (FastCGI directives) given in the *Using NGINX with PHP-FPM* section in *Chapter 6, The NGINX HTTP Server*.	Valid context: http Default value: -
fastcgi_cache_revalidate	Whether the If-Modified-Since and If-None-Match headers should be used to revalidate expired cache entries.	Valid contexts: http, server, and location Default value: off
fastcgi_cache_use_stale	The cases under which it is acceptable to serve stale cached data when an error occurs while accessing the FastCGI server. The updating parameter indicates the case when fresh data are being loaded.	Valid contexts: http, server, and location Default value: off

Directive	Explanation	Context / default value
fastcgi_cache_valid	Indicates the length of time for which a cached response with response code 200, 301, or 302 is valid. If an optional response code is given before the time parameter, this time is only for that response code. The special parameter, any, indicates that any response code should be cached for that length of time.	Valid contexts: http, server, and location Default value: -
fastcgi_connect_timeout	The maximum amount of time NGINX will wait for its connection to be accepted when making a request to a FastCGI server.	Valid contexts: http, server, and location Default value: 60s
fastcgi_force_ranges	Forces byte-range support, irrespective of the value of the Accept-Ranges header.	Valid contexts: http, server, and location Default value: off
fastcgi_hide_header	A list of header fields that should not be passed on to the client.	Valid contexts: http, server, and location Default value: -
fastcgi_ignore_client_abort	If set to on, NGINX will not abort the connection to a FastCGI server if the client aborts the connection.	Valid contexts: http, server, and location Default value: off
fastcgi_ignore_headers	Sets which headers may be disregarded when processing the response from the FastCGI server.	Valid contexts: http, server, and location Default value: -
fastcgi_index	Sets the name of a file to be appended to $fastcgi_script_name that ends with a slash.	Valid contexts: http, server, and location Default value: -
fastcgi_intercept_errors	If enabled, NGINX will display a configured error_page directive instead of the response directly from the FastCGI server.	Valid contexts: http, server, and location Default value: off
fastcgi_keep_conn	Enables the keepalive connections to the FastCGI servers by instructing the server not to immediately close the connection.	Valid contexts: http, server, and location Default value: off
fastcgi_limit_rate	If buffering is enabled, the bytes/s at which the response from the FastCGI server will be read.	Valid contexts: http, server, and location Default value: 0 (disabled)
fastcgi_max_temp_file_size	The maximum size of the overflow file; this directive is written when the response doesn't fit into the memory buffers.	Valid contexts: http, server, and location Default value: 1024m
fastcgi_next_upstream	For more information on this directive, refer to the table (FastCGI directives) given in the *Using NGINX with PHP-FPM* section in *Chapter 6, The NGINX HTTP Server*.	Valid contexts: http, server, and location Default value: error timeout

Directive	Explanation	Context / default value
fastcgi_next_upstream_timeout	The time limit for passing the request to the next server.	Valid contexts: http, server, and location Default value: 0
fastcgi_next_upstream_tries	The number of tries before the request is passed to the next server.	Valid contexts: http, server, and location Default value: 0
fastcgi_no_cache	One or more string variables, which when nonempty or nonzero will instruct NGINX not to save the response from the FastCGI server in the cache.	Valid contexts: http, server, and location Default value: -
fastcgi_param	Sets a parameter and its value to be passed to the FastCGI server. If the parameter should only be passed when the value is nonempty, the additional if_not_empty parameter should be set.	Valid contexts: http, server, and location Default value: -
fastcgi_pass	Specifies the FastCGI server to which the request is passed, either as an address:port combination or as unix:path for a UNIX-domain socket.	Valid contexts: location and if in location Default value: -
fastcgi_pass_header	Overrides the disabled headers set in fastcgi_hide_header, allowing them to be sent to the client.	Valid contexts: http, server, and location Default value: -
fastcgi_pass_request_body	Whether or not the original request body will be passed to the FastCGI server.	Valid contexts: http, server, and location Default value: on
fastcgi_pass_request_header	Specifies whether or not the headers of the original request will be passed to the FastCGI server.	Valid contexts: http, server, and location Default value: on
fastcgi_read_timeout	Specifies the length of time that needs to elapse between two successive read operations from a FastCGI server before the connection is closed.	Valid contexts: http, server, and location Default value: 60s
fastcgi_request_buffering	Whether or not the complete client request body will be buffered before sending the request to the FastCGI server.	Valid contexts: http, server, and location Default value: on
fastcgi_send_lowat	This is a FreeBSD directive. When nonzero, it will tell NGINX to use either the NOTE_LOWAT kqueue method or the SO_SNDLOWAT socket option with the specified size when communicating with an upstream server. This directive is ignored in Linux, Solaris, and Windows.	Valid contexts: http, server, and location Default value: 0

Directive	Explanation	Context / default value
`fastcgi_send_timeout`	The length of time that needs to elapse between two successive `write` operations to a FastCGI server before the connection is closed.	Valid contexts: `http`, `server`, and `location` Default value: `60s`
`fastcgi_split_path_info`	Defines a regular expression with two captures. The first capture will be the value of the `$fastcgi_script_name` variable. The second capture becomes the value of the `$fastcgi_path_info` variable.	Valid context: `location` Default value: -
`fastcgi_store`	Enables storing responses retrieved from a FastCGI server as files on the disk. The on parameter will use the `alias` or `root` directive as the base path under which to store the file. A string may instead be given, to indicate an alternative location to store the files.	Valid contexts: `http`, `server`, and `location` Default value: `off`
`fastcgi_store_access`	Sets file access permissions for the newly-created `fastcgi_store` files.	Valid contexts: `http`, `server`, and `location` Default value: `user:rw`
`fastcgi_temp_file_write_size`	Limits the amount of data buffered to a temporary file at one time so that NGINX will not be blocked for too long on a single request.	Valid contexts: `http`, `server`, and `location` Default value: `8k｜16k` (platform dependent)
`fastcgi_temp_path`	In this directory, temporary files may be buffered as they are proxied from the FastCGI server, optionally multilevel deep. If a second, third, or fourth parameter is given, these parameters specify a subdirectory hierarchy with the parameter value as the number of characters in the subdirectory name.	Valid contexts: `http`, `server`, and `location` Default value: `fastcgi_temp`
`flv`	Activates the `flv` module for this location.	Valid context: `location` Default value: -

Directive	Explanation	Context / default value
geo	Defines a new context, in which a variable is set to a specified value, dependent on the IP address found in another variable. If no other variable is specified, `$remote_addr` is used to determine the IP address. The format of the context definition is as follows: `geo [$address-variable] $variable-to-be-set { … }` The following parameters are recognized within the context: • `delete`: Deletes the specified network • `default`: The variable will be set to this value if no IP address matches • `include`: Includes a file of address-to-value mappings • `proxy`: Defines an address or network of a direct connection from which the IP address will be taken from the `X-Forwarded-For` header • `proxy_recursive`: Works with proxy to specify that the last address in a multi-valued `X-Forwarded-For` header will be used • `ranges`: When defined, it indicates that the following addresses are specified as ranges	Valid context: `http` Default value: -
geoip_city	The path to a GeoIP database file containing IP address-to-city mappings. The following variables then become available: • `$geoip_city_country_code`: Two-letter country code • `$geoip_city_country_code3`: Three-letter country code • `$geoip_city_country_name`: Country name • `$geoip_region`: Country region name • `$geoip_city`: City name • `$geoip_postal_code`: Postal code	Valid context: `http` Default value: -

Directive	Explanation	Context / default value
geoip_country	The path to a GeoIP database file containing the IP address-to-country mappings. The following variables then become available: • `$geoip_country_code`: Two-letter country code • `$geoip_country_code3`: Three-letter country code • `$geoip_country_name`: Country name	Valid context: `http` Default value: -
geoip_org	The path to a GeoIP database file containing the IP address-to-organization mappings. The following variable then becomes available: • `$geoip_org`: Organization name	Valid context: `http`. Default value: -
geoip_proxy	Defines an address or network of a direct connection from which the IP address will be taken from the `X-Forwarded-For` header.	Valid context: `http` Default value: -
geoip_proxy_recursive	Works with `geoip_proxy` to specify that the last address in a multivalued `X-Forwarded-For` header will be used.	Valid context: `http` Default value: `off`
gunzip	Enables the decompression of the `gzip` files when the client doesn't support `gzip`.	Valid contexts: `http`, `server`, and `location` Default value: `off`
gunzip_buffers	Specifies the number and size of buffers used for decompressing a response.	Valid contexts: `http`, `server`, and `location` Default value: `32 4k|16 8k` (platform dependent)
gzip	Enables or disables the compression of responses.	Valid contexts: `http`, `server`, `location`, and `if in location` Default value: `off`
gzip_buffers	Specifies the number and size of buffers used for compressing a response.	Valid contexts: `http`, `server`, and `location` Default value: `32 4k|16 8k` (platform dependent)
gzip_comp_level	The `gzip` compression level (1-9).	Valid contexts: `http`, `server`, and `location` Default value: `1`
gzip_disable	A regular expression of user-agents that shouldn't receive a compressed response. The special value, `msie6`, is a shortcut for `MSIE [4-6]\.`, excluding `MSIE 6.0; ... SV1`.	Valid contexts: `http`, `server`, and `location` Default value: -

Directive	Explanation	Context / default value
gzip_http_version	The minimum HTTP version of a request before compression is considered.	Valid contexts: http, server, and location Default value: 1.1
gzip_min_length	The minimum length of a response before compression is considered, determined by the Content-Length header.	Valid contexts: http, server, and location Default value: 20
gzip_proxied	Refer to the table (The Gzip module directives) in the *Compressing data* section in *Chapter 5, Reverse Proxy Advanced Topics*.	Valid contexts: http, server, and location Default value: off
gzip_static	Enables checking for precompressed files to be delivered directly to clients that support the gzip compression.	Valid contexts: http, server, and location Default value: off
gzip_types	The MIME types that should be compressed with gzip, in addition to the default text/html value. It may be * to enable all MIME types.	Valid contexts: http, server, and location Default value: text/html
gzip_vary	Enables or disables the response header, Vary: Accept-Encoding, if gzip or gzip_static is active.	Valid contexts: http, server, and location Default value: off
hash	The key that is used to map to the upstream server for each request. To use the ketama consistent hashing algorithm instead of rehashing when servers are added or removed, specify the consistent parameter.	Valid context: upstream Default value: -
http	Sets up a configuration context in which the HTTP server directives are specified.	Valid context: main Default value: -
http2_chunk_size	Sets the maximum chunk size for the response body.	Valid contexts: http, server, and location Default value: 8k
http2_idle_timeout	The amount of time with no activity after which the connection is closed.	Valid contexts: http and server Default value: 3m
http2_max_concurrent_streams	Sets the number of HTTP/2 streams that may be active in a single connection.	Valid contexts: http and server Default value: 128
http2_max_field_size	Sets the maximum size of the compressed request header field.	Valid contexts: http and server Default value: 4k
http2_max_header_size	Sets the maximum size of the uncompressed request headers.	Valid contexts: http and server Default value: 16k
http2_recv_buffer_size	The size of the input buffer for each worker.	Valid context: http Default value: 256k

Directive	Explanation	Context / default value
http2_recv_timeout	The amount of time a client has to send data before the connection is closed.	Valid contexts: http and server Default value: 30s
if	Refer to the table (The rewrite module directives) given in the *Introducing the rewrite module* section in *Appendix B, The Rewrite Rule Guide*.	Valid contexts: server and location Default value: -
if_modified_since	Controls how the modification time of a response is compared to the value of the If-Modified-Since request header: • off: The If-Modified-Since header is ignored • exact: An exact match is made (default) • before: The modification time of the response is less than or equal to the value of the If-Modified-Since header	Valid contexts: http, server, and location Default value: exact
ignore_invalid_headers	Disables ignoring headers with invalid names. A valid name is composed of ASCII letters, numbers, the hyphen, and possibly the underscore (controlled by the underscores_in_headers directive).	Valid contexts: http and server Default value: on
image_filter	Refer to the table (The image filter directives) given in the *Generating images* section in *Chapter 7, NGINX for the Application Developer*.	Valid context: location Default value: -
image_filter_buffer	The size of the buffer used to process images. If more memory is needed, the server will return a 415 error (Unsupported Media Type).	Valid contexts: http, server, and location Default value: 1M
image_filter_interlace	Whether or not to interlace images produced by this filter.	Valid contexts: http, server, and location Default value: off
image_filter_jpeg_quality	The quality of the resulting JPEG image, after processing. The value is not recommended to exceed 95.	Valid contexts: http, server, and location Default value: 75
image_filter_sharpen	Increases the sharpness of a processed image by this percentage.	Valid contexts: http, server, and location Default value: 0
image_filter_transparency	Disables preserving the transparency of the transformed GIF and PNG images. The default value, on, preserves transparency.	Valid contexts: http, server, and location Default value: on

Directive	Explanation	Context / default value
imap_auth	Sets the supported client authentication mechanism. It can be one or more of login, plain, or cram-md5.	Valid contexts: mail and server Default value: plain
imap_capabilities	The IMAP4 capabilities that are supported by the backend server.	Valid contexts: mail and server Default value: IMAP4 IMAP4rev1 UIDPLUS
imap_client_buffer	Sets the size of the read buffer for the IMAP commands.	Valid contexts: mail and server Default value: 4k | 8k (platform dependent)
include	The path to a file containing additional configuration directives. It may be specified as glob to include multiple files.	Valid context: any Default value: -
index	Defines the file that will be served to the client when a URI ending with / is received. It may be multivalued.	Valid contexts: http, server, and location Default value: index.html
internal	Specifies a location that can only be used for internal requests (redirects defined in other directives, the rewrite requests, and similar request processing directives).	Valid context: location Default value: -
ip_hash	Ensures the distribution of clients evenly over all server contexts by hashing the IP address, keying on its class C network.	Valid context: upstream Default value: -
keepalive	The number of connections to the upstream servers that are cached per worker process. When used with the HTTP connections, proxy_http_version should be set to 1.1 and proxy_set_header to Connection.	Valid context: upstream Default value: -
keepalive_disable	Disables the keepalive requests for certain browser types.	Valid contexts: http, server, and location Default value: msie6
keepalive_requests	Defines how many requests may be made over one keepalive connection before it is closed.	Valid contexts: http, server, and location Default value: 100
keepalive_timeout	Specifies how long a keepalive connection will stay open. A second parameter may be given, to set a Keep-Alive header in the response.	Valid contexts: http, server, and location Default value: 75s
large_client_header_buffers	Defines the maximum number and size of a large client request header.	Valid contexts: http and server Default value: 4 8k

Directive	Explanation	Context / default value
`least_conn`	Activates the load-balancing algorithm where the server with the least number of active connections is chosen for the next new connection.	Valid context: `upstream` Default value: -
`limit_conn`	Specifies a shared memory zone (configured with `limit_conn_zone`) and the maximum number of connections that are allowed per key value.	Valid contexts: `http`, `server`, and `location` Default value: -
`limit_conn_log_level`	When NGINX limits a connection due to the `limit_conn` directive, this directive specifies at which log level that limitation is reported.	Valid contexts: `http`, `server`, and `location` Default value: `error`
`limit_conn_status`	Which response code to send to the client when the request is rejected.	Valid contexts: `http`, `server`, and `location` Default value: `503`
`limit_conn_zone`	Specifies the key to be limited in `limit_conn` as the first parameter. The second parameter, `zone`, indicates the name of the shared memory zone used to store the key and current number of connections per key and the size of that zone (`name:size`).	Valid context: `http` Default value: -
`limit_except`	Will limit a location to the specified HTTP verb(s) (`GET` also includes `HEAD`).	Valid context: `location` Default value: -
`limit_rate`	Limits the rate (in bytes per second) at which clients can download content. The rate limit works on a connection level, meaning that a single client could increase their throughput by opening multiple connections.	Valid context: `http`, `server`, `location`, and `if` in `location` Default value: `0`
`limit_rate_after`	Starts the `limit_rate` directive after this number of bytes has been transferred.	Valid contexts: `http`, `server`, `location`, and `if` in `location` Default value: `0`
`limit_req`	Sets a limit with bursting capability on the number of requests for a specific key in a shared memory store (configured with `limit_req_zone`). The burst may be specified with the second parameter. If there shouldn't be a delay in between requests up to the burst, a third parameter, `nodelay`, needs to be configured.	Valid context: `http`, `server`, and `location` Default value: -

Directive	Explanation	Context / default value
limit_req_log_level	When NGINX limits the number of requests due to the limit_req directive, this directive specifies at which log level that limitation is reported. A delay is logged at a level one less than the one indicated here.	Valid contexts: http, server, and location Default value: -
limit_req_status	Which response code to send to the client when the request is rejected.	Valid contexts: http, server, and location Default value: 503
limit_req_zone	Specifies the key to be limited in limit_req as the first parameter. The second parameter, zone, indicates the name of the shared memory zone used to store the key and current number of requests per key and the size of that zone (name:size). The third parameter, rate, configures the number of requests per second (r/s) or per minute (r/m) before the limit is imposed.	Valid context: http Default value: -
limit_zone	Deprecated. Use limit_conn_zone instead.	Valid context: http Default value: -
lingering_close	This directive specifies how a client connection will be kept open for more data.	Valid contexts: http, server, and location Default value: on
lingering_time	In connection with the lingering_close directive, this directive will specify how long a client connection will be kept open for processing more data.	Valid contexts: http, server, and location Default value: 30s
lingering_timeout	Also in conjunction with lingering_close, this directive indicates how long NGINX will wait for additional data before closing the client connection.	Valid contexts: http, server, and location default value: 5s
listen (http)	Refer to the table (the listen parameters) given in the *The virtual server section* in *Chapter 2, A Configuration Guide*.	Valid context: server Default value: *:80 | *:8000
listen (mail)	The listen directive uniquely identifies a socket binding under NGINX. It takes the following parameter: • bind: Makes a separate bind() call for this address:port pair	Valid context: server Default value: -
location	Defines a new context based on the request URI.	Valid contexts: server and location Default value: -

Directive	Explanation	Context / default value
lock_file	The prefix name for the lock files. Depending on the platform, a lock file may be needed to implement accept_mutex and shared memory access serialization.	Valid context: main Default value: logs/nginx.lock
log_format	Specifies which fields should appear in the log file and what format they should take.	Valid context: http Default value: combined $remote_addr - $remote_user [$time_local], "$request" $status $body_bytes_sent, and "$http_referer""$http_user_agent"'
log_not_found	Disables reporting of 404 errors in the error log.	Valid contexts: http, server, and location Default value: on
log_subrequest	Enables the logging of subrequests in the access log.	Valid contexts: http, server, and location Default value: off
mail	Sets up a configuration context in which the mail server directives are specified.	Valid context: main Default value: -
map	Defines a new context, in which a variable is set to a specified value, dependent on the value of a source variable. The format of the context definition is as follows: map $source-variable $variable-to-be-set { … } The string or strings to be mapped may also be regular expressions. The following parameters are recognized within the context: • default: Sets a default value for the variable if the value of the source variable didn't match any of the strings or regular expressions specified • hostnames: Indicates that the source values may be hostnames with a prefix or suffix, glob • include: Includes a file with string-to-value mappings	Valid context: http Default value: -
map_hash_bucket_size	The bucket size used to hold the map hash tables.	Valid context: http Default value: 32|64|128
map_hash_max_size	The maximum size of the map hash tables.	Valid context: http Default value: 2048

Directive	Explanation	Context / default value
`master_process`	Determines whether or not to start worker processes.	Valid context: `main` Default value: on
`max_ranges`	Sets the maximum number of ranges allowed in a byte-range request. Specifying 0 disables the byte-range support.	Valid contexts: `http`, `server`, and `location` Default value: -
`memcached_bind`	Specifies which address should be used for outgoing connections to a `memcached` server.	Valid contexts: `http`, `server`, and `location` Default value: -
`memcached_buffer_size`	The size of the buffer for the response from `memcached`. This response is then sent synchronously to the client.	Valid contexts: `http`, `server`, and `location` Default value: `4k`│`8k`
`memcached_connect_timeout`	The maximum length of time NGINX will wait for its connection to be accepted when making a request to a `memcached` server.	Valid contexts: `http`, `server`, and `location` Default value: `60s`
`memcached_gzip_flag`	Specifies a value, when found in the response from a `memcached` server, which will set the `Content-Encoding` header to `gzip`.	Valid contexts: `http`, `server`, and `location` Default value: -
`memcached_next_upstream`	Refer to the table (The `memcached` module directives) given in the *Caching in the database* section in *Chapter 7, NGINX for the Application Developer*.	Valid contexts: `http`, `server`, and `location` Default value: `error timeout`
`memcached_next_upstream_timeout`	How much time can pass before the request is passed to the next server. (The default value is `disabled`.)	Valid contexts: `http`, `server`, and `location` Default value: `0`
`memcached_next_upstream_tries`	How many tries are made before the request is passed to the next server. (The default value is `disabled`.)	Valid contexts: `http`, `server`, and `location` Default value: `0`
`memcached_pass`	Specifies the name or address of a `memcached` server and its port. It may also be a server group, as declared in an upstream context.	Valid contexts: `location` and `if` in `location` Default value: -
`memcached_read_timeout`	This directive specifies the length of time that needs to elapse between two successive `read` operations from a `memcached` server before the connection is closed.	Valid contexts: `http`, `server`, and `location` Default value: `60s`
`memcached_send_timeout`	The length of time that needs to elapse between two successive `write` operations to a `memcached` server before the connection is closed.	Valid contexts: `http`, `server`, and `location` Default value: `60s`
`merge_slashes`	Disables the removal of multiple slashes. The default value of `on` means that NGINX will compress two or more / characters into one.	Valid contexts: `http` and `server` Default value: on

Directive	Explanation	Context / default value
min_delete_depth	Allows the WebDAV DELETE method to remove files when at least this number of elements is present in the request path.	Valid contexts: http, server, and location Default value: 0
modern_browser	Specifies a browser and version parameter, which together will indicate that the browser is considered modern by setting the $modern_browser variable to modern_browser_value. The browser parameter may take one of the following values: msie, gecko, opera, safari, or konqueror. An alternative parameter unlisted may be specified to indicate that any browser not found in ancient_browser nor in modern_browser or has a missing User-Agent header is considered modern.	Valid contexts: http, server, and location Default value: -
modern_browser_value	The value to which the $modern_browser variable will be set.	Valid contexts: http, server, and location Default value: 1
mp4	Activates the mp4 module for this location.	Valid context: location Default value: -
mp4_buffer_size	Sets the initial buffer size for delivering the MP4 files.	Valid contexts: http, server, and location Default value: 512K
mp4_max_buffer_size	Sets the maximum size of the buffer used to process the MP4 metadata.	Valid contexts: http, server, and location Default value: 10M
msie_padding	Enables the disabling of adding comments to responses with a status greater than 400 for the MSIE clients, in order to pad the response size to 512 bytes.	Valid contexts: http, server, and location Default value: on
msie_refresh	This directive enables the sending of a refresh instead of a redirect for the MSIE clients.	Valid contexts: http, server, and location Default value: off
multi_accept	Instructs a worker process to accept all new connections at once. This directive is disregarded if the kqueue event method is used because kqueue reports the number of new connections waiting to be accepted.	Valid context: events Default value: off
open_file_cache	Configures a cache that can store open file descriptors, directory lookups, and file lookup errors.	Valid contexts: http, server, and location Default value: off

Directive	Explanation	Context / default value
open_file_cache_errors	Enables the caching of the file lookup errors by the open_file_cache directive.	Valid contexts: http, server, and location Default value: off
open_file_cache_min_uses	Configures the minimum number of uses for a file within the inactive parameter to open_file_cache for that file descriptor to remain open in the cache.	Valid contexts: http, server, and location Default value: 1
open_file_cache_valid	Specifies the time interval between the validity checks for the items in the open_file_cache directive.	Valid contexts: http, server, and location Default value: 60s
open_log_file_cache	For more information on this directive, refer to the table (HTTP logging directives) given in the *Logging in NGINX* section in *Chapter 6, The NGINX HTTP Server*.	Valid contexts: http, server, and location Default value: off
override_charset	Indicates whether the charset specified in the Content-Type header of a response received from a proxy_pass or fastcgi_pass request should be converted or not. If the response comes as a result of a subrequest, conversion to the main request's charset will always be performed.	Valid contexts: http, server, location, and if in location Default value: off
pcre_jit	Enables just-in-time compilation of Perl-compatible regular expressions known at configuration time. JIT support needs to be enabled in the PCRE library to make use of this speedup.	Valid context: main Default value: off
perl	Activates a Perl handler for this location. The argument is the name of the handler or a string describing a full subroutine.	Valid contexts: location and limit_except Default value: -
perl_modules	Specifies an additional search path for Perl modules.	Valid context: http Default value: -
perl_require	Indicates a Perl module that will be loaded at each NGINX reconfiguration. It may be specified multiple times for separate modules.	Valid context: http Default value: -
perl_set	Installs a Perl handler to set the value of a variable. The argument is the name of the handler or a string, describing a full subroutine.	Valid context: http Default value: -
pid	The file where the process ID of the main process will be written, overwriting the compiled-in default.	Valid context: main Default value: nginx.pid

Directive	Explanation	Context / default value
pop3_auth	Sets the supported client authentication mechanism. It can be one or more of plain, apop, or cram-md5.	Valid contexts: mail and server Default value: plain
pop3_capabilities	Indicates the POP3 capabilities that are supported by the backend server.	Valid contexts: mail and server Default value: TOP USER UIDL
port_in_redirect	Determines whether or not the port will be specified in a redirect method issued by NGINX.	Valid contexts: http, server, and location Default value: on
postpone_output	Specifies the minimum size of data for NGINX to send to the client. If possible, no data will be sent until this value is reached.	Valid contexts: http, server, and location Default value: 1460
protocol	Indicates the protocol that is supported by this mail server context. It may be one of imap, pop3, or smtp.	Valid context: server Default value: -
proxy	Enables or disables e-mail proxying.	Valid context: server Default value: -
proxy_bind	Specifies the address that should be used for outgoing connections to a proxied server.	Valid contexts: http, server, and location Default value: -
proxy_buffer	Allows setting the size of the buffer used for the mail proxy connection beyond the default of one page.	Valid contexts: mail and server Default value: 4k | 8k (platform dependent)
proxy_buffer_size	The size of the buffer used for the first part of the response from the upstream server, in which the response headers are found.	Valid contexts: http, server, and location Default value: 4k | 8k (platform dependent)
proxy_buffering	Activates the buffering of proxied content; when switched off, responses are sent synchronously to the client as soon as they are received.	Valid contexts: http, server, and location Default value: on
proxy_buffers	The number and size of buffers used for responses from upstream servers.	Valid contexts: http, server, and location Default value: 8 4k | 8k (platform dependent)
proxy_busy_buffers_size	The total size of buffer space allocated to sending the response to the client while still being read from the upstream server. This is typically set to two proxy_ buffers.	Valid contexts: http, server, and location Default value: 8k | 16k (platform dependent)
proxy_cache	Defines a shared memory zone to be used for caching.	Valid contexts: http, server, and location Default value: off

Directive	Explanation	Context / default value
proxy_cache_bypass	One or more string variables, which when nonempty or nonzero, will cause the response to be taken from the upstream server instead of the cache.	Valid contexts: http, server, and location Default value: -
proxy_cache_convert_head	Converts HEAD to GET when caching.	Valid contexts: http, server, and location Default value: on
proxy_cache_key	A string used as the key for storing and retrieving cache values.	Valid contexts: http, server, and location Default value: $scheme$proxy_host$request_uri
proxy_cache_lock	Enabling this directive will prevent multiple requests from making an entry into the same cache key.	Valid contexts: http, server, and location Default value: off
proxy_cache_lock_age	How long to wait for the proxy_cache_lock directive before passing the request to the upstream server.	Valid contexts: http, server, and location Default value: 5s
proxy_cache_lock_timeout	The length of time a request will wait for an entry to appear in the cache or for the proxy_cache_lock directive to be released.	Valid contexts: http, server, and location Default value: 5s
proxy_cache_methods	Which methods indicate that a request will be cached.	Valid contexts: http, server, and location Default value: GET HEAD
proxy_cache_min_uses	The number of requests for a certain key needed before a response is cached.	Valid contexts: http, server, and location Default value: 1
proxy_cache_path	For more information on this directive, to the table (Proxy module caching directives) given in the *Caching data* section in *Chapter 5, Reverse Proxy Advanced Topics.*	Valid context: http Default value: -
proxy_cache_revalidate	Enables revalidation, depending on the values of the If-Modified-Since and If-None-Match headers.	Valid contexts: http, server, and location Default value: off
proxy_cache_use_stale	The cases under which it is acceptable to serve stale cached data when an error occurs accessing the upstream server. The updating parameter indicates the case when fresh data are being loaded.	Valid contexts: http, server, and location Default value: off

Directive	Explanation	Context / default value
`proxy_cache_valid`	Indicates the length of time for which a cached response with the response code, `200`, `301`, or `302`, is valid. If an optional response code is given before the `time` parameter, this time is only for that response code. The special parameter, `any`, indicates that any response code should be cached for that length of time.	Valid contexts: `http`, `server`, and `location` Default value: -
`proxy_connect_timeout`	The maximum amount of time NGINX will wait for its connection to be accepted when making a request to an upstream server.	Valid contexts: `http`, `server`, and `location` Default value: `60s`
`proxy_cookie_domain`	Replaces the domain attribute of the `Set-Cookie` header from the upstream server; the domain to be replaced can either be a string or a regular expression, or reference a variable.	Valid contexts: `http`, `server`, and `location` Default value: `off`
`proxy_cookie_path`	Replaces the path attribute of the `Set-Cookie` header from the upstream server; the path to be replaced can either be a string or a regular expression, or reference a variable.	Valid contexts: `http`, `server`, and `location` Default value: `off`
`proxy_force_ranges`	Forces byte-range support irrespective of the value of the `Accept-Ranges` header.	Valid contexts: `http`, `server`, and `location` Default value: `off`
`proxy_header_hash_bucket_size`	The bucket size used to hold proxy header names (one name cannot be longer than the value of this directive).	Valid contexts: `http`, `server`, `location`, and `if` Default value: `64`
`proxy_header_hash_max_size`	The total size of headers received from the upstream server.	Valid contexts: `http`, `server`, and `location` Default value: `512`
`proxy_hide_header`	A list of header fields that should not be passed on to the client.	Valid contexts: `http`, `server`, and `location` Default value: -
`proxy_http_version`	The HTTP protocol version used to communicate with upstream servers (use `1.1` for `keepalive` connections).	Valid contexts: `http`, `server`, and `location` Default value: `1.0`
`proxy_ignore_client_abort`	If set to on, NGINX will not abort the connection to an upstream server if the client aborts the connection.	Valid contexts: `http`, `server`, and `location` Default value: `off`
`proxy_ignore_headers`	Sets the headers that may be disregarded when processing the response from the upstream server.	Valid contexts: `http`, `server`, and `location` Default value: -

Directive	Explanation	Context / default value
proxy_intercept_errors	If enabled, NGINX will display a configured error_page instead of the response directly from the upstream server.	Valid contexts: http, server, and location Default value: off
proxy_limit_rate	If buffering is enabled, the bytes/s at which the response from the upstream server will be read.	Valid contexts: http, server, and location Default value: 0 (disabled)
proxy_max_temp_file_size	The maximum size of the overflow file, written when the response doesn't fit into memory buffers.	Valid contexts: http, server, and location Default value: 1024m
proxy_method	The HTTP method to substitute when proxying to the upstream server.	Valid contexts: http, server, and location Default value: -
proxy_next_upstream	Indicates the conditions under which the next upstream server will be selected for the response. This won't be used if the client has already been sent something. The conditions are specified using the following parameters: • error: An error occurred while communicating with the upstream server • timeout: A timeout occurred while communicating with the upstream server • invalid_header: The upstream server returned an empty or otherwise invalid response • http_500: The upstream server responded with a 500 error code • http_503: The upstream server responded with a 503 error code • http_504: The upstream server responded with a 504 error code • http_404: The upstream server responded with a 404 error code • off: Disables passing the request to the next upstream server when an error occurs	Valid contexts: http, server, and location Default value: error timeout
proxy_next_upstream_timeout	The number of seconds that pass before giving the request to the next server.	Valid contexts: http, server, and location Default value: 0 (disabled)

Directive	Explanation	Context / default value
proxy_next_upstream_tries	The number of tries before passing the request to the next server.	Valid contexts: http, server, and location Default value: 0 (disabled)
proxy_no_cache	Defines the conditions under which the response will not be saved to the cache. The parameters are string variables, which evaluate to something nonempty and nonzero to not cache.	Valid contexts: http, server, and location Default value: -
proxy_pass	Specifies the upstream server to which the request is passed, in the form of a URL.	Valid contexts: location, if in location, and limit_except Default value: -
proxy_pass_error_message	Useful in situations where the backend authentication process emits a useful error message to the client.	Valid contexts: mail and server Default value: off
proxy_pass_header	Overrides the disabled headers set in proxy_hide_header, allowing them to be sent to the client.	Valid contexts: http, server, and location Default value: -
proxy_pass_request_body	Prevents sending the body of the request to the upstream server if set to off.	Valid contexts: http, server, and location Default value: on
proxy_pass_request_headers	Prevents sending the headers of the request to the upstream server if set to off.	Valid contexts: http, server, and location Default value: on
proxy_read_timeout	Specifies the length of time that needs to elapse between the two successive read operations from an upstream server before the connection is closed.	Valid contexts: http, server, and location Default value: 60s
proxy_redirect	Rewrites the Location and Refresh headers received from the upstream servers; this directive is useful for working around assumptions made by an application framework.	Valid contexts: http, server, and location Default value: default
proxy_request_buffering	Whether or not the complete client request body will be buffered before sending the request to the upstream server.	Valid contexts: http, server, and location Default value: on
proxy_send_lowat	If non-zero, NGINX will try to minimize the number of send operations on outgoing connections to a proxied. It is ignored in Linux, Solaris, and Windows.	Valid contexts: http, server, and location Default value: 0
proxy_send_timeout	The length of time that needs to elapse between two successive write operations to an upstream server before the connection is closed.	Valid contexts: http, server, and location Default value: 60s

Directive	Explanation	Context / default value
proxy_set_body	The body of a request sent to an upstream server may be altered by setting this directive.	Valid contexts: http, server, and location Default value: -
proxy_set_header	Rewrites the contents of the headers sent to an upstream server; this directive may also be used to not send certain headers by setting its value to the empty string.	Valid contexts: http, server, and location Default value: Host $proxy_host and Connection close
proxy_ssl_certificate	The path to a PEM-encoded file of the certificate to use for authenticating with an HTTPS upstream server.	Valid contexts: http, server, and location Default value: -
proxy_ssl_certificate_key	The path to a PEM-encoded file of the secret key to use to use for authenticating with an HTTPS upstream server.	Valid contexts: http, server, and location Default value: -
proxy_ssl_session_reuse	Sets whether or not SSL sessions may be reused when proxying.	Valid contexts: http, server, and location Default value: on
proxy_store	Enables storing responses retrieved from an upstream server as files on disk. The on parameter will use the alias or root directive as the base path under which to store the file. A string may instead be given to indicate an alternative location to store the files.	Valid contexts: http, server, and location Default value: off
proxy_store_access	Sets file access permissions for the newly-created proxy_store files.	Valid contexts: http, server, and location Default value: user:rw
proxy_temp_file_write_size	Limits the amount of data buffered to a temporary file at one time so that NGINX will not be blocked for too long on a single request.	Valid contexts: http, server, and location Default value: 8k|16k (platform dependent)
proxy_temp_path	A directory where temporary files may be buffered as they are proxied from the upstream server, optionally multilevel deep. If a second, third, or fourth parameter is given, these specify a subdirectory hierarchy with the parameter value as the number of characters in the subdirectory name.	Valid contexts: http, server, and location Default value: proxy_temp
proxy_timeout	If a timeout beyond the default of 24 hours is required, this directive can be used.	Valid contexts: mail and server Default value: 24h
random_index	Activates randomly choosing a file to be served to the client when a URI ending with / is received.	Valid context: location Default value: off

Directive	Explanation	Context / default value
read_ahead	If possible, the kernel will preread files up to the size parameter. This directive is supported on current FreeBSD and Linux (the size parameter is ignored on Linux).	Valid contexts: http, server, and location Default value: 0
real_ip_header	Sets the header whose value is used as the client IP address when set_real_ip_from matches the connecting IP.	Valid contexts: http, server, and location Default value: X-Real-IP
real_ip_recursive	Works with set_real_ip_from, to specify that the last address in a multivalued real_ip_header header will be used.	Valid contexts: http, server, and location Default value: off
recursive_error_pages	Enables doing more than one redirect using the error_page directive (default is off).	Valid contexts: http, server, and location Default value: off
referer_hash_bucket_size	The bucket size of the valid referers hash tables.	Valid contexts: server and location Default value: 64
referer_hash_max_size	The maximum size of the valid referers hash tables.	Valid contexts: server and location Default value: 2048
request_pool_size	Fine tunes per-request memory allocation.	Valid contexts: http and server Default value: 4k
reset_timedout_connection	With this directive enabled, connections that have been timed out will immediately be reset, freeing all associated memory. The default value is to leave the socket in the FIN_WAIT1 state, which will always be the case for the keepalive connections.	Valid contexts: http, server, and location Default value: off
resolver	Configures one or more name servers to be used to resolve upstream server names into IP addresses. An optional valid parameter overrides the TTL of the domain name record (now commercial).	Valid contexts: http, server, and location Default value: -
resolver_timeout	Sets the timeout for name resolution (now commercial).	Valid contexts: http, server, and location Default value: 30s

Directive	Explanation	Context / default value
return	Stops processing and returns the specified code to the client. The nonstandard code, 444, will close the connection without sending any response headers. If a code additionally has text accompanying it, the text will be placed in the response body. If instead, a URL is given after the code, this URL will be the value of the Location header. A URL without a code is treated as a code 302.	Valid contexts: server, location, and if Default value: -
rewrite	For more information on this directive, refer to the table (The rewrite module directives) given in the *Introducing the rewrite module* section in *Appendix B, The Rewrite Rule Guide*.	Valid contexts: server, location, and if Default value: -
rewrite_log	Activates notice level logging of rewrites to the error_log.	Valid contexts: http, server, if in server, location, and if in location Default value: off
root	Sets the path to the document root. Files are found by appending the URI to the value of this directive.	Valid contexts: http, server, location, and if in location Default value: html
satisfy	Allows access if all or any of the access or auth_basic directives grant access. The default value, all, indicates that a user must come from a specific network address and enter the correct password.	Valid contexts: http, server, and location Default value: all
satisfy_any	This is deprecated. Use the any parameter of the satisfy directive.	Valid contexts: http, server, and location Default value: off
secure_link_secret	A salt used to compute the MD5 hash of a URI.	Valid context: location Default value: -
send_lowat	If non-zero, NGINX will try to minimize the number of send operations on client sockets. This directive is ignored in Linux, Solaris, and Windows.	Valid contexts: http, server, and location Default value: 0
send_timeout	This directive sets a timeout between two successive write operations for a client receiving a response.	Valid contexts: http, server, and location Default value: 60s
sendfile	Enables using sendfile(2) to directly copy data from one file descriptor to another.	Valid contexts: http, server, location, if in location Default value: off

Directive	Explanation	Context / default value
`sendfile_max_chunk`	Sets the maximum size of data to copy in one `sendfile(2)` call to prevent a worker from seizing.	Valid contexts: `http`, `server`, and `location` Default value: `0`
`server (http)`	Creates a new configuration context, defining a virtual host. The `listen` directive specifies the IP address(es) and port(s); the `server_name` directive lists the `Host` header values that this context matches.	Valid context: `http` Default value: -
`server (upstream)`	For more information on this directive, refer to the table (The `upstream` module directives) given in the *The upstream module* section in *Chapter 4, NGINX as a Reverse Proxy*.	Valid context: `upstream` Default value: -
`server (mail)`	Creates a new configuration context, defining a `mail` server. The `listen` directive specifies the IP address(es) and port(s); the `server_name` directive sets the name of the server.	Valid context: `mail` Default value: -
`server_name (http)`	Configures the names that a virtual host may respond to.	Valid context: `server` Default value: `""`
`server_name (mail)`	Sets the name of the server, which is used in the following ways: • The POP3/SMTP server greeting • The salt for SASL CRAM-MD5 authentication • The EHLO name when using `xclient` to talk to an SMTP backend	Valid contexts: `mail` and `server` Default value: `hostname`
`server_name_in_redirect`	Activates using the first value of the `server_name` directive in any redirect issued by NGINX within this context.	Valid contexts: `http`, `server`, and `location` Default value: `off`
`server_names_hash_bucket_size`	The bucket size used to hold the `server_name` hash tables.	Valid context: `http` Default value: `32	64	128` (processor dependent)
`server_names_hash_max_size`	The maximum size of the `server_name` hash tables.	Valid context: `http` Default value: `512`
`server_tokens`	Disables sending the NGINX version string in error messages and the `Server` response header (default value is on).	Valid contexts: `http`, `server`, and `location` Default value: `on`
`set`	This directive sets a given variable to a specific value.	Valid context: `server`, `location`, and `if` Default value: -

Directive	Explanation	Context / default value
set_real_ip_from	Defines the connecting address(es) from which the client IP will be extracted from the real_ip_ header directive. The value, unix:, means that all connections from the UNIX-domain sockets will be treated this way.	Valid contexts: http, server, and location Default value: -
slice	The size of the slice to use when splitting a request into smaller, cacheable subrequests.	Valid contexts: http, server, and location Default value: 0
smtp_auth	Sets the supported SASL client authentication mechanism. It can be one or more of login, plain, or cram-md5.	Valid contexts: mail and server Default values: login and plain
smtp_capabilities	Indicates the SMTP capabilities that are supported by the backend server.	Valid contexts: mail and server Default value: -
so_keepalive	Sets the TCP keepalive parameter on the socket connection to the proxied server.	Valid contexts: mail and server Default value: off
source_charset	Defines the charset of a response. If it is different from the defined charset, a conversion is performed.	Valid contexts: http, server, location, and if in location Default value: -
split_clients	Creates a context in which variables appropriate to A/B (or split) testing are set. The string specified in the first parameter is hashed using MurmurHash2. The variable specified in the second parameter is then set to a value based on how the string falls within the range of hash values. The match is specified as either a percentage or * to place weights on the values.	Valid context: http default value: -
ssi	Enables the processing of SSI files.	Valid contexts: http, server, location, and if in location Default value: off
ssi_min_file_chunk	Sets the minimum size of a file above which it should be sent using sendfile(2).	Valid contexts: http, server, and location Default value: 1k
ssi_silent_errors	Suppresses the error message normally output when an error occurs during SSI processing.	Valid contexts: http, server, and location Default value: off
ssi_types	Lists the MIME types of a response in addition to text/html in which the SSI commands are processed. It may be * to enable all MIME types.	Valid contexts: http, server, and location Default value: text/html

Directive	Explanation	Context / default value
`ssi_value_length`	Sets the maximum length of values for parameters used in Server Side Includes.	Valid contexts: `http`, `server`, and `location` Default value: `256`
`ssl (http)`	Enables the HTTPS protocol for this virtual server.	Valid contexts: `http` and `server` Default value: `off`
`ssl (mail)`	Indicates if this context should support the SSL/TLS transactions.	Valid contexts: `mail` and `server` Default value: `off`
`ssl_buffer_size`	The size of the buffer to use for sending data. Set `low` to minimize `Time To First Byte`.	Valid contexts: `http` and `server` Default value: `16k`
`ssl_certificate (http)`	The path to the file containing the SSL certificate for this `server_name` in the PEM format. If intermediate certificates are required, they need to be added in order after the certificate corresponding to the `server_name` directive, up to the root, if necessary.	Valid contexts: `http` and `server` Default value: -
`ssl_certificate (mail)`	The path to the PEM-encoded SSL certificate(s) for this virtual server.	Valid contexts: `mail` and `server` Default value: -
`ssl_certificate_key (http)`	This directive specifies the path to the file containing the SSL certificate's secret key.	Valid contexts: `http` and `server` Default value: -
`ssl_certificate_key (mail)`	The path to the PEM-encoded SSL secret key for this virtual server.	Valid contexts: `mail` and `server` Default value: -
`ssl_ciphers`	The ciphers that should be supported in this virtual server context (OpenSSL format).	Valid contexts: `http` and `server` Default value: `HIGH:!aNULL:!MD5`
`ssl_client_certificate`	The path to the file containing the PEM-encoded public CA certificate(s) of the certificate authorities used to sign client certificates.	Valid contexts: `http` and `server` Default value: -
`ssl_crl`	The path to the file containing the PEM-encoded certificate revocation list (CRL) for the client certificates that are to be verified.	Valid contexts: `http` and `server` Default value: -
`ssl_dhparam`	The path to a file containing the DH parameters, used for the EDH ciphers.	Valid contexts: `http` and **server** Default value: -
`ssl_ecdh_curve`	The curve to use for the ECDHE ciphers.	Valid contexts: `http` and `server` Default value: `prime256v1`
`ssl_engine`	Specifies a hardware SSL accelerator.	Valid context: `main` Default value: -

Directive	Explanation	Context / default value
`ssl_password_file`	The path to a file, which contains passphrases for the secret keys used, one per line.	Valid contexts: `http` and `server` Default value: -
`ssl_prefer_server_ciphers` `(http)`	Indicates that the server's ciphers are to be preferred over the client's ciphers when using the SSLv3 and TLS protocols.	Valid contexts: `http` and `server` Default value: `off`
`ssl_prefer_server_ciphers` `(mail)`	Indicates that SSLv3 and TLSv1 server ciphers are preferred over the client's ciphers.	Valid contexts: `mail` and `server` Default value: `off`
`ssl_protocols (http)`	Indicates the SSL protocols that should be enabled.	Valid contexts: `http` and `server` Default value: `TLSv1`, `TLSv1.1`, and `TLSv1.2`
`ssl_protocols (mail)`	Indicates the SSL protocols that should be enabled.	Valid contexts: `mail` and `server` Default value: `TLSv1`, `TLSv1.1`, and `TLSv1.2`
`ssl_session_cache (http)`	Sets the type and size of the SSL cache to store the session parameters. A cache can be one of the following types: • off: Clients are told that sessions won't be reused at all • none: Clients are told that sessions are reused, but they aren't really • builtin: An OpenSSL builtin cache used by only one worker with a size specified in sessions • shared: A cache shared by all worker processes, given a name and session size specified in megabytes	Valid contexts: `http` and `server` Default value: `none`

Directive	Explanation	Context / default value
ssl_session_cache (mail)	Sets the type and size of the SSL cache to store session parameters. A cache can be one of the following types: • off: In this cache, clients are told that sessions won't be reused at all • none: In this cache, clients are told that sessions are reused, but they aren't really • builtin: In this cache, an OpenSSL built-in cache used by only one worker with a size specified in sessions • shared: This cache is shared by all worker processes, and is given a name and session size specified in megabytes	Valid contexts: mail and server Default value: none
ssl_session_timeout (http)	This directive specifies how long the client can use the same SSL parameters, provided they are stored in the cache.	Valid contexts: http and server Default value: 5m
ssl_session_timeout (mail)	This directive specifies how long the client can use the same SSL parameters, provided they are stored in the cache.	Valid contexts: mail and server Default value: 5m
ssl_stapling	This directive enables the stapling of OCSP responses. The CA certificate of the server's issuer should be contained in the file specified by ssl_trusted_certificate. A resolver should also be specified to be able to resolve the OCSP responder hostname.	Valid contexts: http and server Default value: off
ssl_stapling_file	This directive specifies the path to a DER-formatted file containing the stapled OCSP response.	Valid contexts: http and server Default value: -
ssl_stapling_responder	This directive specifies a URL specifying the OCSP responder. Only URLs beginning with http:// are currently supported.	Valid contexts: http and server Default value: -
ssl_stapling_verify	This directive enables the verification of OCSP responses.	Valid contexts: http and server Default value: -
ssl_trusted_certificate	This directive specifies the path to a file containing PEM-formatted SSL certificates of the CA's signing client certificates and OCSP responses when ssl_stapling is enabled.	Valid contexts: http and server Default value: -

Directive	Explanation	Context / default value
ssl_verify_client	Enables the verification of SSL client certificates. If the optional parameter is specified, a client certificate will be requested and, if present, verified. If the optional_no_ca parameter is specified, a client certificate is requested, but doesn't require it to be signed by a trusted CA certificate.	Valid contexts: http and server Default value: off
ssl_verify_depth	Sets how many signers will be checked before declaring the certificate invalid.	Valid contexts: http and server Default value: 1
starttls	Indicates whether or not STLS/STARTTLS are supported and/or required for further communication with this server.	Valid contexts: mail and server Default value: off
sub_filter	The string to be matched without regards to case and the string to be substituted into that match. The substitution string may contain variables.	Valid contexts: http, server, and location Default value: -
sub_filter_once	Setting this directive to off will cause the match in sub_filter to be made as many times as the string is found.	Valid contexts: http, server, and location Default value: on
sub_filter_types	Lists the MIME types of a response in addition to text/html in which a substitution will be made. It may be * to enable all MIME types.	Valid contexts: http, server, and location Default value: text/html
tcp_nodelay	Enables or disables the TCP_NODELAY option for keepalive connections.	Valid contexts: http, server, and location Default value: on
tcp_nopush	This directive is relevant only when the sendfile directive is used. This directive enables NGINX to attempt to the send response headers in one packet, as well as sending a file in full packets.	Valid contexts: http, server, and location Default value: off
threadpool	A named thread pool used for file I/O, so worker processes don't block.	Valid context: main Default value: default threads=32 maxqueue=65536
timeout	The amount of time NGINX will wait before a connection to the backend server is finalized.	Valid contexts: mail and server Default value: 60s
timer_resolution	Specifies how often gettimeofday() is called instead of each time a kernel event is received.	Valid context: main Default value: -

Directive	Explanation	Context / default value
`try_files`	Tests the existence of files given as parameters. If none of the previous files are found, the last entry is used as a fallback, so ensure that this path or named location exists.	Valid contexts: `server` and `location` Default value: -

`types`	Sets up a map of MIME types to filename extensions. NGINX ships with a `conf/mime.types` file that contains most MIME type mappings. Using `include` to load this file should be sufficient for most purposes.	Valid contexts: `http`, `server`, and `location`
		Default value: This value is as follows:
		`text/html html;`
		`image/gif gif;`
		`image/jpeg jpg`

`types_hash_bucket_size`	The bucket size used to hold the types hash tables.	Valid contexts: `http`, `server`, and `location` Default value: 32 | 64 | 128 (processor dependent)
`types_hash_max_size`	The maximum size of the types hash tables.	Valid contexts: `http`, `server`, and `location` Default value: 1024
`underscores_in_headers`	Enables the use of the underscore character in client request headers. If left at the default value `off`, evaluation of such headers is subject to the value of the `ignore_invalid_headers` directive.	Valid contexts: `http` and `server` Default value: `off`
`uninitialized_variable_warn`	Controls whether or not warnings about uninitialized variables are logged.	Valid contexts: `http`, `server`, `location`, and `if` Default value: `on`
`upstream`	Sets up a named context in which a group of servers is defined.	Valid context: `http` Default value: -
`use`	The `use` directive indicates the connection processing method that should be used. This will overwrite the `compiled-in` default value, and must be contained in an `events` context, if used. It is especially useful when the `compiled-in` default value is found to produce errors over time.	Valid context: `events` Default value: -
`user`	The user and group under which the worker processes will run is configured using this parameter. If the group is omitted, a group name equal to that of the user will be used.	Valid context: `main` Default value: `nobody nobody`

Directive	Explanation	Context / default value
userid	Activates the module, according to the following parameters: • on: Setsversion 2 cookies and logs those received • v1: Sets version 1 cookies and logs those received • log: Disables the setting of cookies, but enables the logging of them • off: Disables both the setting of cookies and the logging of them	Valid contexts: http, server, and location Default value: off
userid_domain	Configures a domain to be set in the cookie.	Valid contexts: http, server, and location Default value: none
userid_expires	Sets the age of the cookie. If the keyword max is used, this directive translates to 31 Dec 2037 23:55:55 GMT.	Valid contexts: http, server, and location Default value: -
userid_mark	Sets the first character of the tail of the base64 representation of the userid_name cookie.	Valid contexts: http, server, and location Default value: off
userid_name	Sets the name of the cookie.	Valid contexts: http, server, and location Default value: uid
userid_p3p	Configures the P3P header.	Valid contexts: http, server, and location Default value: -
userid_path	Defines the path set in the cookie.	Valid contexts: http, server, and location Default value: /
userid_service	Identity of the service that set the cookie. For example, the default value for Version 2 cookies is the IP address of the server that set the cookie.	Valid contexts: http, server, and location Default value: The IP address of the server

Directive	Explanation	Context / default value
valid_referers	Defines the values of the Referer header that will cause the $invalid_referer variable to be set to an empty string. Otherwise, it will be set to 1. The parameters can be one or more of the following: • none: There is no Referer header • blocked: The Referer header is present, but empty or lacking a scheme • server_names: The Referer value is one of the server_names parameters • arbitrary string: The value of the Referer header is a server name with or without URI prefixes and ★ at the beginning or end • regular expression: Matches the text after the scheme in the Referer header's value	Valid context: server and location Default value: -
variables_hash_bucket_size	The bucket size used to hold the remaining variables.	Valid context: http Default value: 64
variables_hash_max_size	The maximum size of the hash that holds the remaining variables.	Valid context: http Default value: 1024
worker_aio_requests	The number of open asynchronous I/O operations for a single worker process when using aio with epoll.	Valid context: events Default value: 32
worker_connections	This directive configures the maximum number of simultaneous connections that a worker process may have open. This includes, but is not limited to, the client connections and connections to upstream servers.	Valid context: events Default value: 512
worker_cpu_affinity	Binds worker processes to CPU sets, as specified by a bitmask. This directive is only available on FreeBSD and Linux.	Valid context: main Default value: -
worker_priority	Sets the scheduling priority for worker processes. This directive works like the nice command, with a negative number being a higher priority.	Valid context: main Default value: 0

Directive	Explanation	Context / default value
worker_processes	This is the number of worker processes that will be started. These processes will handle all connections made by clients. Choosing the right number is a complex process; a good rule of thumb is to set this equal to the number of CPU cores.	Valid context: main Default value: 1
worker_rlimit_core	Changes the limit on core file size of a running process.	Valid context: main Default value: -
worker_rlimit_nofile	Changes the limit on the number of open files of a running process.	Valid context: main Default value: -
worker_rlimit_sigpending	Changes the limit on the number of pending signals of a running process when using the rtsig connection processing method.	Valid context: main Default value: -
working_directory	The current working directory for worker processes. It should be writable by the worker to produce core files.	Valid context: main Default value: -
xclient	The SMTP protocol allows checking based on the IP, HELO, or LOGIN parameters, which are passed via the XCLIENT command. This directive enables NGINX to communicate this information.	Valid contexts: mail and server Default value: on
xml_entities	The path to the DTD that declares the character entities referenced in the XML to be processed.	Valid contexts: http, server, and location default value: -
xslt_last_modified	Whether or not to preserve the Last-Modified header when doing an XSLT transformation.	Valid contexts: http, server, and location Default value: off
xslt_param	Parameters passed to the stylesheets, whose values are the XPath expressions.	Valid contexts: http, server, and location Default value: -
xslt_string_param	Parameters passed to the stylesheets, whose values are strings.	Valid contexts: http, server, and location Default value: -
xslt_stylesheet	The path to an XSLT stylesheet used to transform an XML response. Parameters may be passed as a series of key/value pairs.	Valid context: location Default value: -
xslt_types	Lists the MIME types of a response in addition to text/xml, in which a substitution will be made. It may be * to enable all MIME types. If the transformation results in an HTML response, the MIME type will be changed to text/html.	Valid contexts: http, server, and location Default value: text/xml

B
The Rewrite Rule Guide

This appendix is meant to introduce the `rewrite` module in NGINX and serve as a guide for creating new rules as well as translating legacy Apache rewrite rules into NGINX's format. In this appendix, we will discuss the following topics:

- Introducing the `rewrite` module
- Creating new rewrite rules
- Translating from Apache

Introducing the rewrite module

The `rewrite` module of NGINX is a simple regular expression matcher combined with a virtual stack machine. The first part of any rewrite rule is a regular expression. As such, it is possible to use parentheses to define certain parts as **captures**, which can later be referenced by positional variables. A positional variable is one in which its value depends on the order of the capture in the regular expression. They are labeled by number, so positional variable `$1` references what is matched by the first set of parentheses, `$2` references what is matched by the second set, and so on. For example, refer to the following regular expression:

```
^/images/([a-z]{2})/([a-z0-9]{5})/(.*)\.(png|jpg|gif)$
```

The first positional variable, `$1`, references a two-letter string, which comes immediately after the `/images/` string at the beginning of the URI. The second positional variable, `$2`, refers to a five-character string composed of lowercase letters and the numbers from 0 to 9. The third positional variable, `$3`, is presumably the name of a file. And the last variable to be extracted from this regular expression, `$4`, is one of `.png`, `.jpg`, or `.gif`, which appears at the very end of the URI.

The second part of a rewrite rule is the URI to which the request is rewritten. The URI may contain any positional variable captured in the regular expression indicated by the first argument, or any other variable valid at this level of NGINX's configuration:

```
/data?file=$3.$4
```

If this URI does not match any of the other locations in the NGINX configuration, it is returned to the client in the `Location` header with either a `301` (`Moved Permanently`) or a `302` (`Found`) HTTP status code, indicating the type of redirect that is to be performed. This status code may be specified explicitly if `permanent` or `redirect` is the third parameter.

This third parameter to the rewrite rule may also be either `last` or `break`, indicating that no further `rewrite` module directives will be processed. Using the `last` flag will cause NGINX to search for another `location` matching the rewritten URI:

```
rewrite '^/images/([a-z]{2})/([a-z0-9]{5})/(.*)\.(png|jpg|gif)$'
  /data?file=$3.$4 last;
```

The `break` parameter may also be used as a directive on its own to stop the `rewrite` module directive processing within an `if` block, or any other context in which the `rewrite` module is active. The following snippet presumes that some external method is used to set the `$bwhog` variable to a nonempty and nonzero value when a client has used too much bandwidth. The `limit_rate` directive will then enforce a lower transfer rate. The `break` parameter is used here because we entered the `rewrite` module with `if`, and we don't want to process any further such directives:

```
if ($bwhog) {

  limit_rate 300k;

  break;

}
```

Another way to stop the processing of the `rewrite` module directives is to `return` control to the main `http` module processing the request. This may mean that NGINX returns information directly to the client, but `return` is often combined with `error_page` to either present a formatted HTML page to the client or activate a different module to finish processing the request. The `return` directive may indicate a status code, a status code with some text, or a status code with a URI. If a bare URI is the sole parameter, the status code is understood to be a `302`. When the text is placed after the status code, this text becomes the body of the response. If a URI is used instead, this URI becomes the value of the `Location` header, to which the client will then be redirected.

As an example, we want to set a short text as the output for a file not found error in a particular location. We specify `location` with an equals sign (=) to exactly match this URI:

```
location = /image404.html {

  return 404 "image not found\n";

}
```

Any call to this URI would then be answered with an HTTP code of `404` and the text `image not found\n`. So, we can use `/image404.html` at the end of a `try_files` directive or as an error page for the image files.

In addition to directives relating to the act of rewriting a URI, the `rewrite` module also includes the `set` directive to create new variables and set their values. This is useful in a number of ways, from creating flags when certain conditions are present, to passing named arguments on to other locations and logging what was done.

The following example demonstrates some of these concepts and the usage of the corresponding directives:

```
http {

  # a special log format referencing variables we'll define later
  log_format imagelog '[$time_local] ' $image_file ' ' $image_type
    ' ' $body_bytes_sent ' ' $status;

  # we want to enable rewrite-rule debugging to see if our rule
    does
  # what we intend
  rewrite_log on;

  server {

    root /home/www;

    location / {

      # we specify which logfile should receive the rewrite-rule
        debug
      # messages
      error_log logs/rewrite.log notice;

      # our rewrite rule, utilizing captures and positional
        variables
```

```
    # note the quotes around the regular expression - these
      are
    # required because we used {} within the expression
      itself
    rewrite '^/images/([a-z]{2})/([a-z0-9]{5})/(.*)\.
      (png|jpg|gif)$' /data?file=$3.$4;

    # note that we didn't use the 'last' parameter above; if
      we had,
    # the variables below would not be set because NGINX
      would
    # have ended rewrite module processing

    # here we set the variables that are used in the custom
      log
    # format 'imagelog'
    set $image_file $3;

    set $image_type $4;

}

location /data {

    # we want to log all images to this specially-formatted
      logfile
    # to make parsing the type and size easier
    access_log logs/images.log imagelog;

    root /data/images;

    # we could also have used the $image-variables we defined
    # earlier, but referencing the argument is easier to read
    try_files /$arg_file /image404.html;

}

location = /image404.html {

    # our special error message for images that don't exist
    return 404 "image not found\n";

}

}

}
```

The following table summarizes the `rewrite` module directives we discussed in this section:

Rewrite module directives	Explanation
`break`	Ends the processing of the `rewrite` module directives found within the same context.
`if`	Evaluates a condition, and if `true`, this directive follows the `rewrite` module directives specified within the context set up using the following format: `if (condition) { … }` The condition may be any of the following cases: • **A variable name**: `false` if the variable name is empty or any string starting with `0` • **String comparison**: The `=` and `!=` operators • **Regular expression matching**: The `~` (case-sensitive) and `~*` (case-insensitive) positive operators and their negative counterparts, `!~` and `!~*` • **File existence**: The `-f` and `! -f` operators • **Directory existence**: The `-d` and `! -d` operators • **File, directory, or symbolic link existence**: The `-e` and `! -e` operators • **File executability**: The `-x` and `! -x` operators
`return`	Stops processing and returns the specified code to the client. The nonstandard code, `444`, will close the connection without sending any response headers. If a code additionally has text accompanying it, the text will be placed in the response body. If a URL is given after the code instead, this URL will be the value of the `Location` header. A URL without a code is treated as a code `302`.
`rewrite`	Changes the URI from the one matched by the regular expression in the first parameter to the string in the second parameter. If a third parameter is given, it is one of the following flags: • `last`: Stops processing the `rewrite` module directives and searches for a location matched by the changed URI • `break`: Stops processing the `rewrite` module directives • `redirect`: Returns a temporary redirect (code `302`), used when the URI does not begin with a scheme • `permanent`: Returns a permanent redirect (code `301`)
`rewrite_log`	Activates the `notice` level logging of `rewrite` to `error_log`.

Rewrite module directives	Explanation
`set`	Sets a given variable to a specific value.
`unitialized_ variable_warn`	Controls whether or not warnings about uninitialized variables are logged.

Creating new rewrite rules

When creating new rules from scratch, just as with any configuration block, plan out exactly what needs to be done. Some questions to ask yourself are as follows:

- What pattern(s) do I have in my URLs?
- Is there more than one way to reach a particular page?
- Do I want to capture any parts of the URL into variables?
- Am I redirecting to a site not on this server, or could my rule be seen again?
- Do I want to replace the query string arguments?

In examining the layout of your website or application, it should be clear what patterns you have in your URLs. If there is more than one way to reach a certain page, create a rewrite rule to send a permanent redirect back to the client. Using this knowledge, you can construct a canonical representation of your website or application. This not only makes for cleaner URLs, but also helps your site to be found more easily.

For example, if you have a `home` controller to handle default traffic, but can also reach that controller through an index page, you could have users getting to the same information using the following URIs:

```
/
/home
/home/
/home/index
/home/index/
/index
/index.php
/index.php/
```

It would be more efficient to direct requests containing the name of the controller and/or the index page back to the root:

```
rewrite ^/(home(/index)?|index(\.php)?)/?$ $scheme://$host/
  permanent;
```

We specified the $scheme and $host variables because we're making a permanent redirect (code 301) and want NGINX to construct the URL using the same parameters that reached this configuration line in the first place.

If you would like to be able to log individual parts of the URL separately, you can use captures on the URI in the regular expression. Then, assign the positional variables to the named variables, which are then part of a log_format definition. We saw an example of this in the previous section. The components are essentially as follows:

```
log_format imagelog '[$time_local] ' $image_file ' ' $image_type '
  ' $body_bytes_sent ' ' $status;

rewrite '^/images/([a-z]{2})/([a-z0-9]{5})/(.*)\.(png|jpg|gif)$'
  /data?file=$3.$4;

set $image_file $3;

set $image_type $4;

access_log logs/images.log imagelog;
```

When your rewrite rule leads to an internal redirect or instructs the client to call a location in which the rule itself is defined, special care must be taken to avoid a rewrite loop. For example, a rule may be defined in the server context with the last flag, but must use the break flag when defined within the location it references:

```
server {

  rewrite ^(/images)/(.*)\.(png|jpg|gif)$ $1/$3/$2.$3 last;
  location /images/ {

    rewrite ^(/images)/(.*)\.(png|jpg|gif)$ $1/$3/$2.$3 break;

  }

}
```

Passing new query string arguments as part of a rewrite rule is one of the objectives of using the rewrite rules. However, when the initial query string arguments should be discarded, and only the ones defined in the rule should be used, place a ? character at the end of the list of new arguments:

```
rewrite ^/images/(.*)_(\d+)x(\d+)\.(png|jpg|gif)$
  /resizer/$1.$4?width=$2&height=$3? last;
```

Translating from Apache

There is a long history of writing rewrite rules for the powerful `mod_rewrite` module of Apache, and most resources on the Internet are focused on these rules. When encountering the rewrite rules in Apache's format, they can be translated into a form that NGINX can parse by following a few simple rules.

Rule #1 – Replacing directory and file existence checks with try_files

Encounter an Apache rewrite rule of the following form:

```
RewriteCond %{REQUEST_FILENAME} !-f

RewriteCond %{REQUEST_FILENAME} !-d

RewriteRule ^(.*)$ index.php?q=$1 [L]
```

This can best be translated into an NGINX configuration as follows:

```
try_files $uri $uri/ /index.php?q=$uri;
```

These rules state that when the filename specified in the URI is neither a file nor a directory on disk, the request should be passed to the `index.php` file lying in the current context's root and given the `q` argument with a value matching the original URI.

Before NGINX had the `try_files` directive, there would be no choice but to use `if` to test for the existence of the URI:

```
if (!-e $request_filename) {

  rewrite ^/(.*)$ /index.php?q=$1 last;

}
```

Don't do this. You may see configurations on the Internet that recommend doing exactly this, but they are outdated or are copies of an outdated configuration. While not strictly a rewrite rule, because `try_files` belongs to the core `http` module, the `try_files` directive is much more efficient at performing this task and this is exactly what it was created for.

Rule #2 – Replacing matches against REQUEST_URI with a location

Many Apache rewrite rules are made to be placed into the `.htaccess` files because, historically, users would most likely have access to these files themselves. A typical shared hoster would not enable their users' direct access to the virtual host configuration context responsible for their website, but would instead offer the ability to place nearly any kind of configuration into an `.htaccess` file. This led to the situation we have today, with a proliferation of the `.htaccess-file-specific` rewrite rules.

While Apache also has a `location` directive, it is rarely used to solve the problem of matching the URI because it may only be used in either the main server configuration or the configuration of a virtual host. So, instead we see a proliferation of rewrite rules that match `REQUEST_URI`:

```
RewriteCond %{REQUEST_URI} ^/niceurl

RewriteRule ^(.*)$ /index.php?q=$1 [L]
```

This is best handled in NGINX by using `location`:

```
location /niceurl {

    include fastcgi_params;

    fastcgi_index index.php;

    fastcgi_pass 127.0.0.1:9000;

}
```

Of course, what is inside the `location` context is dependent upon your setup, but the principle remains the same; matches against the URI are best served by `location`.

This principle also applies to `RewriteRules` that have an implicit `REQUEST_URI`. These are typically bare `RewriteRules` that transform the URI from an older format to a newer one. In the following example, we see that `show.do` is no longer necessary:

```
RewriteRule ^/controller/show.do$ http://example.com/controller
    [L,R=301]
```

This code translates to an NGINX configuration as follows:

```
location = /controller/show.do {

  rewrite ^ http://example.com/controller permanent;

}
```

Not to get too carried away with creating locations whenever we see `RewriteRule`, we should keep in mind that regular expressions translate directly.

Rule #3 – Replacing matches against HTTP_HOST with a server

Related closely to the rule mentioned in the *Rule #2 – Replacing matches against REQUEST_URI with a location* section, this rule takes configurations into account that try to either remove or add a www onto a domain name. These types of rewrite rule are often found in `.htaccess` files or in virtual hosts with overloaded `ServerAliases`:

```
RewriteCond %{HTTP_HOST} !^www

RewriteRule ^(.*)$ http://www.example.com/$1 [L,R=301]
```

Here, we translate the case where no www is found at the beginning of the `Host` part of the URL to the variant with a www there:

```
server {

  server_name example.com;

  rewrite ^ http://www.example.com$request_uri permanent;

}
```

In the opposite case, where no www is desired, we enter the following rule:

```
RewriteCond %{HTTP_HOST} ^www

RewriteRule ^(.*)$ http://example.com/$1 [L,R=301]
```

This rule translates to the following NGINX configuration:

```
server {

  server_name www.example.com;

  rewrite ^ http://example.com$request_uri permanent;

}
```

What is not shown is the `server` context for the variant that has been redirected. This has been left out because it's not relevant to the rewriting itself.

 This same principle applies to more than just matching www or lack thereof. It can be used in dealing with any `RewriteCond` that uses `%{HTTP_HOST}`. These rewrites are best done in NGINX by using multiple `server` contexts, one each to match the desired condition.

For example, we have the following multisite configuration in Apache:

```
RewriteCond %{HTTP_HOST} ^site1

RewriteRule ^(.*)$ /site1/$1 [L]

RewriteCond %{HTTP_HOST} ^site2

RewriteRule ^(.*)$ /site2/$1 [L]

RewriteCond %{HTTP_HOST} ^site3

RewriteRule ^(.*)$ /site3/$1 [L]
```

This basically translates to a configuration that matches by hostname and has a different `root` configuration per host:

```
server {

  server_name site1.example.com;
  root /home/www/site1;

}
```

```
server {

  server_name site2.example.com;

  root /home/www/site2;

}

server {

  server_name site3.example.com;

  root /home/www/site3;

}
```

These are essentially different virtual hosts, so it is best to treat them as such in the configuration as well.

Rule #4 – Replacing RewriteCond with if for variable checks

This rule applies only after having applied the rules mentioned in the *Rule #1 – Replacing directory and file existence checks with try_files*, *Rule #2 – Replacing matches against REQUEST_URI with a location*, and *Rule #3 – Replacing matches against HTTP_HOST with a server* sections. If there are any remaining conditions not covered by those rules, if may be applied to test the values of variables. Any HTTP variable may be used by prefixing the lowercased name of the variable with $http_. If there are hyphens (-) in the name, these are translated into underscores (_).

The following example (taken from Apache's documentation on the mod_rewrite module at http://httpd.apache.org/docs/2.2/mod/mod_rewrite.html) is used to decide the page that should be delivered to a client based on the User-Agent header:

```
RewriteCond %{HTTP_USER_AGENT} ^Mozilla

RewriteRule ^/$ /homepage.max.html [L]

RewriteCond %{HTTP_USER_AGENT} ^Lynx
RewriteRule ^/$ /homepage.min.html [L]

RewriteRule ^/$ /homepage.std.html [L]
```

This rule can be translated to an NGINX configuration as follows:

```
if ($http_user_agent ~* ^Mozilla) {

  rewrite ^/$ /homepage.max.html break;

}

if ($http_user_agent ~* ^Lynx) {

  rewrite ^/$ /homepage.min.html break;

}

index homepage.std.html;
```

If there are any special variables that are available only under Apache's mod_rewrite, these of course can't be checked in NGINX.

Summary

We explored the rewrite module of NGINX in this appendix. There are only a few directives associated with the module, but these can be used to create some complex configurations. Taking the process of creating new rewrite rules step by step has hopefully demonstrated how rewrite rules can be made easily. An understanding of regular expressions, how to read and construct them, is needed before creating the rewrite rules of any complexity. We rounded this appendix off by examining how to translate the Apache-style rewrite rules into a configuration that NGINX can parse. In doing so, we discovered that quite a few Apache rewrite rule scenarios can be solved differently in NGINX.

C

The NGINX Community

NGINX is not only supported by a vibrant community, but also has a company to back it. Igor Sysoev, the original author of NGINX, cofounded NGINX, Inc. in 2011 to offer professional support to companies using NGINX. He and the other NGINX developers are still available to the community, though. This appendix provides a brief overview of the community resources available online.

The following topics are covered in this appendix:

- NGINX Plus
- Mailing list
- IRC channel
- Web resources
- Writing a proper bug report

NGINX Plus

NGINX, Inc. offers a commercial product called **NGINX Plus**. It is intended for users that need more advanced load-balancing features, more control over media streaming capabilities, or dynamic configuration. You can see more details at `https://www.nginx.com/products/feature-matrix/`. If you find that these features match your needs, you can try it for free or contact sales directly.

Mailing list

The mailing list at `nginx@nginx.org` has been active since 2005. Subscribing to the list and seeing what kinds of question are asked and how they are answered is the best way to get an idea of how to get help from the list. Before asking a question, search online for an answer. There is also an FAQ at `https://www.nginx.com/resources/wiki/community/faq/`. See if someone has already asked the question recently by searching the archives at `http://mailman.nginx.org/pipermail/nginx/`. It's not only embarrassing for you if the same question has been asked recently, but it's also annoying to the readers of the list. Be patient; you may not receive an answer immediately. Above all, be polite. Volunteers answer questions in their free time.

IRC channel

The IRC channel, `#nginx`, at `http://irc.freenode.net/` is a real-time resource for those interested in getting to know the developers and having helpful responses to short queries. Please do follow IRC etiquette when visiting the channel. Larger blocks of text, such as configuration files or compilation output, should go into a Pastebin and only the URL copied into the channel. More details about the channel can be found at `https://www.nginx.com/resources/wiki/community/irc/`.

Web resources

The wiki at `https://www.nginx.com/resources/wiki/` has been a useful resource for a number of years. Here you will find a complete directive reference, a module listing, and a number of configuration examples. Keep in mind though, that this is a wiki, and the information found on it is not guaranteed to be accurate, up-to-date, or to fit your needs exactly. As we have seen throughout this book, it is always important to think about what you want to accomplish before setting out to derive the solution.

NGINX, Inc. maintains the official reference documentation located at `http://nginx.org/en/docs/`. There are some documents introducing NGINX, as well as how-to guides and pages describing each module and directive.

Writing a good bug report

When searching for help online, it is useful to be able to write a good bug report. You will find that an answer is much more easily forthcoming if you can formulate the problem in a clear, reproducible way. This section will help you do just that.

The most difficult part of a bug report is actually defining the problem itself. It will help you to first think about what it is you are trying to accomplish. State your goal in a clear, concise manner as follows:

```
I need all requests to subdomain.example.com to be served from
    server1.
```

Avoid writing reports in the following manner:

```
I'm getting requests served from the local filesystem instead of
    proxying them to server1 when I call subdomain.example.com.
```

Do you see the difference between these two statements? In the first case, you can clearly see that there is a specific goal in mind. The second case describes more the result of the problem than the goal itself.

Once the problem has been defined, the next step is describing how that problem can be reproduced:

```
Calling http://subdomain.example.com/serverstatus yields a "404
    File Not Found".
```

This line will help whoever is looking into this problem try to solve it. It ensures that there is a non-working case that can be shown to be working once the problem is solved.

Next, it is helpful to describe the environment in which this problem was observed. Some bugs only surface when running under certain operating systems or with a particular version of a dependent library.

Any configuration files necessary to reproduce the problem should be included in the report. If a file is found in the software archive, a reference to that file is enough.

Read your bug report before sending it off. Often, you will find that some information has been left out. Sometimes, you will find that you have even solved the problem yourself, just by defining it clearly!

Summary

In this appendix, we learned a bit about the community behind NGINX and what the commercial offers are. We saw who the major players are and what resources are available online. We also got an in-depth look at writing a bug report that should be helpful in finding the solution to a problem.

D
Persisting Solaris Network Tunings

In *Chapter 9, Troubleshooting Techniques*, we saw how to change different network tuning parameters for different operating systems. This appendix details what is necessary to persist these changes on Solaris 10 and above.

The following script is what is actually run by the **Service Management Framework (SMF)** to set the network parameters with ndd. Save it as /lib/svc/method/network-tuning.sh and make it executable so that it can be run at any time on the command line to test:

```
# vi /lib/svc/method/network-tuning.sh
```

The following snippet is the content of the /lib/svc/method/network-tuning.sh file:

```
#!/sbin/sh
# Set the following values as desired
ndd -set /dev/tcp tcp_max_buf 16777216
ndd -set /dev/tcp tcp_smallest_anon_port 1024
ndd -set /dev/tcp tcp_largest_anon_port 65535
ndd -set /dev/tcp tcp_conn_req_max_q 1024
ndd -set /dev/tcp tcp_conn_req_max_q0 4096
ndd -set /dev/tcp tcp_xmit_hiwat 1048576
ndd -set /dev/tcp tcp_recv_hiwat 1048576
# chmod 755 /lib/svc/method/network-tuning.sh
```

The following manifest serves to define the network tuning service and will run the script at boot time. Note that we specify the duration of transient to let SMF know that this is a run-once script and not a persistent daemon.

Place it in /var/svc/manifest/site/network-tuning.xml and import with the following command:

```
# svccfg import /var/svc/manifest/site/network-tuning.xml
```

You will see the following output:

```
<?xml version="1.0"?>
<!DOCTYPE service_bundle SYSTEM
  "/usr/share/lib/xml/dtd/service_bundle.dtd.1">
<service_bundle type='manifest' name='SUNW:network_tuning'>

  <service
    name='site/network_tuning'
    type='service'
    version='1'>

      <create_default_instance enabled='true' />

    <single_instance />

    <dependency
      name='usr'
      type='service'
      grouping='require_all'
      restart_on='none'>
      <service_fmri value='svc:/system/filesystem/minimal' />
    </dependency>

    <!-- Run ndd commands after network/physical is plumbed. -->
    <dependency
      name='network-physical'
      grouping='require_all'
      restart_on='none'
      type='service'>
      <service_fmri value='svc:/network/physical' />
    </dependency>

    <!-- but run the commands before network/initial -->
    <dependent
      name='ndd_network-initial'
```

```
      grouping='optional_all'
      restart_on='none'>
      <service_fmri value='svc:/network/initial' />
    </dependent>

    <exec_method
      type='method'
      name='start'
      exec='/lib/svc/method/network-tuning.sh'
    timeout_seconds='60' />

    <exec_method
      type='method'
      name='stop'
      exec=':true'
    timeout_seconds='60' />

    <property_group name='startd' type='framework'>
      <propval name='duration' type='astring'
        value='transient' />
    </property_group>

    <stability value='Unstable' />

    <template>
      <common_name>
        <loctext xml:lang='C'>
          Network Tunings
        </loctext>
      </common_name>

    </template>
  </service>

</service_bundle>
```

This service is intentionally kept simple for demonstration purposes.

 The interested reader can explore SMF in the Solaris man pages
(https://docs.oracle.com/cd/E26502_01/html/E29043/smf-
5.html) and online resources (https://github.com/natefoo/smf-
nettune/blob/master/README.md).

Index

Symbols

A

B

C

www.ingramcontent.com/pod-product-compliance
Lightning Source LLC
Chambersburg PA
CBHW080929060326
40690CB00042B/3221